"This Gospel . . . Shall Be Preached":

A History and Theology of Assemblies of God Foreign Missions Since 1959—Volume 2

Gary B. McGee

D1468880

Gospel Publishing House
Springfield, Missouri

02–0673

Library of Congress Cataloging-in-Publication Data

(Revised for vol. 2)
McGee, Gary B., 1945-
  This Gospel—shall be preached.

Vol. 1 originally presented as the author's thesis (doctoral—St. Louis University)
  Includes bibliographies and indexes.
  1. Assemblies of God—Missions—History.
2. Pentecostal churches—Missions—History. I. Title.
BV2595.A8M36 1986 266'.994 86-80015
ISBN 0-88243-511-6 (v. 1 : soft)
ISBN 0-88243-673-2 (v. 2)

Printed in the United States of America

In honor of J. Philip Hogan executive director of the Assemblies of God Division of Foreign Missions (1960–1989)

Keen observer of world events

Restless promoter of global evangelization

Contents

Foreword

The history of Assemblies of God foreign missions represents a modern day application of apostolic Christianity. As a 20th century revival movement, Pentecostals have not only rediscovered the *apostolic message* and received the *apostolic power*—they have also returned to the *apostolic patterns* of making Jesus known in the power of the Holy Spirit. This is nowhere more obvious than in their practice of world evangelization, which has resulted in an unprecedented harvest of souls, evident in the most phenomenal expansion of experiential Christianity in religious history. During the last few decades Pentecostals have outgrown all traditional Protestant denominations—in the words of an outside observer, "burying last year's statistics under a mass of new adherents, new churches, new territories."

In this second volume of *This Gospel Shall Be Preached*, Dr. McGee brings the remarkable story of the foreign missionary enterprise of the Assemblies of God (USA) up to the present. He illustrates the agency's consistency with its original objectives as well as its advancement in understanding a Pentecostal theology of missions; the record reflects an increased maturity and understanding of what "partnership in mission" means. This second volume also shows how the Assemblies of God has excelled in lay involvement in missions and how modern, efficient vehicles for the spreading of the Good News came into existence. At the same time, the many roles of the modern missionary and the complexity of the new challenges before him are not overlooked.

Dr. J. Philip Hogan is the dean of Pentecostal mission executives, a perceptive administrator and key strategist of the program. Through three decades of extraordinary growth he has profoundly shaped its course. The book is rightfully dedicated to him, for it is a history of the "Hogan Era."

Hogan himself would give all the credit to the Holy Spirit. In a plenary address at the historic International Congress on World Evangelization in Lausanne in 1974 (described by *Time* magazine as a "formidable forum, possibly the widest ranging meeting of Christians ever held"), Hogan explained what this book records: "Make no mistake, the missionary venture of the Church, no matter how well planned, how finely administered, or how fully supported, would fail like every other vast human enterprise were it not that where human instrumentality leaves off, a blessed ally takes over. It is the Holy Spirit who calls, it is the Holy Spirit who inspires, it is the Holy Spirit who reveals, and it is the Holy Spirit who administers."

Dr. McGee's two volumes of *This Gospel Shall Be Preached* illustrate what can be achieved for the kingdom of God when "human instrumentality" cooperates in a biblical fashion with the "blessed ally." The Assemblies of God exemplifies how that difficult and delicate balance between Spirit-born spontaneity and organizational accountability is attained. Clearly, before they had a program they had a passion. Thank God that their program did not replace that passion—as so often happens—but channeled it into a spectacular yet biblically sound, structurally viable and stable worldwide movement.

Like the first volume, this book is thoroughly researched and documented, clearly organized and written. For historians and theologians of missions it will be an indispensable resource on present Pentecostal practice and thinking. For anyone whose heart is in missions it will be interesting and exciting reading.

PETER KUZMIČ, DR.THEOL.
DIRECTOR
BIBLICAL THEOLOGICAL INSTITUTE
OSIJEK, YUGOSLAVIA

Acknowledgments

The preparation of this second volume on the history and theology of Assemblies of God foreign missions has depended on help from several individuals, whose contributions I readily acknowledge. I am particularly grateful to J. Philip Hogan, executive director of the Division of Foreign Missions, and to his administrative assistant, Norman L. Correll, for the value they have placed on Assemblies of God missions history and their generous assistance in making this book possible. I am also indebted to President H. Glynn Hall and other officers of the Assemblies of God Theological Seminary for granting me a leave of absence for the 1987–1988 academic year. This made available valuable time for research and writing in order to have the book ready for the denomination's 75th anniversary in 1989.

My research has been greatly expedited by the resources and services of the Assemblies of God Archives in Springfield, Missouri, and the helpful assistance of Wayne E. Warner, director, and his assistants, Joyce Lee and Glenn W. Gohr. The librarians of the Cordas C. Burnett Library at the Assemblies of God Theological Seminary and the Myer Pearlman Library at Central Bible College (both in Springfield) also came to my rescue on several occasions. Indispensable sources of missions documentation, which proved invaluable in my work, have been collected and preserved within the Division of Foreign Missions by Adele Flower Dalton and Gloria Robinett. The contributions of Mrs. Dalton to preserving the missionary heritage of the Assemblies of God cannot be overestimated. I also wish to thank Eleanor E. Parry for her indexing of the *Pentecostal Evangel,* saving me untold hours of research.

For the quality of editing and preparing a manuscript for publication, the book editing of Gospel Publishing House stands second to none. The exacting work of Glen Ellard, book editor, and his assistants, notably Jean Lawson and Donna Ketcherside, have vastly improved the quality of the manuscript. Glenn W. Gohr skillfully prepared the index.

The editors of the *Pentecostal Evangel, Mountain Movers,* and *Advance* magazines have generously allowed me to quote from their publications. Permission to quote from my articles has been received from the editors of *Missiology* for "Assemblies of God Overseas Missions: Foundations for Recent Growth" and the editors of *International Bulletin of Missionary Research* for "The Azusa Street Revival and Twentieth-Century Missions."

Pictures have been provided by the offices of the following: Assemblies of God Archives, Division of Foreign Missions of the Assemblies of God, Assemblies of God Theological Seminary, National Association of Evangelicals, *Pentecostal Evangel,* School of World Mission at Fuller Theological Seminary, Assemblies of God Office of Information, Southern California District Council, Center for Ministry to Muslims, and HealthCare Ministries; the picture of Roland Allen was supplied by The Living Church Foundation, Inc., Milwaukee, Wisconsin; pictures were also provided by the following people: J. Philip and Virginia Hogan, Daniel Munshi, James E. Richardson, Charles E. Greenaway, Harold Schmitt, George Assad, Alfred J. Perna, Sr., Morris O. Williams, Sandra G. Clopine, Herman N. van Amerom, G. Edward Nelson, and Delia M. Mora.

Finally, my wife, Alice, and two daughters, Angela and Catherine, have been an encouragement to me throughout the entire process of research and writing.

Introduction

Since the 1950s, the Assemblies of God mission enterprise has grown to become a major leader in the Christian world mission. As one of the strongest agencies among conservative Christian organizations, its theological foundations and missiological perspectives, as well as the rapid growth of some of its fraternally-related churches overseas, have increasingly caught the attention of church leaders, church growth analysts, and missiologists. During the same years, important developments occurred in the leadership of the Division of Foreign Missions, the missionary personnel, and general operation.

Key changes in the denominational leadership in 1960 have had far-reaching consequences for the world mission of the church. J. Philip Hogan, elected as executive director of Foreign Missions and following in the steps of Noel Perkin, has overseen one of the most aggressive attempts of the 20th century to fulfill the Great Commission. His willingness to pragmatically consider new avenues of evangelism, church planting, and leadership training opened the door for such creative initiatives as the International Correspondence Institute, International Media Ministries, and other important endeavors abroad. Closely associated with him in leadership positions have been missionaries having lengthy and fruitful experience in working with national churches.

For the home base, the administration of General Superintendent Thomas F. Zimmerman, also begun in 1960, bolstered the vision and confidence of the American constituency to aggressively pursue evangelism and expedite efforts in planting more churches. Zimmerman's concerns for increasing lay opportunities in ministry, whether at home or abroad, strengthened the base for the ever expanding initiatives of the Division of Foreign Missions. Not surprisingly, the Zimmerman and Hogan tenures witnessed the linking of lay ministries (e.g., Mobilization and Placement Service) with the work of missionaries and national churches for the furtherance of the mission of the church.

A new generation of missionaries has also come to the fore, enjoying the benefits of improved transportation and living conditions, greater care for the well-being of the family abroad, new opportunities for missiological training, and improved promotions of their ministries by the Division of Foreign Missions. At the same time, they have faced the familiar challenges of missionary service, including the strenuous responsibility of raising their own financial support among the local congregations. Though inflation in some countries has added to their burden, the missionaries have kept in close contact with Assemblies of God congregations through itineration, stirring them with passionate messages to support the cause of world evangelization in the last days before the return of Christ.

No less dedicated than their predecessors, these missionaries have focused on strategic planning in evangelism, recognized the benefits of team work, pursued the use of electronic media communications, pioneered new discipleship training programs, faithfully prepared men and women for leadership positions, and encouraged the development of strong indigenous "New Testament" churches. These objectives, paralleled by the demise of the colonial empires in the last 40 years, have revolutionized their position as missionaries, altering their responsibilities from those of oversight to partnership.

They exhibit, nevertheless, a continuing commitment to the spiritual foundations of their Pentecostal heritage. Planning may be necessary, and indeed Assemblies of God missionaries and missions executives have excelled at strategizing, but in their estimation, the Holy Spirit—His dynamic presence, guidance, and power—remains the key to church growth. The carefully coordinated Good News Crusades, whether utilizing missionaries, missionary-evangelists, or national evangelists, have epitomized the benefits of human planning and dependence on the Spirit to accompany the proclamation of the gospel with "signs and wonders." Progress has also been made in the exposition of Pentecostal missiology. Led by the prolific Melvin L. Hodges, others have further articulated Pentecostal distinctives and missiology.

The entire operation of the Division of Foreign Missions has become increasingly more complex since 1959. From a little more than $6 million, the Division's budget has grown beyond the $84 million mark, which includes the contributions of the Women's Ministries Department, Light-for-the-Lost, Speed-the-Light, and Boys and Girls Missionary Crusade. Retaining only a small percentage to cover administrative costs, the Division works under a huge burden to properly disburse all funds. The endeavors of five international ministries, whose activities cross many borders, are superintended by directors responsible to the Division's Foreign Missions Committee. Increased administrative responsibilities have necessitated the addition of area representatives to help shoulder the loads of the field directors. Oversight is also shared by missionary field fellowship chairmen who assist in coordinating missionary efforts with the various ministries of national churches.

To survey and interpret the years between 1959 and 1989, I have placed the chapters in four divisions. The first division, "Preparations for Advance," focuses on the maturation of the Pentecostal missions enterprise, foundations for growth, and leadership changes. The second division is titled "Global Conquest (1959–1967)," after the popular promotional theme during most of the 60s. Promotions, evangelistic efforts abroad, contributions of support agencies, missiological perspectives, and missionary life are given consideration. The third division, "Evangelism, Education, and Expansion (1968–1977)," addresses missiological training, Good News Crusades, and new ventures in education, among other topics. The publication of Melvin L. Hodges' *Theology of the Church and Its Mission* in 1977, the most extensive exposition of Pentecostal missiology to that time, marks the end of this unit. The fourth and final division, "Into the 80s (1978–1989)," reviews international ministries, missiological training, evangelism, partnership perspectives, and the increased emphasis on ministries of compassion.

Consistent with my approach in the first volume, I believe that the development of the mission enterprise of the Assemblies of God is best understood when historical and theological factors are considered together. Although this book is not a theology of mission per se, its tracing of missiological perspectives since 1959 will hopefully contribute to future studies in the theology of Pentecostal missions.

Several terms especially deserve clarification to benefit the reader. When using the word "mission," I have tried to reserve it for speaking of the church's missionary task. "Missions" in the plural is best used in regard to the efforts of mission agencies. In addition, I attempt to link titles to their historical contexts. Thus, "field secretaries" are commonly referred to in the years before 1978 and "field directors" afterward. "Foreign Missions Department" is the preferred term for the agency before 1972, superseded that year by "Division of Foreign Missions."

From modest beginnings the Pentecostal movement, with its restorationist longing for the apostolic signs and wonders to appear with evangelism, has prompted one of the most vigorous expansions of the church in the history of Christianity. As an integral part of that undertaking, the Assemblies of God has pointedly recognized the merit of establishing indigenous "New Testament" churches overseas, capable of aggressive evangelism themselves. By so doing, it has reached the hoped-for level of maturity characterized by fraternal relationships. With this bonding intact, the Assemblies of God (U.S.A.) and the national churches abroad continue striving in their team efforts to catch up with the strategy of the Spirit for worldwide evangelization: "You will receive power when the Holy Spirit comes on you; and you will be my witnesses . . . to the ends of the earth" (Acts 1:8, NIV).

Part One

Preparations for Advance

1

Pentecostal Missions Mature

A Worldwide Missionary Movement

Spiritual awakenings and missionary zeal have long been associated on the American religious scene—from the Haystack Prayer Meeting and the formation of the American Board of Commissioners for Foreign Missions (1810) to the Mount Hermon Conference and the founding of the Student Volunteer Movement for Foreign Missions (1888). Spiritual renewals have triggered fresh attempts to fulfill the Great Commission.

To these awakenings should be added the Pentecostal revival of the 20th century. In part, this worldwide revival stemmed from spiritual activity that began at Charles F. Parham's Bethel Bible School in Topeka, Kansas, on January 1, 1901—for it eventually triggered revivals around the world. Foremost among them was the Azusa Street Revival of 1906–1909 in Los Angeles, California.[1] News of this revival traveled across the United States as leaders published thousands of copies of the *Apostolic Faith* (a newspaper distributed occasionally between September 1906 and May 1908). From coast to coast and overseas, expectant believers avidly read the testimonies and teachings in the pages of this and similar periodicals. Indigenous Pentecostal revivals also occurred abroad, although they have not yet received the historical analysis they deserve.

Those who attended the revival services on Azusa Street believed that the apostolic "signs and wonders" that had characterized the advance of the early Christians in the Book of Acts had been restored in the last days. The gifts of the Spirit, including tongues, interpretations, prophecies, miracles, faith, and divine healings, were given to aid in the advancement of the gospel. This emphasis on the work of the Holy Spirit, although rejected by many, constituted a unique position regarding the Christian world mission. Reliance was to be upon the Spirit, not the mechanical formulations of mission strategists. Such a wholesale return to the apostolic pattern of the first century was without parallel on the missionary landscape. Their enthusiasm for world evangelization propelled a diaspora of new missionaries even though the leaders of the revival did not organize a missionary society.

The first "missionary manifesto" among independent American Pentecostals, calling for the establishment of a missionary society, surfaced in 1908 at the Pentecostal Camp Meeting in Alliance, Ohio, under the direction of Levi R. Lupton, a holiness-oriented Quaker who experienced the Pentecostal baptism in December 1906. Although those attending the meeting had no interest in starting another ecclesiastical organization, they asserted that "such an affiliation of Pentecostal Missions is desirable as will preserve and increase the tender sweet bond of love and fellowship now existing and guard against abuse of legitimate liberty."[2] In the following year, the Pentecostal Missionary Union in the United States of America was formed (modeled after an organization of the same name founded in Great Britain in January 1909), headquartered in Alliance. This effort, however, collapsed a year later.[3] Nevertheless, whether through their own initiative or with the encouragement of this agency, over 185 Pentecostals had traveled overseas to engage in missionary evangelism by 1910 and could be found in Africa, China, India, Japan, Latin America, and the Middle East. More influential and successful missionaries soon followed in their footsteps.[4]

Pentecostal Missionary Agencies After 1910

Claiming that the apostolic power of the early Christian church had been restored, however, did not insulate Pentecostals from the vexations of missionary turnover, financial support, inadequate legal recognition, issues of training and strategy, as well as the need for effective communication with the supporting constituencies. The first major Pentecostal missionary agency to appear in America was the Pentecostal Mission in South and Central Africa, organized in 1910 by the Bethel Pentecostal Assembly of Newark, New Jersey.[5] The Assemblies of God, founded at Hot Springs, Arkansas, in 1914, soon represented missionaries ministering not only in Africa, but in the Middle East, India, China, and Latin America as well. Among the reasons for calling the first Council, the conveners had stated:

> We come together . . . that we may get a better understanding of the needs of each foreign field, and may know how to place our money in such a way that one mission or missionary shall not suffer, while another not any more worthy, lives in luxuries. Also that we may discourage wasting money on those who are running here and there accomplishing nothing, and may concentrate our support on those who mean business for our king.[6]

Five years later, the Assemblies of God created the "Missionary Department" to coordinate and promote its burgeoning overseas enterprise. Closely connected to the American Assemblies of God in its earliest years, the Pentecostal Assemblies of Canada, incorporating separately in 1922, also sponsored a far-flung missionary program.[7]

For various reasons, other Pentecostal denominations were slower in developing their overseas endeavors. The Pentecostal Holiness Church had set up a "missionary board" in 1904, but did not realize permanent achievements until the mid-1920s.[8] The Church of God (Cleveland, Tennessee) traces its missionary heritage back to the voyage of R. M. Evans to the Bahama Islands in 1910.[9] However, not until 1926—after the disruptions of World War I, inadequate financial support, and internal unrest in 1923—was a mission board appointed. Once in place, decades of steady growth followed. The leadership of J. H. Ingram through his worldwide travels effectively linked the organization to the efforts of independent Pentecostal pioneer missionaries who united with it.[10]

Contemporary with these efforts were those of the Russian and Eastern European Mission (1927),[11] the Apostolic Faith Movement (Portland, Oregon; first missionary sent in 1911),[12] the Pentecostal Church of God (1919),[13] the Evangelization Society of the Pittsburgh Bible Institute founded by Charles Hamilton Pridgeon (1920),[14] the Church of God of Prophecy (1923),[15] the Church of God in Christ (1897; first Home and Foreign Missions Board in 1925),[16] the Fellowship of Christian Assemblies (1922, 1951),[17] the Independent Assemblies of God International (1922, 1951),[18] the Pentecostal Assemblies of Newfoundland (1925),[19] the International Church of the Foursquare Gospel (1927),[20] the Christian Church of North America (1929),[21] the Elim Fellowship (1933),[22] and the Open Bible Standard Churches (1935).[23] The Oneness Pentecostal church organizations, resulting from a division in the Assemblies of God in 1916, also sponsored important mission endeavors.[24]

Europeans banded together to sponsor, among others, the Congo Evangelistic Mission (later the Zaire Evangelistic Mission) founded by William F. P. Burton and James Salter (1915),[25] the Pentecostal Mission Alliance in the Netherlands founded by G. R. Polman (1920),[26] and the mission initiatives of the Scandinavian Pentecostal churches.[27] In addition to the work of such organizations, missionaries sometimes served independently, depending on supporting congregations for financial assistance. Many of these ventures also proved successful.

Although no formal Pentecostal agency coordinated the efforts of the various organizations or those of independent missionaries, limited ecumenism did prevail in some fields, such as Liberia and India. By the outbreak of World War II, hundreds of Pentecostal missionaries had been sent overseas.

The Third Force

Along with other evangelical mission agencies, denominational missions programs and independent efforts experienced dramatic growth after World War II.[28] They also reflected growing sophistication in organization and promotions, increased missionary longevity, and growing financial stability.

While the Pentecostal missionary expansion went largely unnoticed by contemporary historians of the expansion of Christianity, observers began to comment early in the 1950s that a new movement of unparalleled significance had emerged within Christendom, representing a fresh and distinctive thrust that could no longer be ignored.[29] Its uniqueness became increasingly apparent with its worldwide growth.

Although Pentecostal missionaries from America and Europe had laid important foundations through the younger churches they helped to establish, indigenous Pentecostal movements (some with worship patterns and perspectives similar to classical Pentecostalism) also represented large segments of this growth.

In 1953, Bishop Lesslie Newbigin of the Church of South India identified a "third stream of Christian tradition," which he labeled as Pentecostal, noting its emphasis on "that which is to be known and recognized in present experience—the power of the ever-living Spirit of God."[30] Five years later, Henry P. Van Dusen, then president of Union Theological Seminary in New York, also referred to a "third force" in Christendom. In an article in *Life* magazine, he praised the mission successes of Pentecostals as well as those of Holiness, Adventist, and Church of Christ groups.[31] This positive reference encouraged the Pentecostals to refer to themselves exclusively as the third major segment of Christianity.

During the same year, Donald Grey Barnhouse, a prominent American Presbyterian and editor of *Eternity* magazine, visited the headquarters of the Assemblies of God in Springfield, Missouri. Barnhouse praised the organization for its commitment to evangelical doctrines and, although he disagreed with its Pentecostal theology, reflected on its remarkable advance in missions overseas.[32]

The Pentecostals clearly enjoyed being in the spotlight and testifying to their beliefs. But David J. du Plessis, an international Pentecostal leader, insisted, in the *International Review of Missions* in 1958,

> The Pentecostal revival of this century is different. In the first place, there is no man who can claim to have been the founder of this great worldwide Christian revival. In the second place, there has been no new emphasis on any special doctrine. Rather, the emphasis is upon an experience. . . .
>
> The Pentecostal revival today is merely a restoration of a personal experience of a life-changing salvation followed by the receiving of the baptism in the Holy Spirit with the evidence or confirmation of the initial manifestation of speaking in unknown tongues, which in turn is usually followed by experiences of power to cast out devils, heal the sick and miracles.[33]

As Pentecostal churches thrived overseas, their doctrines and methods increasingly attracted the attention of church leaders, missiologists, historians, and other analysts.

Cooperation With Evangelicals

Significantly, this growing recognition came at a time of increasing identity with American evangelicals. Pentecostals received invitations to join the National Association of Evangelicals (NAE) when it was formed in 1942. As a result, Assemblies of God church leaders rubbed shoulders with other Pentecostal and evangelical executives for the first time. The missions arm of the NAE, the Evangelical Foreign Missions Association (EFMA), began in 1945 and included four Pentecostal organizations among its charter members: Assemblies of God, Church of God (Cleveland, Tennessee), Open Bible Standard Churches, and the Pentecostal Holiness Church. The Christian Church of North America, International Church of the Foursquare Gospel, and Pentecostal Assemblies of Canada joined later.[34]

While the NAE and EFMA affiliations brought benefits to the Pentecostals, the criticisms by fundamentalists associated with the rival American Council of Christian Churches proved to be painful for several years.[35] In 1952 the American Council condemned as heretics the Pentecostals, along with Universalists, Seventh Day Adventists, and Roman Catholics.

In spite of these tensions, the Assemblies of God, the largest Pentecostal denomination represented, remained in the NAE, although its Foreign Missions Department withdrew from the EFMA for a short time (1950–1953).[36] The denomination also joined the World Evangelical Fellowship, founded in Woudschoten, Holland, in 1951. After attending the annual conference in 1953, J. Philip Hogan, a representative of the Promotions Division of the missions department at the time, stated that before the hostile forces of communism, liberalism, atheism, and others, "we do not stand as Pentecostals, but as Evangelicals. In many areas the liberty to propagate the gospel hangs by a slender thread. That liberty can only be preserved by united evangelical action on a world level; hence the importance of the World Evangelical Fellowship."[37] This positive opinion of unity with evangelicals became common among many Pentecostals.

With the broader church world, official contact continued on a limited basis for some years: Since 1920 the Assemblies of God had held membership in the Foreign Missions Conference of North

America, an interdenominational agency providing needed services for mission agencies since 1893. However, when the conference became the Division of Overseas Missions of the National Council of Churches (NCC),[38] the Assemblies of God altered its status to that of a consultant agency in 1950. But 11 years later it broke off contact altogether when the International Missionary Council (of which the Division of Overseas Missions of the NCC was a constituent) became fully integrated with the World Council of Churches. This final break coincided with the first term (1960–1961) of Thomas F. Zimmerman, newly-elected general superintendent of the Assemblies of God, as president of the NAE and the sharply growing identification of the denomination with NAE activities and agencies.[39]

In the years that followed, member Pentecostal mission boards and the EFMA had a long and warm relationship. This important cooperative relationship with other evangelicals demonstrated that Pentecostals were gaining respect and stature in the church world. No longer isolated, they were beginning to enjoy the benefits of increased cooperation.

With the growing acceptance of Pentecostals by the evangelical mainstream, the feelings of isolation and rejection began to subside. Pentecostals had proudly viewed their mission efforts as a resumption of "the Lord's Pentecostal missionary movement," having begun on the Day of Pentecost. They also concluded that "the professing church is largely in apostasy, neither cold nor hot, and is nearly ready to be spued out."[40] The 1963 publication of *Our World Witness: A Survey of Assemblies of God Foreign Missions* by Noel Perkin and John Garlock, however, reflected a far more charitable view of other evangelical mission efforts. The writers identified a great surge in world evangelization contemporary to the beginning of the Pentecostal movement in the early 1900s. While part of this surge could be attributed to the birth of the movement, they nevertheless noted that "even in those churches which did not accept the Pentecostal experience there was a spiritual stirring which resulted in greater missionary activity."[41]

By midcentury, major Pentecostal mission agencies had addressed serious problems in their operations, initiated important contacts with each other and evangelicals, and taken a more balanced view of their role in the Christian world. Within a few years, one perceptive Roman Catholic scholar would write, "[W]hen speaking of Pentecostals, we are not now dealing with an obscure 'sect,' born almost seventy years ago in a small Midwest town, but with a world-embracing movement. . . ."[42]

Henry P. Van Dusen, president of Union Theological Seminary in New York City, identified Pentecostals with an emerging "third force" in Christendom through an article published in *Life* magazine in 1958.

Clyde W. Taylor served as an officer of the National Association of Evangelicals and the Evangelical Foreign Missions Association for many years. A warm friend of the Division of Foreign Missions, he was often asked to speak at the annual School of Missions.

The National Association of Evangelicals emerged from the National Conference for United Action Among Evangelicals that met at the Hotel Coronado in St. Louis, Missouri, April 7–9, 1942. Among the delegates were representatives of the Assemblies of God (on the right, near the rear): Ernest S. Williams, J. Roswell Flower, Noel Perkin, Stanley H. Frodsham, Ralph Riggs, and Thomas F. Zimmerman.

2

Foundations for Recent Growth

The world missionary enterprise of the General Council of the Assemblies of God began on an unassuming scale in 1914 when independent Pentecostals gathered in Hot Springs, Arkansas, to organize their efforts and bring a semblance of order to the initiatives of the missionaries they supported. In their minds, the anticipated premillennial return of Christ mandated every possible effort to achieve the evangelization of the world in the shortest possible time. To accomplish this task, the Holy Spirit had empowered them through Spirit-baptism, an experience subsequent to conversion and evidenced initially by glossolalia, to proclaim the gospel.[1] Therefore the spiritual dynamics of the Apostolic Church, notably healings, exorcisms, and the manifestations of the gifts of the Spirit, would naturally follow.[2] Accordingly, when the last nation had heard the gospel (Matthew 24:14), Christ would return. Even though the Pentecostals shared a common millennial vision with other Christians at the time (as well as firm beliefs in the entire trustworthiness of the Bible and justification by faith), their restorationist claims received ridicule from many quarters. To some outsiders, such claims reflected a psychological aberration resulting in hysteria.[3] Few could have imagined the impact that the new movement would have on world Christianity.

Notwithstanding the predictions of doom, the Pentecostal movement in general and the Assemblies of God in particular grew, and has continued to expand abroad. Final statistics for Assemblies of God missions in 1988 cite 1,575 missionaries working in 120 countries, 329 theological training institutions educating 32,628 students, 94,706 national ministers and 13,364 layworkers serving national constituencies, conservatively estimated at 16,269,817, in 117,450 churches.[4] The total annual giving of the American Assemblies of God to missions reached the considerable sum of $82,834,346, representing one of the largest budgets among Protestant mission agencies.

Beginning inauspiciously, however, the mission program of the Assemblies of God struggled in the years after 1914 to support its administrative operation, distribute funds equitably, reorient many formerly independent missionaries to a cooperative effort, establish policies, promote the enterprise effectively, and articulate a Pentecostal missiology. On the foreign fields, many successful ventures in planting indigenous national churches were achieved by missionaries who tempered their millennial expectations with long-range planning. Nevertheless, missionaries often followed the paternalistic practices of other denominational representatives in controlling the younger churches.[5] American Pentecostal missionaries, like their Protestant and Catholic counterparts, added their own cultural baggage to the gospel message.

When World War II forced a large number of missionaries to return to the United States, the leadership of the denomination's Foreign Missions Department began to boldly plan for the postwar period. This signalled the beginning of strategic planning for the entire operation. With this turn of events, important foundations (some of long standing) made possible the remarkable growth that began in the 1960s. These included (1) the ardent Pentecostal belief that the apostolic signs and wonders of the Holy Spirit will follow the proclamation of the gospel, (2) the application of indigenous church principles will result in the planting of New Testament churches, (3) the training of national leaders must receive high priority, and (4) the popular support of the home churches must be nurtured and efficiently channeled.

Signs and Wonders

The prevailing mood among Assemblies of God church members was that God had raised them up specifically (along with other Pentecostals) to fulfill the Great Commission—thus, they were a people with a clear destiny.[6] To achieve this, the Holy Spirit had been recently "outpoured" to enable them to effectively witness for Christ. They took encouragement especially from the longer ending of the Gospel of Mark (16:17,18): "These signs shall follow them that believe; In my name shall they cast out devils; they shall speak with new tongues; they shall take up serpents; and if they drink any deadly thing, it shall not hurt them; they shall lay hands on the sick, and they shall recover."[7]

Men, women, boys, and girls could all receive the baptism in the Holy Spirit. Melvin L. Hodges, field secretary for Latin America and the West Indies, contended that this diminishing of the gap between clergy and laity was the key to restoring the New Testament church.[8] This important leveling factor has been basic to the advance of Pentecostalism. Reflecting on its development in Latin America, Alan Walker, an Australian Methodist visiting the region, observed that "the secret of the growth of Pentecostalism is its use of lay men and women. . . . [E]very Pentecostalist is an evangelist, and his church grows."[9]

With the combination of Spirit-baptism and the sense of Christ's imminent return, Assemblies of God missionaries have held tenaciously to the necessity of the "born-again" conversion to rescue the perishing, regardless of prior religious affiliation or the lack of it. In spite of the urgency to "pluck brands from the burning," Robert C. Cunningham, editor of the *Pentecostal Evangel*, the official voice of the organization, stated that "our missionary program cannot be built on a mere sympathy for the perishing souls of men. It must be founded on a deep love for the Lord of the harvest, and on a loyal obedience to His command, 'Go ye into all the world and preach the gospel to every creature.' "[10] Not surprisingly, leanings toward universalism among the missionary personnel have been rare.

With the heightened awareness of spiritual power came a dependency on the directives of the Holy Spirit to accomplish the task. Noel Perkin, director of Assemblies of God foreign missions for 32 years, maintained that effective endeavors must be undergirded with intense personal spirituality. Indeed, prayer is the key to successful power encounters with the forces of evil.[11] Such an atmosphere of spirituality generated courage to exorcise demons, pray for deliverances from chemical addictions, and believe God to heal the sick. As an example, Harmon A. Johnson, a missionary to Brazil with the Independent Assemblies of God, stated, "The emphasis on Christ's conquering power takes the Christian message out of the realm of the theoretical and addresses itself to the problems that are vexing Brazilians."[12] This vital willingness to challenge evil forces and expect divine interventions has been a noted ingredient of Pentecostal success.

A casual examination of Assemblies of God periodicals before 1960 (*Pentecostal Evangel, Missionary Challenge, World Challenge*) finds thousands of testimonies of healings and deliverances. In the 1950s and 1960s the overseas crusades conducted by American evangelists linked to the salvation/healing movement, which swept the United States, played an important role in church growth.[13] However, evangelistic efforts were by no means limited to visiting evangelists; in fact, missionaries, national ministers, and layworkers carried most of the burden. Kenneth Godbey, a missionary to Nigeria, recounted that extensive evangelism in the Obudu area resulted in many outstanding healings and observed that "it was like the Bible says it will be when we believe—signs and wonders followed the preaching of His Word."[14]

This restorationist perspective on evangelism has proven to be a significant component in the rapid advance of Pentecostalism, although it did not diminish the value of human planning. With planning, however, came increased administrative structures and policies. As a result, the "private vision" of some missionaries preferring to be led solely by the Spirit and the "global vision" of mission officials superintending a worldwide network of missionaries have at times required patient negotiations to resolve.

While missionaries prayed and believed God to demonstrate supernatural power in evangelistic endeavors, related theological issues sometimes did not receive the attention they deserved (e.g., the sovereignty of God and the role of signs and wonders in evangelism and local congregations). Keen observers sounded words of caution and challenged their readers to face the problems.[15]

Planting New Testament Churches

In embryo form the commitment to planting indigenous churches abroad can be traced to the third General Council, in 1915. The commitment of the delegates to evangelize the heathen by New Testament methods undoubtedly reflected their examination of the Book of Acts, containing what appeared to be independent congregations evangelizing their own vicinities under the direction of the Spirit. Assemblies of God leaders and missionaries were also affected by the writings of Roland Allen, William Owen Carver, John L. Nevius, and William Taylor (influences stemming in part from the former affiliation of some members with the Christian and Missionary Alliance [CMA]).

The articulation of a Pentecostal missiology, however, developed at a painfully slow pace. Two major reasons stood behind this: (1) Pentecostals focused on accomplishing their task, rather than interpreting it, and (2) the Bible institute training that missionary candidates increasingly received did not lend itself to missiological research and writing.

Apart from their own study of the New Testament, the most significant influence came from the pen of Roland Allen, whose book *Missionary Methods: St. Paul's or Ours?* (1912) had great appeal to them, even though he was an ardent sacramentarian.[16] Alice E. Luce, a former missionary to India with the Church Missionary Society, had been deeply influenced by this publication and authored several articles that appeared in the *Pentecostal Evangel* several months before the ninth General Council meeting in St. Louis, Missouri, in 1921.[17] These writings set the stage for the important missiological statement adopted by the Council, endorsing Pauline methods and the three essential characteristics of an indigenous church: self-support, self-propagation, and self-government.[18]

With the permanent appointment of Noel Perkin as missionary secretary in 1927, another exponent of indigenous church principles joined the growing ranks of those who strove to fulfill the ideals formulated in 1915 and 1921. Perkin's counsel in the mid-1930s to beginning missionary Melvin L. Hodges to study the writings of Allen reaped enormous dividends in the publication of Hodges' *Indigenous Church* in 1953, his administrative oversight for Latin America, and subsequent books and articles.

These contributions, demonstrating Hodges' considerable field experience, reflection, and familiarity with Allen, began to appear at one of the most critical moments in the history of the enterprise. The activities of salvation/healing evangelists from America included the tendency of some of them to set up networks of direct financial support for national pastors and evangelists (e.g., T. L. Osborn's Association for Native Evangelism). Although this approach appealed to many on the home front, Hodges, Perkin, J. Philip Hogan, secretary for promotions (1954–1959), and others recognized that such a return to paternalism actually represented a major step backward in the development of national church organizations.[19] The determination of the leadership and many missionaries to maintain their course afforded vital assistance to the younger churches when the sudden demise of the colonial empires ushered in the independence of scores of new nations.

The indigenous church, however, was not the ultimate goal in the minds of its advocates. Rather, it was the founding of New Testament churches in every land; only through them could the evangelization of the world be achieved. In the words of Melvin Hodges, "We follow these principles not because they are indigenous, but because they are Biblical."[20] The awareness about the nature of a truly indigenous and "New Testament" church—with its far-reaching, and to some, threatening implications—came gradually and not without dissent (some paid only lip service to the ideal). To Morris Williams, a missionary to Malawi, indigenous church principles disallowed racism in any form. He wrote in 1957 that

> self-supporting, self-administrating and self-propagating is the right way . . . the indigenous way . . . but let's not put a nationalistic or racial interpretation on the word "self." That "self" should refer to the combined members of the local church regardless of color or nationality. When this is done it becomes, not "your" church, but "our" church . . . no matter who is talking! Let us teach the national how to run and support God's work without mentioning nationality . . . thereby upholding the Bible principle of "oneness" in Christ, the middle wall of partition between us having been broken down and the enmity abolished! Nationalistic feeling must not get into the church.[21]

In the 1950s, Assemblies of God missionaries increasingly clarified their missiology, rejoiced in the fruit from the seed of pioneer indigenous efforts, and resolved to pursue their objectives with all haste.

Training National Leaders

For many of the earliest Pentecostals, formal theological training smacked of arid intellectualism and was to be avoided at all costs since it would inevitably stifle the Spirit-filled life. As the Pentecostal movement grew and was racked by theological issues and practical problems, Bible institutes came into existence to provide needed instruction for future clergy and laity. In some cases those who had received training at, or were impressed with, such institutions (e.g., the Missionary Training Institute at Nyack, New York) founded similar ones. At the inaugural meeting of the Assemblies of God, its leaders called for the establishment of a Bible training school. Graduates of Nyack and former members of the CMA played a particularly important role in the development of Assemblies of God Bible institutes such as the Bethel Bible Training School, Newark, New Jersey (1916; independent, but A/G—related); Central Bible Institute, Springfield, Missouri (1922; College after 1965); Glad Tidings Bible Institute, San Francisco, California (1919; later, Bethany Bible College); and Southern California Bible School, Los Angeles, California (1920; later, Southern California College).[22] All of these institutions produced an impressive number of missionaries.

This interest in Bible institute education, paralleling the growing number of similar evangelical and fundamentalist schools in the United States, naturally carried over to the mission field, and schools were begun there for the same reasons: provision of an intense biblical education, a dynamic spiritual atmosphere through daily chapel services and prayer meetings, a practical experience in evangelism while enrolled, and a speedy entry into the ministry. Furthermore, it is historically accurate to say that the development of overseas training has closely mirrored the ministerial training programs offered stateside by the parent body.

As Bible institutes began to flourish in the Assemblies of God in the 1920s and 1930s, missionaries (often graduates of these schools) began to establish them abroad. Perhaps the earliest attempt to found a foreign training school was a Bible institute operating in North China by 1922. The longest-standing overseas school, however, is the Bethel Bible Institute in Mavelikara, India, founded by John H. Burgess in 1927. Arthur E. Wilson, a visionary pioneer to Upper Volta (now Burkina Faso), reported that "a trained native ministry is the cheapest, the most effective, the quickest, and the only way to thoroughly evangelize any field."[23] Later, he observed that "from the beginning, our native evangelists have been supported by native funds, the tithes and offerings in both money and farm produce given by Christians."[24] The rewards of training and teaching self-support readily paid off in some fields.

Assemblies of God Bible institutes welcomed students regardless of their social standing (although they were usually from the lower classes) and offered various levels of training, pragmatically based on their previous educational background. In some schools, prospective pastors and evangelists had to be taught to read. Other schools hoped for an elementary or high school education in the applicants. The operation of the schools varied widely, some holding classes for 4, 6, or 8 months a year.

Since the missionaries usually had severely limited budgets, the schools often began in primitive facilities. Missionaries and students often constructed or renovated facilities with their own hands, making bunkbeds, tables, chairs, and other necessary items. Success depended on adaptability. When a hurricane destroyed the buildings at the Instituto Biblico Pentecostal in Manacas, Cuba, classes and chapel services were held in a "rabbit house," which had been hurriedly cleaned. Field Secretary Henry C. Ball noted that "the Bible institute in Cuba has a record for working under handicaps. Commodious quarters for teachers and students have been nonexistent from the very beginning."[25]

With approximately 85 percent of the graduates entering the ministry, the value of Bible training schools had become so apparent by 1959 that one missionary called their usage "The Crowning Missionary Method."[26] Perkin's successor, J. Philip Hogan called it "the greatest contribution to a national ministry. . . . These Bible schools are the heart of modern missions."[27]

By the 1950s the founding of overseas Bible institutes was accelerating rapidly. At the end of the decade, the Assemblies of God operated 61 such schools, half having been started in that 10-year period. Associations were formed to coordinate programs, study minimum requirements, standardize curriculums, and to study other needs.[28] In addition, half of the missionary personnel and budget of the Foreign Missions Department was committed to theological education. In two-thirds of the schools, national ministers constituted majorities or shared equally with the missionaries on the boards of directors.[29]

Not until a member of the Southern Baptist Convention informed the department did the leadership know that it led all other Protestant agencies in sponsoring theological training institutions abroad. By 1959, the facilities in many of these schools were cramped and potential students were being turned away. Missionary Louise Jeter Walker (Latin America) reported that for every graduate of the school where she taught, there were two begging to enroll.[30] Urgent appeals were made to American supporters to contribute funds for expansion. With the introduction in 1959 of the Global Conquest promotional campaign (an accelerated emphasis on literature production, national workers training, and evangelism), the Assemblies of God added greater momentum to a proven method.

Popular Support

Throughout the course of Assemblies of God history, its missionary endeavor has carried a triumphalist strain.[31] The Global Conquest theme accurately reflected the long-standing purpose of the organization: fulfillment of the Great Commission before the return of Christ. Visiting missionaries, pastors, evangelists, and district and national officers heralded the need for world evangelism and emphasized that it could not be accomplished without prayer, financial sacrifice, and for some, the willingness to follow the call of God for service abroad. Not surprisingly, this revivalistic atmosphere has fed a stream of new recruits throughout its history.

Official advertisement of the mission enterprise first appeared in the organization's weekly and monthly publications: the *Christian Evangel* (after 1919, the *Pentecostal Evangel*) and the *Word and Witness*. Letters from missionaries were published along with articles that highlighted their efforts.

Since early missionaries frequently had closer ties to supporting congregations than the department, they corresponded with members of these churches, advising them of their needs and successes. As time passed, the promotion of the work extended beyond letters and articles in church publications to books and booklets, sometimes privately published. Missionaries were also encouraged to visit their supporting churches when home on furlough in order to hold "missions conventions." By the 1950s the itineration of missionaries in local churches across the United States between terms of service overseas had become a normal mode of promoting missions. Whatever criticisms may be leveled about the "wear and tear" of such activity on the missionaries and their families, it has doubtlessly been one of the most effective means of generating grass-roots enthusiasm and support that could have been devised.

The Foreign Missions Department began its own magazine, the *Missionary Challenge,* in 1944. Five years later, the Promotions Division was started to handle the publishing needs, and eventually it established closer cooperation with the church's districts. Regional missions conventions were also planned. Representatives of the Division crisscrossed the country, raising mission awareness in local churches through preaching and showing films about missionary activities. Pastors and congregations were also told that giving to missions was a key to local church growth.[32]

Even before the creation of the Promotions Division, the supporting constituents had begun to harness their mutual efforts in supporting missionaries. The Women's Missionary Council (Women's Ministries Department after 1975) began in 1925 through the initiative of Etta Calhoun, a member of a congregation in Houston, Texas. This agency provided valuable, practical assistance to missionaries in the way of food and clothing for orphans, bandages for lepers, as well as assistance for various relief projects.[33] Ralph W. Harris, national secretary of the denomination's youth department, launched Speed-the-Light, a fund-raising plan to assist missionary transportation (bicycles, cars, jeeps, airplanes, motorboats, etc.), in 1944. Within fifteen years, the youth of the Assemblies of God had raised over $3 million for such vehicles.[34] Boys and Girls Missionary Crusade was introduced at the National Sunday School Convention in 1949 to offer children the opportunity to give as well; within 10 years, nearly $100,000 had been donated to provide gospel literature for overseas evangelism.[35] Enthusiastic support at every age level for overseas missions became a hallmark of Assemblies of God congregations.

Through his books, *Missionary Methods: St. Paul's or Ours?* and *The Spontaneous Expansion of the Church,* Anglican missiologist Roland Allen unexpectedly exerted a profound influence on the course of Assemblies of God foreign missions.

Church members at Bethel Temple Assembly of God, Fort Worth, Texas, contribute to World Evangelism Day offering in 1953

Students leaving a chapel service at Cuban Bible Institute (ca. 1953)

Kiyoma Yumiyama served as general superintendent of the Assemblies of God in Japan for many years. This picture was taken in 1961.

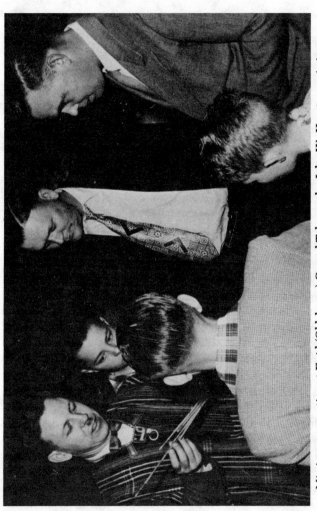

Missions convention at Enid (Oklahoma) Gospel Tabernacle. John W. Hurston, missionary to Liberia, explains native-made arrows to interested observers at the African display.

3

The Transition Team

The 1959 General Council of the Assemblies of God, held in San Antonio, Texas, proved to be a watershed in the history of the organization. The departure of Ralph M. Riggs as general superintendent and the retirements of J. Roswell Flower and Noel Perkin signalled an important change in leadership. The elections of Thomas F. Zimmerman as general superintendent and J. Philip Hogan as executive director of foreign missions (as well as assistant general superintendent, a title also held by four other executives at the time) demonstrated that a new generation of leaders had moved to the helm to pilot the denomination.

Within a few months of taking office, Hogan began to make major changes in the office staff of the Foreign Missions Department. His new appointments of Wesley R. Hurst, Harold Mintle, Raymond T. Brock, and Charles E. Greenaway were balanced by the continuing leadership of the field secretaries from the Perkin administration: Maynard L. Ketcham (Far East), Everett L. Phillips (Africa), and Melvin L. Hodges (Latin America and the West Indies). Victor G. Greisen, a former district superintendent and missionary, became the first new field secretary in the Hogan administration. The revamped office of foreign missions secretary went to Robert T. McGlasson, a veteran administrator of the department's New York City office. Noel Perkin himself continued to serve: as consultant and dean of the School of Missionary Orientation (later renamed School of Missions). Gladys Newbill, a longtime employee of headquarters, became financial secretary. Thus members of the transition team reflected considerable experience and stability as well as promising energetic and aggressive promotion of the enterprise. The crucial roles they played at this juncture of Assemblies of God mission history warrants an examination of their backgrounds.

Executive Director of Foreign Missions

The election of J. Philip Hogan to the top post of the Foreign Missions Department constituted one of the most significant events at the San Antonio General Council. Coming from the third echelon of departmental leadership and being a relatively youthful 43, his selection may have surprised some, but closer analysis reveals that he was the natural choice to follow Noel Perkin.

James Philip Hogan was born on a ranch near Olathe, Colorado, in December 1915. The Morton sisters (Bessie Bell and Eva Edith), traveling evangelists from Florence, Colorado, brought the Pentecostal message to that part of the state around 1920. A short time later, the ministry of other evangelists led to the establishment of a body of believers, services initially being conducted in the homes of members (including that of the Hogans). In this atmosphere of revival in 1922, Hogan, though not quite 7, surrendered his life to Christ and about 2 years later received the baptism in the Holy Spirit.[1]

His parents, recognizing the call of God on both of their sons, Phil as well as Gene, moved to Springfield, Missouri, in 1933 to enable them to enter Central Bible Institute (CBI) to prepare for the ministry. In addition to his studies, Phil became heavily involved in practical ministry, pastoring the Assemblies of God church in the nearby town of Republic. While at CBI, he also met and became engaged to Mary Virginia Lewis, the daughter of Gayle and Mary Lewis (at that time Gayle Lewis served as superintendent of the Central District[2]). After graduation in 1936, Hogan traveled for a year as an evangelist. Upon Virginia's graduation the following year, they were married in Youngstown, Ohio, on December 28, 1937. Itinerant ministry continued, and for a brief period the Hogans evangelized in several states. He received ordination from the Central District in 1938.

A more permanent ministry developed when Bert Webb, pastor of Springfield's Central Assembly of God, invited them to pastor a new local church that Central was mothering, Eastside Assembly. Other pastorates followed in Painesville, Ohio, and River Rouge (near Detroit), Michigan. These early years of ministry reflected the energy of his personality. Never content with the status quo, Hogan constantly looked for more effective means to expand the work of God. When they moved to River Rouge, the church was located on a dead-end street, housed in the basement of a proposed building, and close to the river. Recognizing that growth would be severely limited because of the church's location and facilities, Hogan gradually won the confidence of the congregation and suggested they move to a better site. By the end of his 3-year pastorate, the church had prepared to purchase property and erect a new building in Lincoln Park (later called Bethel Assembly of God).

The Detroit pastorate proved to be a turning point in their lives. During a missions convention at the church in 1944, two missionaries, Leonard Bolton[3] (China) and Willis G. Long (North India), were the featured speakers. After Bolton preached, a woman in the congregation gave Virginia an opportunity to pray at the altar by taking her baby, Phyllis Lynn, to the church nursery (a son, Richard, had been born to them in 1938; he died in an automobile accident in 1956). While praying, she heard the Lord say to her, "This [China] is the place." She responded somewhat hesitantly, hoping that her husband would hear the same call. On the way home in the car, Hogan talked to Bolton, who was staying in their home, about China, indicating that he too had been stirred about missionary service.

In the following months, Hogan avidly read every book on China that he could find in the Detroit public libraries, including books by Edgar Snow and Madame Chiang Kai-shek. He was also fascinated with biographies of missionary heroes such as J. Hudson Taylor, C. T. Studd, and John G. Paton.[4] For a time he also ministered on Sunday afternoons in a Chinese mission in downtown Detroit.

At Christmastime (1945), the Hogan family journeyed to Springfield to visit his parents and to consult with Noel Perkin. After meeting with him for less than 30 minutes, they were tentatively appointed to China. Howard C. Osgood, the recently appointed field secretary for China, was also on hand to endorse the need for them on his field. After returning home, the Hogans soon resigned from their church and enrolled at the Chinese Language Institute at the University of California at Berkeley. There, with other prospective missionaries (e.g., the Garland Benintendis) and military officers, the Hogans studied Mandarin and Chinese culture. Although they had raised some support by itinerating in churches, they also depended on the standard missionary allowance of $150 per month from the Foreign Missions Department.

Notice of their formal appointment finally arrived on December 15, 1946, and in February 1947 they sailed to the Far East aboard the *Marine Lynx* (a troop ship); their final destination was the coastal city of Ningpo, China. The Pentecostal work there had been pioneered by Nettie Danks Nichols (1875–1940). Nichols had been trained at A. B. Simpson's Missionary Training Institute at Nyack, New York, and she opened the Bethel Mission in Ningpo in 1912. In her later years, she turned over the pastorate to a national minister, Joshua Bang, who also assisted her in administration. When she died, the work included a church, 10 outstations, a Bible institute, and an orphanage.[5] However, in the years immediately following her death, the mission began to suffer from a lack of effective leadership.

The arrival of the Hogans in March 1947 was designed to bring about changes at the Bethel Mission and Bible Institute. They received a tumultuous welcome (which included firecrackers as well as city officials). Problems at the mission stemming from prior dependence on American financial assistance and failure to firmly follow indigenous church principles soon became apparent.[6] Added to these difficulties was the encroaching presence of communism. Consequently, ministry in Ningpo proved to be disillusioning and short-lived. Nevertheless, the Hogans supervised the construction of a new church building, taught in the Bible institute, and engaged in evangelistic ministry in the region.

One event in particular made a lasting impression about the meaning of commitment. Since the area of Ningpo had been heavily overrun by communists, the Nationalist Chinese authorities, prior to their defeat on the mainland and hasty departure to Taiwan, summarily executed many Chinese youths who were known sympathizers. Observing the executions, Hogan later recounted, "I saw them stacked up like cordwood beside the road. I saw their bodies strewn across the green rice fields. As I stood over them, moved with great emotion, I said to myself, What is the strange god of these young people that will cause them to make this kind of sacrifice? It is going to cost us something to preach Jesus around the world in this hour."[7] In Hogan's later writing and preaching ministry, the need for the church's total commitment to the Great Commission constantly surfaces.

After 18 months, the Hogans retired to the missionary rest home in Shanghai, where they enjoyed the company of the Howard Osgoods and the Garland Benintendis. Hearing of believers in Taiwan and the opportunity to begin a Pentecostal work, the Hogans and Benintendis embarked in mid-1948 for ministry there. A physical problem required Virginia to return to Shanghai for surgery at the China Inland Mission Hospital; meanwhile, the political and military situation worsened on the mainland and required the evacuation of foreigners. Her perilous return to Taiwan is a remarkable account of suffering and faith.[8]

Protestant missions on Taiwan had originally been sponsored by English and Canadian Presbyterians. Dr. James and Lillian Dickson, distinguished American Presbyterian missionaries working in Taipei, gladly helped the two families get settled and locate interpreters.[9] Through street preaching and tract distribution, a small nucleus of believers emerged. However, the threat of an imminent communist invasion disrupted the new venture. After prayer, Phil and Virginia Hogan agreed that she and their two children would accompany the Benintendi family home to the States in November 1949. Virginia and the children returned to Springfield, where her mother and father (now an assistant general superintendent) resided. She and the children made their home in Mission Village.

Hoping for 6 more months on the island, Phil Hogan stayed behind to shepherd the new body of believers. During these few months he ministered in the little chapel the church used, trained the secretary of the YMCA to carry on the work after his departure, baptized about 15 believers, and witnessed firsthand some of the political upheavals on Taiwan.

The efforts of the Hogans and Benintendis represented the first Pentecostal, evangelistic efforts on the island. When the Benintendis later returned to Taiwan, they discovered that the church and its pastor had persevered in their faith.

Six months after Virginia had left, Phil finally arrived in Springfield and was reunited with his family; he visited the office of the Foreign Missions Department only to learn that meetings had been arranged for him for the next 6 months—beginning the following Sunday.

After a year of itinerant ministry on behalf of missions, the strain of this new schedule, following the previous 6 months of separation, took a heavy toll on the family. In June 1951, the Hogans accepted the pastorate of Bethel Temple Assembly of God in Florence, South Carolina. While there he supervised the building of a new church edifice, but exhibited a certain restlessness, taking advantage of every opportunity to preach at missions conventions in other churches.

After meeting with Noel Perkin in Atlanta at a convention, Hogan accepted an invitation to return to Springfield to serve as a field representative for the Promotions Division beginning in 1952, later becoming the secretary (head) of the Division (1954–1959). Hogan recognized that many churches in the Assemblies of God failed to support the program and that missions conventions were often sponsored only by larger congregations. Clearly, the need for missions education in the churches was acute. During these years, Hogan and his associates traveled widely across the country promoting Assemblies of God missions in local churches, district gatherings, regional missions conventions, and General Council meetings. Whether through showing missionary films, writing his influential "Call to Action" column in the *Pentecostal Evangel,* or his preaching ministry, he attempted to correct the imbalance and energetically stressed the imperative of world evangelization for all. In addition, he helped formulate the Global Conquest strategy that caught the imagination of the General Council membership in 1959.[10]

After the announced retirement of Noel Perkin, the General Presbytery recommended three names to the General Council for the office of executive director of foreign missions: Emil A. Balliet, an administrative assistant to Perkin having a respected pastoral background; Melvin L. Hodges, field secretary for Latin America and the West Indies and author on indigenous church principles; and not surprisingly, J. Philip Hogan.

Apparently many of the missionaries attending the Council wanted a leader who had been a missionary and would aggressively promote world missions and protect the department from any influence that might try to compromise its objectives and prominence. However, Balliet had never been a missionary and Hodges' demeanor may have been too quiet and gentle. After Hogan's election, Balliet returned to pastoring and later served with distinction as president of Southern California College, Costa Mesa, California (1970–1975).[11] Hodges continued his work as field secretary and missiologist.

Although Hogan's election as executive director of Assemblies of God missions came as somewhat of a surprise to him, he willingly accepted the new challenge.[12] Having been a pastor, evangelist, and missionary, as well as an enthusiastic promoter of world evangelization, he brought important leadership gifts to the enterprise at a pivotal time in its history.

Foreign Missions Secretary

The 1959 General Council also took steps to bring the organization of the Foreign Missions Department more into line with other departments at the headquarters. The title for the department head (foreign missions secretary) was changed to executive director of foreign missions, and a new position was created to assist him with the administration of the department. The Council authorized that the title of the person in the new position would be the old title of foreign missions secretary.[13]

To fill this new position, Hogan recommended Robert T. McGlasson to the Executive Presbytery. McGlasson, a 1932 graduate of CBI, and his wife, Thelma, had pastored churches in Pennsylvania, New York, and New Jersey. He was elected secretary-treasurer of the New York-New Jersey District in 1944; at the same time, Noel Perkin approached him about setting up and directing the new Eastern Office of the Foreign Missions Department. Given the title eastern secretary, McGlasson opened the office in 1945; at the end of the year, he resigned his district position to devote his efforts full-time to missions.

The responsibilities of the eastern secretary were extensive because New York City was the embarkation point for most missionaries heading overseas. McGlasson and his assistant, Stephen Walegir,[14] helped with securing visas; purchasing equipment for missionaries; packing and shipping; transportation arrangements; meeting missionaries arriving by air, ship, and train; maintaining the missionary rest home in the Bronx; and representing the department to the Foreign Missions Conference of North America, the Church World Service, the State Department Advisory Committee on Voluntary Foreign Aid, and the American Council of

Voluntary Agencies for Foreign Service. They also assisted Gustav Kinderman (field secretary for Europe [1946–1954], secretary for relief and rehabilitation [1951–1962]) with European relief efforts. Refugee settlement also required their attention, for the Assemblies of God sponsored U.S. settlement of approximately 7,000 refugees from Europe as well as White Russian refugees from China (via Hong Kong and the Philippines).[15]

Soon after Hogan's election as executive director, he tapped the knowledgeable and experienced eastern secretary for the redefined post of foreign missions secretary. In this capacity, McGlasson assisted with the administration of the department, now consisting of 56 employees: stenographers, secretaries, file clerks, statisticians, bookkeepers, and related assistants.[16]

Field Secretaries

Next to the executive director, the field secretaries held the weightiest responsibilities within the department. Their work included promotion of missions in the U.S., administrative oversight of missionaries scattered over vast regions overseas, and the maintenance of cordial relationships with fraternal church organizations. Such activities required extensive travel and included representing the department before officials of foreign governments. In 1960 four field secretaries served the following global regions: Africa; the Far East; Latin America and the West Indies; and Europe, the Middle East, and Southern Asia.

Although Hogan became the new executive director, the previously appointed field secretaries remained in place. At the time, the man having the longest tenure was Maynard L. Ketcham. A graduate of Beulah Heights Bible and Missionary Training Institute and Taylor University, Ketcham and his wife, Gladys, were the first Assemblies of God missionaries to the Bengali-speaking area of Eastern India, including Calcutta. After their arrival in 1926, they worked to implement indigenous church principles in the development of a national church organization. In 1951 he was appointed field secretary for Southern Asia and reassigned to the Far East region in 1955.[17]

Melvin L. Hodges had served as field secretary for Latin America and the West Indies since 1954. With his wife, Lois, he went to

Central America in 1936. While there, he worked for a time with Ralph D. Williams in church planting, Bible institute teaching, and building strong national church organizations.[18] His first book, *The Indigenous Church* (1953), contained valuable instruction for the development of New Testament churches based on indigenous church principles.[19] Hogan referred to him as "the department expert on the building of the indigenous church overseas."[20]

Field secretary for Africa was Everett L. Phillips. The departure of the Phillipses for Africa as missionaries in 1940 came in response to a letter from some Nigerians who were baptized in the Holy Spirit after reading the *Pentecostal Evangel*. While there the Phillipses opened a Bible school and assisted in the founding of 120 churches; Everett also served as superintendent of the Nigerian Assemblies of God. In 1954 he became field secretary for Africa.[21]

Victor G. Greisen had served as superintendent of the Kansas district of the Assemblies of God (1938–1955) and missionary to his native land of Denmark before accepting the invitation to become field secretary for Europe, the Middle East, and Southern Asia in 1960. While in Denmark he had taught at the Bible school in Mariager and with his wife, Esther, visited other parts of Europe in ministry.[22]

Promotions and Finance

The biggest changes in personnel came in the Promotions Division. Wesley R. Hurst (1922–1987) succeeded Hogan as secretary of promotions. Wesley and June Hurst had been missionaries to Tanganyika (later Tanzania) since 1953 when he accepted this new assignment. His responsibilities included missions conventions, itineraries for furloughed missionaries, public relations, and statistics. Besides having been a pastor, evangelist, and one-time district youth leader, Hurst also brought valuable missionary experience to this strategic post.[23]

Serving under Hurst were Harold Mintle, Raymond T. Brock, and Charles E. Greenaway. Mintle had served with the Nebraska District before moving to Springfield to work in publications. His responsibilities included promoting the new *Global Conquest* magazine.[24]

Having been a missionary to Nigeria for a short time (1953–1955),

Raymond T. Brock brought missionary experience as well as academic expertise (M.A., University of Tulsa) to the job of editor in chief. His task included editing *Global Conquest* and the *Missionary Forum,* supplying articles on foreign missions to the *Pentecostal Evangel,* and overseeing the publication of other types of literature.[25]

Charles E. Greenaway had been a church planter in Togo-Dahomey (later Togo, and Benin), Upper Volta (later Burkina Faso), and Senegal. Over the years he became widely known throughout the Assemblies of God for his preaching and missions promotion. Accepting an extended furlough from his duties in Africa, he became a traveling representative for the Global Conquest initiative.[26]

By 1960 the Foreign Missions Department was responsible for the distribution of millions of dollars each year. In one respect it was a large banking operation with hundreds of accounts. Gladys Newbill, a bookkeeper with 10 years in the department, was assigned the office of financial secretary.

The Missionary Personnel

While the leadership of the department reflected a changing of the guard, the same was also true of the overseas missionary force, now numbering more than 800. A growing list of first generation missionaries had passed off the scene by 1960; a new generation had come to the forefront. These missionaries also carried the pioneering spirit, but in contrast to some of their predecessors, most had received Bible institute education, recognized the value of teamwork abroad, and were more committed to the implementation of indigenous church principles. They also had the advantage of specialized missiological training through the introduction of the School of Missionary Orientation, enriched by the growing volume of articles and books from the pen of Melvin Hodges. Great strides had also been made in expediting their transportation on the mission fields and providing Christian literature for their ministries. In addition, growing attention was being given to the general welfare of the missionaries and the quality of their family life.

Conclusion

Pentecostal mission agencies by midcentury reflected an emerging maturity, evidenced by the growing stability of their missionary personnel, continuing support from the home constituencies, and increasing contacts with evangelical and other Pentecostal leaders. Having the largest and most successful Pentecostal missions program, the Assemblies of God began to receive the attention of other mission agencies and missions scholars.

The commitment of the Assemblies of God to world evangelization never flagged in the years after 1914, but issued in prayer, sacrificial giving, creative methods for assisting the endeavor, and the willingness of some to devote their lives in service overseas to the gospel. Publications and promotional work served to enhance the enthusiasm that revivalism encouraged. The ideal of establishing New Testament churches through the implementation of indigenous church principles remained a guiding principle of development. With these foundations securely in place, unprecedented growth soon followed.

The year 1960 ushered in a new era in Assemblies of God missions. Young leaders, exemplified by J. Philip Hogan, arose to direct the burgeoning mission enterprise. Associates of Hogan brought valuable experience to their posts and exhibited determination to mobilize the entire American constituency to the cause of world evangelization. Significantly, the timing of their appointments coincided with important changes taking place in the ranks of the missionary personnel.

The

Fields

Are

White

The

Laborers

Few

Here

Am

I

Send

Me

REV. & MRS. J. PHILIP HOGAN
PHYLLIS LYNNE - RICHARD

Address:
Foreign Missions Dept.
336 W. Pacific
Springfield, Missouri

Prayer reminder for the J. Philip Hogan family, appointed missionaries to China, 1946

J. Philip and Virginia Hogan (left) with students at the Bethel Bible School, Ningpo, China, 1947

Robert T. McGlasson served as foreign missions secretary from 1959–1977. This picture was taken at the Atlanta Regional Missions Convention in 1967.

Maynard L. Ketcham, longtime missionary to India, served as field secretary for the Far East from 1955 to 1970.

Kansas District Superintendent Victor G. Greisen later served as field secretary for Europe, the Middle East, and Southern Asia, 1959–1963.

Everett L. Phillips, field secretary for Africa (1954–1970), preaching the dedicatory sermon at Calvary Temple, Arusha, Tanzania. His interpreter is at left.

Part Two

Global Conquest
(1959–1967)

4

Unprecedented Promotion and Progress

On August 30, 1959, at the General Council meeting in San Antonio, Texas, the Assemblies of God launched Global Conquest to advance worldwide evangelization. This three-pronged program, calling for increased literature production, national workers training, and evangelism, represented the most ambitious promotional campaign that the denomination (or any other Pentecostal organization) had ever attempted. The symbol of the initiative used in publications pictured the world overlaid with the shadow of a cross; circling the world was a rocket bearing the inscription Global Conquest; a caption read, "A 'Crash' Program for World Evangelism." In vivid terms and symbols the program challenged Assemblies of God church members to put forth every effort to fulfill the Great Commission (Matthew 28:16–20) before the return of Christ, a theme easily traced to the beginnings of the Pentecostal movement. An examination of Global Conquest, therefore, is essential for understanding the development of Assemblies of God missions in the early 1960s.

The Promotional Theme

The unprecedented promotional effort of Global Conquest sought to utilize every possible means to present the challenge of missions, whether through the printed page, the classroom, or the pulpit. The members of the General Council, believing that world evangelization was their destiny and being encouraged by successful reports from overseas, responded enthusiastically to the call.

Missions education in the local churches now became a top priority of the Foreign Missions Department, giving publications additional emphasis. A special missions education study committee coordinated the endeavor. John Garlock, a former missionary to Africa and newly-appointed foreign missions editor (succceeding Raymond T. Brock in 1963) listed three objectives that guided their efforts:

1. To *help* the local church understand the purpose and current expression of Assemblies of God foreign missions

2. To *inspire* individual dedication that leads to complete stewardship as it relates to foreign missions

3. To *illustrate* these purposes by: (a) Reporting the activities of our missionaries and national workers in their indigenous church ministries. (b) Describing their activities in relation to the lands, peoples, cultures, and religions of our foreign mission fields.[1]

Thus missions education—having the goal that local congregations would be able to understand, and identify themselves with, the work of world evangelization—took on the dual role of informing as well as inspiring.

Beginning in 1959, the monthly *Global Conquest* magazine advertised the new program to the denomination. Beginning with 225,000 copies a month, in 2 years the magazine's circulation had increased by 100,000. Another monthly publication of the department, *Call to Action,* contained the addresses and pictures of missionaries celebrating birthdays current for the month of the periodical's issue. Fourteen thousand free copies of each issue were distributed in 1961. The department also produced scores of pamphlets, describing the work of the missionaries on various fields.

To emphasize the rich heritage of the enterprise, a series of missionary biographies entitled *Heroes of the Conquest* were printed, beginning in 1960. Twenty biographies were eventually printed and distributed in booklet form. The biographies recounted the experiences of, among others, Blanche Appleby (South China), Leonard Bolton (Southwest China), Beulah Buchwalter (Ghana), Frank Isensee (Peru), Carl Juergensen (Japan), Fred Merian (India), Oren Munger (Nicaragua), Joseph Nilson (Congo), and Florence Steidel (Liberia). Executive Director J. Philip Hogan remarked, "While we honor these pioneers, we also rejoice that God is sending more and more volunteers—young people who, we believe with all our hearts, will prove themselves to be as dedicated and self-sacrificing as their predecessors."[2]

Additional promotional literature included special offering envelopes, missionary posters, and church bulletin covers.[3] The Foreign Missions Department also continued to publish *Key,* a quarterly bulletin for district missionary secretaries that kept them up-to-date on finances, policies, and personnel.

Other publications played important parts as well: The *Pentecostal Evangel* continued its long tradition of supporting overseas missions through news accounts and feature stories; the Sunday School Department promoted missions through the Boys and Girls Missionary Crusade (BGMC); and missionary stories appeared in the *Word of Life* Sunday school curriculum produced by the Church School Literature Division of Gospel Publishing House. In addition, overseas missions were highlighted in *WMC Slant* and *Missionette Memos,* published by the Women's Missionary Council; youth leaders received information through the *C.A. Guide;* and missionary challenge and inspiration in the tract format enabled a general distribution.

To expedite the development of missions education materials, the department appointed Gwen Jones, former editor of the *Sunday School Counselor,* to the staff as missions education editor in 1963 to assist John Garlock.[4] In this capacity she replaced Marian Craig. They were later succeeded in 1965 by David A. Womack as foreign missions editor and Rex Jackson as missions education editor.[5]

Under the leadership of Garlock and Jones, the Promotions Division, in cooperation with Gospel Publishing House, sponsored two important projects related to classroom instruction. First, Noel Perkin and John Garlock co-authored *Our World Witness* (1963), a survey of Assemblies of God foreign missions. This 118-page book, accompanied by an instructor's guide by missionaries George and Billie Davis, served as the 1964 textbook for the Workers Training Program for Assemblies of God Sunday schools, offering the first opportunity for congregations across the nation to study foreign missions together.[6] In 10 chapters the authors discussed the biblical basis of missions, the history of missions, ministries and goals of Assemblies of God missions, methods of teaching missions, and the partnership of believers and local churches with world missions.

The second project was a study series of six books entitled *What*

Is a Missionary?, graded for children, youth, and adults. Gwen Jones edited the three student texts as well as the teacher supplements.[7] They were designed to give "a personal dimension rather than a geographic or statistical approach" to missions and to be used by laypeople and ministers in local congregations.[8] The annual missions convention at Central Bible College, Springfield, Missouri, presented the first opportunity to use the adult textbook, and John Garlock commented that "the eager enthusiasm and the spirit of learning with which the course was received were a great encouragement to those . . . who . . . spent months in its preparation."[9]

The department also produced missionary films through its audiovisual service. Available rentals included filmstrips, slides, and 16 mm sound films. By 1963 the agency offered 28 films that it produced, as well as recommended films from nondenominational sources.[10]

The distribution of magazines and textbooks, as well as the production of films and slides, were complemented by the planning of missions conventions, featuring furloughed missionaries and Global Conquest representatives. Norman Correll, who succeeded Charles E. Greenaway in 1962 as Global Conquest representative, gave advice in the *Missionary Forum* to missionaries on how to hold successful conventions. He placed considerable responsibility for success on the attitude of the missionary. In reference to the missionary's sermons, he suggested telling them "about your country (not a dry travelogue) and about your missionary ministries. Spice your report generously with personal experiences, sweeten it with humorous happenings, and above all strongly emphasize the spiritual results." In addition, the missionary should keep his message within the time limit because "many a speaker has hung himself in the noose of 'long windedness.' "[11] Upon request, the department also made available to churches a missions convention packet, furnishing guidelines for planning and information about available resources, including flags of various foreign countries.

Occasionally, the successful accounts of such conventions were printed in the *Pentecostal Evangel* or *Key*. One story highlighted a united convention sponsored in 1961 by 11 churches in the Oakland Bay area of California. One participating church, First Assembly of God in Vallejo, built decorated display booths to represent areas of missionary outreach such as literature, communications, and Bible schools. The missionaries brought souvenirs for display from the countries where they served. Home missionary outreach among the American Indians also received recognition. Each church held nightly services for a little more than a week, featuring a different missionary each night. This afforded the smaller churches the opportunity to enjoy the benefits of a full-fledged convention. A closing rally, including a parade of missionaries in national costume and special music by the Russian Radio Choir from San Francisco, was held at the Full Gospel Temple in Richmond. After a sermon by Charles Greenaway, a total of $1,000 was pledged for the missionaries; the cash offerings from all the churches totaled more than $4,000.[12]

The Foreign Missions Department also encouraged the implementation of the Faith Promise Plan in missions conventions to foster regular support for overseas evangelism. A faith promise was defined as a commitment to God, thus requiring no monthly statement from the church citing the unpaid balance. Donors were encouraged to put their faith in the Lord and trust in his provision to complete the pledge.[13] Churches were also assured that God would bless any congregation that gave to overseas missions. J. Philip Hogan, writing in the *Pentecostal Evangel,* stated:

> I have been selling missions to churches on a money-back guarantee for many years. I have been bold enough to tell people that, no matter what their obligations are at home, if they set aside a portion for the lost abroad God will help them in the local outreach.[14]

Ample testimonies of God's miraculous provision in such circumstances were readily given.[15]

Leading churches in giving received awards for their achievements. Special plaques were presented by district missionary secretaries at district councils to pastors whose churches led in giving. Statistics were also tabulated on the districts that excelled in contributions as well as the top 10 churches nationally. Officers of the Foreign Missions Department presented the appropriate awards at General Council meetings. Wesley R. Hurst, secretary for promotions, reported that the Southern California District led all other districts in 1966 by giving $1,083,161.23. First among churches for contributions that year was Calvary Temple, Seattle, Washington, with offerings totaling $51,238.58. Although more than 7,000 churches gave at least one offering a year to foreign missions, of these, 1,557 gave less than $100 (738 churches sent nothing).[16] Nevertheless, this represented a considerable advance in giving over previous years.

General Council gatherings also provided important opportunities to emphasize missions, featuring colorful parades of missionaries in national dress and stirring messages of notable preachers. During the Sunday afternoon Global Conquest Rally at the 1961 General Council in Portland, Oregon, J. Philip Hogan, preaching from John 3:8 ("The wind bloweth where it listeth, and thou hearest the sound thereof, but canst not tell whence it cometh, and whither it goeth: so is every one that is born of the Spirit"), proclaimed that the Holy Spirit was sovereignly moving in many countries and now was the time to reach them with the gospel. Missionary evangelist Willard Cantelon followed by challenging the delegates to give generously in the Global Conquest offering. A reporter for the *Pentecostal Evangel* noted "there was weeping and crying out as the people gave themselves, as well as their money, to the Lord." By midnight the cash offering and the pledged contributions (telephoned in from around the country) reached $55,640.[17]

Many Assemblies of God preachers and church members rose to the challenge presented by the various promotional means of Global Conquest. More than ever before, the heartbeat of missions could be heard in local congregations.

The Strategic Endeavor

Global Conquest targeted the need for evangelism in the major cities of the world, although not to the exclusion of important ministries in remote areas. Through its financial assistance, it also undergirded the well-proven methods of existing operations and helped to expand new ones. The program focused on three areas for aid: distribution of gospel literature, training national leaders, and establishing evangelistic centers in key cities.

Literature Distribution

The production of gospel literature is a long-standing tradition in the Pentecostal movement. From the movement's beginning, leaders printed and circulated periodicals to evangelize and indoctrinate. In the Assemblies of God, the *Word and Witness, Latter Rain Evangel,* and *Pentecostal Evangel* were formative influences in the development of personal piety, the advancement of home and foreign missions, and building loyalty to the organization.[18] The emphasis on biblical teaching also helped to provide balance and sometimes needed correctives to the experiential dimension of Pentecostalism.

Missionaries had long recognized the need for literature on their fields. By 1959 the Assemblies of God operated 16 print shops around the world and in 7 years the number rose to 20 (publishing operations often utilized local commercial presses as well). By 1966 they produced 25 million pieces of literature in 77 languages annually.[19]

Global Conquest funds now augmented the contributions of auxiliary agencies of the General Council in underwriting literature production. Over a 20-year period, the youth of the Assemblies of God through Speed-the-Light had contributed $339,216 for printing equipment and since 1949 the children of the Assemblies of God had given $1.5 million for literature production. Within 5 years of its creation (1961), the new Light-for-the-Lost program of the Men's Fellowship Department had raised $150,000 for literature saturation campaigns.[20]

One of the most strategic literature investments of the Assemblies of God has been the Spanish Literature Division (Editorial Vida; later Life Publishers International) founded by Henry C. Ball in 1946.[21] Producing magazines, books, hymnals, tracts, and Sunday school literature, by the 1960s it was selling materials to 64 denominations from 34 countries. After considerable study, the Division moved to Miami, Florida, in 1966 "because of its strategic importance as the gateway to Central and South America, and because there are thousands of Spanish-speaking people in Miami—mostly Cuban refugees. . . ."[22] Under the oversight of Melvin L. Hodges, field secretary for Latin America and the West Indies, the staff included Loren Triplett, formerly a missionary to Nicaragua, as coordinator for Spanish literature (succeeding John C. Jackson in 1966); George and Billie Davis, the former as head of the Sunday school division; Louise Jeter Walker, head of the Bible school di-

vision; and David Scott, assistant to Triplett for business administration and distribution.

Two factors stood behind the sudden upsurge in literature through
Global Conquest: the population explosion and the threat of communist literature reaching the masses.[23] Christine Carmichael, a
writer for the Foreign Missions Department, wrote that "whatever
the idea, the printed word will set it marching through the highways
of men's minds."[24]

Missionaries and national ministers found ample use for literature
in their attempts at evangelism and discipling. In Malawi and Tanzania, Blanket-Every-Village Crusades were conducted to distribute
gospel literature, including personal follow-up. Other missionaries
found outlets for Scripture portions and tracts at fairs in large cities,
through bookmobiles, and in Christian bookstores.[25] Additional initiatives involved the growing number of correspondence programs,
such as the Home Study Division of Southern Asia Bible College
in Bangalore, India.

The cost of producing literature abroad sometimes made it in-
expensive for distribution. For example, in the Philippines, Evangel
Press in Manila printed materials in four languages: English, Ta-
galog, Ilocano, and Cebuano. A missionary to the Philippines, Floyd
Horst, reported that $2 would supply "three Christian books which
would sell for a dollar each in America; 200 Gospels of John; 500
gospel tracts; a half day's salary for a colporteur; and gasoline for
twenty-five miles' travel in literature distribution."[26]

Various benefits surfaced through the use of literature in evangelism. Delmer R. Guynes, a missionary to Malaysia, describing a
citywide literature crusade in the capital of Kuala Lumpur, reported
that the event resulted in (1) a greater burden for evangelism among
local believers, (2) a joy among them in knowing that nearly every
home in the city had been given the gospel, (3) a file on interested
individuals for future contact, (4) the accomplishment of a major
evangelistic thrust by the local congregation, (5) the discovery of
population centers that exhibited interest in Christianity, and (6) the
salvation of souls and the groundwork for revival.[27]

Sometimes unusual results came with literature distribution. A
missionary to Latin America, George Davis, recounted the following
story:

> Marcos Murillo, a humble tailor, was working at his sewing machine one day when the wind caused a piece of paper to flutter. He pulled the paper from between the cane poles that made the wall, and found it to be a gospel tract which the former occupant had left there. The tailor was saved through reading the tract and was filled with a desire to witness.

> He gave his house to the church and went out to preach to others. He won hundreds of people to Christ and started several new churches. Many of his converts are pastoring churches which he pioneered.[28]

Murillo later served as the general superintendent of the Assemblies of God in Costa Rica.

A spectacular revival among French Gypsies also came about through a tract published by BGMC funds. Given to the chief of the tribes whose daughter was dying, the tract spoke of Christ's power to heal. When the French pastor who had presented the tract prayed for the girl, she received healing. Within a short time, thousands of Gypsies had been converted, some eventually attending Bible school to train for the ministry.[29]

Training National Leaders

The Assemblies of God took great pride in the increasing number of its overseas Bible institutes—the positive results in subsequent church growth and development of national church organizations had become apparent. The number of these schools continued to climb, from 61 in 1959 to 86 in 1966. As Global Conquest funds became available, monies were designated for buildings, operational expenses, supplies, and equipment.

The schools exhibited three characteristics: adaptability, a direct connection to evangelism, and increasing curricular offerings. The limited financial resources of the national churches and the missionaries often required adaptability as a primary ingredient for offering theological training. Such adaptations helped to overcome problems of geography, resources, and facilities. Ralph D. Williams, a noted missionary to Latin America, taught for a time at the Bible institute in Barquisimeto, Venezuela. Since many interested people lived too far away to attend the school, night Bible schools were opened in Maracaibo and Cabimas, representing a population center of over a million people at the time. All 10 Assemblies of God churches in the area sent students to the schools. The setting up of two new schools enabled persons not owning cars to attend; the school in Cabimas saved students a 2-hour ride and payment of tolls on a bridge 6 miles long. The sponsoring committee in Maracaibo had resources to provide classrooms and equipment, but the committee in Cabimas was not so fortunate. Williams recounted that

> there were no desks, . . . some used iron chairs purchased from an old theater. Also the church designated for the classes had no roof. There is, however, a lean-to annex running down one side of the building which was to serve as the classroom. With the large number of students this narrow annex proved to be too hot and stuffy, so we moved out into the roofless auditorium. We now hold our classes under the starry sky, except for those nights when the rain chases us back under cover.[30]

When the schools opened, 46 students had enrolled in Maracaibo and 28 in Cabimas (much to the surprise of Williams and his colleagues). Thus it was due to the consecration of the students and the ministry of God's Word—not the facilities—that such schools succeeded. Modest beginnings would be superseded by improvements as they trusted in God.[31]

Also contributing to the achievements of the overseas Bible institutes was their emphasis on evangelism. Student activities included preaching assignments, teaching Sunday school classes, street witnessing, distribution of gospel literature, as well as participation in the Christ's Ambassadors youth program, Women's Missionary Council, and Men's Fellowship meetings. Theory was to be complemented by meaningful hands-on experience. Following the apostle Paul's example of instruction at the city of Ephesus in Acts 19:10, every Bible institute would hopefully be an evangelistic center. This combination of classroom instruction and practical ministry produced thousands of new churches overseas, often reflecting the same adaptability in the use of facilities as the Bible institutes.[32]

Studies were made to improve the curricular offerings of these schools as well as the charting of proposed constitutions and bylaws (which pointedly recommended the participation of national ministers and church leaders in governance).[33] In 1960 a special committee of Bible school administrators from Latin America met on the campus of Central Bible College in Springfield to "review our present Bible school operations in Latin America and to offer suggestions and plans to the individual schools which will help increase their efficiency, attain more uniform standards and curriculum, and be a guide in the establishing of new schools."[34] Those who attended included Melvin L. Hodges, field secretary, Elsie F. Blattner (Venezuela), Verne A. Warner (Dominican Republic), and Floyd Woodworth (Cuba). The agenda included such topics as the standardization of curriculum, administration, student activities, relationship of the school to the national church, financial resources, library collection, and preparation of teachers. The committee noted, however, that although it could propose guidelines, it could not formulate a pattern usable everywhere.

To facilitate the development of these schools, the Foreign Missions Committee appointed Louise Jeter Walker, a veteran missionary, as coordinator of Assemblies of God Bible institutes in Latin America. Having served as the director of the Cuban Bible Institute since 1951, Walker was well aware of the needs and problems facing such institutions. With her husband, Alva (formerly a missionary to Africa), she traveled extensively in Latin America, conducting seminars and workshops that ranged in length from 2 days to 3 weeks. She taught in faculty training classes, guided in library acquisitions, and helped plan for night schools, short-term Bible institutes, and extension courses. Walker also wrote and published *El Instituto* ("The Institute") in English and Spanish editions for schools throughout the region. After 6 years she resigned to devote her energies to writing and editing correspondence courses.[35] Her educational contributions have had a major impact on theological education and church growth in Latin America.

Bible institutes flourished in other regions as well, with Global Conquest funds often underwriting the costs of construction or expansion. Three hundred Nigerian students were being trained for ministry in five schools in various parts of that country. The schools were coordinated and supervised by the executive committee of the Nigeria Assemblies of God, most of whom had graduated from these schools. In-service training had been part of their programs since the beginning. Missionary Ralph L. Cimino stated that

[w]hen students have matured spiritually and progressed scholastically so they are capable of pastoring a small church, they are recommended for assignment. Every Friday most students leave the campus by foot, bicycle, train, or bus to conduct services in their churches. Such a weekend usually includes many house-to-house calls, open-air services, Sunday school teachers training classes, morning prayer meetings, and regular services.

When the students return for classes on Monday morning, they are more than eager for the teaching and spiritual help available.[36]

Celebrating its 25th anniversary in 1966, the thriving national church in Nigeria claimed 600 ministers, almost half of whom had graduated from the church's theological training institutions. These graduates formed the mainstay of leadership and promised a bright future for growth.

Evangelism

The imperative of world evangelization represented the primary reason for the organization of the Assemblies of God. At the World Congress on Evangelism in Berlin (1966), Thomas F. Zimmerman, general superintendent of the Assemblies of God, warned that "our generation must be confronted with the fact that God's judgment stands over this wicked world to be meted out when Christ returns to take vengeance on the unevangelized and the Gospel-rejectors, both living and dead."[37]

Within a year of its debut, Global Conquest had assisted in sponsoring Foreign City Crusades (renamed Good News Crusades in 1965) and the building of evangelistic centers. While these crusades represented an important strategy, they also coincided with the salvation/healing movement that had become popular in America in the 1950s. Evangelists such as Jack Coe, Oral Roberts, Clifton O. Erickson, A. A. Allen, and T. L. Osborn crisscrossed the United States holding services in city auditoriums and often in large tents. Although the movement declined after 1958 in the United States, many of these evangelists (e.g., Osborn and Erickson) continued to hold large crusades overseas. Other evangelists followed in their wake, for mass campaigns continued to be an effective means of evangelism.

The Foreign Missions Department had tried to regulate their activities when working with Assemblies of God missionaries and national church organizations in the 1950s, but met with only limited success. Concerns about integrity and financial accountability continued into the next decade. The department made it quite clear that it would work only with those evangelists who would allow them and the missionaries to monitor their activities. Experience had proven that unsupervised campaigns led to strained relations with the national churches and produced little actual church growth. Nevertheless, approved evangelists were encouraged and a list of those who had been endorsed was published in *Key*. The roster included Watson Argue, Loren Cunningham, Lorne Fox, Hal Herman, Mildred Holler, Richard E. Jeffery, Gladys Pearson, Morris Plotts, A. N. Trotter, and Mabel Willetts; the number of women evangelists on the list is significant.[38]

One of the most successful evangelists has been Hal Herman, a former news writer and photo editor for Columbia Studios in Hollywood, California. Beginning with his first meeting in Germany in 1951, Herman had conducted 65 crusades in 24 countries by 1966 and reported many conversions and remarkable healings.[39] Other noteworthy American evangelists included Willard Cantelon, Bob Harrison, Bob Hoskins, and Paul Olson.

While the crusades of American evangelists carried more glamor than those of the missionaries and their national counterparts, the more successful evangelistic efforts (when considering long-term church growth) have been accomplished by missionaries, national ministers, and the thousands of committed Pentecostal Christians in churches from Argentina to Italy and Nyasaland (later Malawi) to the South Seas who have willingly testified to their faith.[40] Missionaries and national evangelists often held city-wide crusades and conducted village evangelism as well. For example, the evangelistic endeavors of Orville Carlson and Lawrence Larson in Fiji and Sam Sasser in the Marshall Islands brought important results in the Western Pacific.[41]

Gifted national evangelists came to include Gideon Bomba,[42] superintendent of the Assemblies of God in Malawi; Paul Yonggi Cho, a prominent pastor (Korea);[43] Charles Osueke, a national evangelist (Nigeria); José María Rico, a former Jesuit priest (Bolivia);[44] and

Eduardo Ríos (Peru).[45] These men possessed cultural and linguistic advantages that American evangelists did not have.

The conservation of the results, however, required extensive follow-up procedures. Increasingly, such crusades received the assistance of Global Conquest funds to cover costs for renting halls and purchasing time on radio and TV stations, Light-for-the-Lost literature for precrusade distribution and follow-up procedures (correspondence courses, etc.), Speed-the-Light vehicles and radio equipment, and educational materials provided by BGMC. Upon establishing themselves as a congregation, believers could look for assistance in building a church to the growing Revolving Loan Fund of the Foreign Missions Department and sometimes to outright gifts from the department or American churches.[46]

The building of evangelistic centers in major cities of the world was another aim of Global Conquest. The pilot project was Seoul, Korea, which the large Yoido Full Gospel Church pastored by Paul Yonggi Cho eventually emerged from. A crusade conducted by Evangelist Sam Todd (an Assemblies of God evangelist [1960–1964] who worked with Gordon Lindsay's Voice of Healing organization) launched the Seoul Evangelistic Center. When the initial revival ended, missionary John Hurston (director) and Paul Yonggi Cho (co-pastor), assisted by other missionaries and national workers, carried on the work. Within a few years, this congregation numbered over 5,000 members, constituting the largest Pentecostal church in Asia. This important development encouraged the ministry of local evangelists as well. Maynard L. Ketcham, field secretary for the Far East, praised the efforts of a "Sister" Kim in particular who pitched a tent for services and within 6 months had a congregation of 150.[47] Other centers were opened in La Paz, Bolivia; Calcutta, India; Dakar, Senegal; Georgetown, Guyana (formerly British Guiana); and Barcelona, Spain, among others. The effort in Seoul was by far the most successful in establishing an evangelistic outreach to an entire nation. Other evangelistic centers often became major churches, but with limited outreach to other regions.

Radio and Television Evangelism

Although few missionaries were engaged in radio broadcasting before 1950, it became a popular avenue for evangelism in many parts of the world in the following decade; television programming was soon added. Global Conquest funds contributed to that development. By 1963, the Assemblies of God was broadcasting in 13 languages, logging 330 broadcast hours per month, and using an annual budget of over $40,000.

By far the most successful venture in radio evangelism developed in Central and South America. Latin American Radio Evangelism (LARE) began in 1955 in the garage of missionary Paul Finkenbinder (son of missionary pioneers Frank and Gladys Finkenbinder) in San Salvador, El Salvador, "with one Webcor tape recorder mounted on a missionary barrel producing a program called 'La Iglesia del Aire' (The Church of the Air)."[48] Beginning with six broadcasts a week and a firm belief that God would supply the needed funds, LARE grew in 7 years to 22 broadcasts in 9 countries. By short wave, the program covered all of Latin America. With partial assistance from Global Conquest funds, the voice of Paul Finkenbinder, "Hermano Pablo" ("Brother Paul"), became well-known all over the continent. LARE sponsored the first daily Latin American network gospel program. Assemblies of God pastors assisted by forming the League of Prayer, a group that prayed for the prayer requests sent in by listeners. Later, a television series, "The Bible in Drama," utilizing biblical costumes and settings and national Christian workers as actors, may possibly have been the first regular presentation of the gospel by means of television in Latin America. Each program closed with a strong evangelistic appeal.[49] (Finkenbinder served as an appointed Assemblies of God missionary from 1947 to 1972, when he left the Foreign Missions Department to seek a broader base for his radio and television ministries.) Other broadcasts, more regional in scope, included *La Hora Evangélica* ("The Gospel Hour") in Cuba and *La Voz de la Fe* ("The Voice of Faith") covering Mexico and Guatemala.[50]

Another notable radio ministry began in San Francisco under the inspiration of Paul Demetrus. Born in Chicago to parents who belonged to the Russian Orthodox Church, the younger Demetrus was converted and graduated from Central Bible Institute in 1942. In the early 1950s, following the establishment of the Far East Broadcasting Company in Manila and the International Broadcasting Association in Stockholm (sponsored by the Swedish Pentecostal churches), he received the opportunity to send the gospel by radio to the Soviet Union and to Russian communities around the world.[51] In his *Voice of Truth* broadcasts, he was assisted by the Russian Radio Choir of San Francisco (where he located his headquarters). The choir was composed of refugees from Russia who had become Pentecostal Christians. Demetrus, who received appointment as a missionary, served not only as the speaker for the Russian broadcast but as producer for other programs that were added. The main speaker for the *Voice of Truth* in the Ukrainian language was Fred Smolchuck, a pastor in Detroit, Michigan, and onetime superintendent of the Ukrainian Branch (district) of the Assemblies of God.[52]

Other important radio ministries included the *Voice of the Assemblies of God* (missionary Lawrence Olson, speaker) and *Words of Life* (missionary Bernhard Johnson, Jr., speaker) in Brazil, and *Vim Kweega* ("The Living Word") in Burkina Faso (general superintendent Lebende Miningou, speaker), among others.[53] For evangelistic outreach to Muslims, the Foreign Missions Department negotiated for programming with a major television station in Beirut, Lebanon, which had a potential audience ranging from Egypt to Iran. In reference to the enlarging radio and television ministries, J. Philip Hogan remarked: "In these days the church of Jesus Christ cannot cautiously peer around the corner of the Twentieth Century while keeping its feet firmly planted in the Nineteenth Century and still witness to this generation. We must be alert to all that modern science has produced that will help us facilitate the spread of this gospel message."[54] This pragmatic attitude toward using new avenues of evangelism has characterized the Assemblies of God mission enterprise, particularly under Hogan's leadership.

Original logo for Global Conquest promotional
campaign

Global Conquest Day at General Council in Memphis, Tennessee,
1963. Missionaries record pledges telephoned from around the country.

The Heroes of the Conquest series provided information on the lives and activities of key missionaries, as well as inspirational reading.

Assemblies of God print shop in Rio de Janeiro, Brazil, founded in 1948

Central Bible Institute of Nigeria

Missionary-Evangelist Hal Herman preaching in Messina, Sicily, with Paolo Calabrese, his interpreter

Missionary Paul Finkenbinder, "Hermano Pablo," helped pioneer radio and televangelism in Latin America.

Paul Demetrus developed an effective radio ministry aimed toward the Soviet Union and other Eastern bloc nations.

An evangelist and church planter, Gideon Bomba became the first general superintendent of the Assemblies of God in Malawi.

Joint meeting of Foreign Missions Board and Laymen's Advisory Council in 1962. Participants were (clockwise around the table): H. C. Noah, Emmett Peterson, Edward Johnson, Emil Balliet, R. T. McGlasson, E. M. McNab, E. C. Sumrall, Melvin L. Hodges, Bert Webb, J. Philip Hogan, Mrs. Irene Ruthroff (secretary), Deroy Owings, D. V. Terry, Rollin Severance, G. Raymond Carlson, V. G. Greisen, and D. Leroy Sanders.

5

The Role of Support Agencies

In 1961 the Women's Missionary Council (WMC; after 1975, the Women's Ministries Department) chose the theme "Freely Give" for National WMC Day on February 27th. This theme, taken from Matthew 10:8 ("Heal the sick, cleanse the lepers, raise the dead, cast out devils: freely ye have received, freely give"), accurately summarizes the work of important auxiliary programs in the General Council. Although the WMC, Light-for-the-Lost, Speed-the-Light, Boys and Girls Missionary Crusade, Mobilization and Placement Service, and Ambassadors in Mission were not the result of the Global Conquest program, they closely cooperated with it to expedite the work of missions.

Women's Missionary Council

The work of Assemblies of God women in supporting foreign missions, home missions, and benevolence ministries is easily traced to the ministry of Etta Calhoun, who organized the first Women's Missionary Council in Houston, Texas, in 1925. Although she had wanted to be a missionary, the care of her invalid mother prevented her from going overseas. Nevertheless, in beginning this practical program of prayer for and assistance to missionaries, she exerted a profound impact on the course of Assemblies of God missions, matched by few women. To Calhoun, if "such work was done 'in the Spirit,' and 'for the love of God,' He could and would bless it, but if workers resorted to formality and human activity alone the work would amount to nothing."[1]

By 1951 most districts had set up their own WMC agencies. During the General Council gathering in 1951, the delegates passed a resolution to create a national office for coordinating the work of the district WMC departments. Edith Whipple, a long time employee at the headquarters in Springfield, was chosen as national secretary. When she left office 8 years later, WMC representation could be found in every district of the denomination and nationwide membership stood at 62,000.

Whipple was succeeded by Mildred Smuland, who directed the program from 1959 until 1972. Since her late husband, Roy, had served as the superintendent of the New England District, Mrs. Smuland had gained considerable leadership experience, working as the Sunday school representative and district WMC president. In addition to these qualifications, Smuland had taught at Central Bible College and, most recently, served as representative for the national WMC office.[2]

The late 1950s proved to be especially important years in the development of this endeavor. Four reasons stand out: publications, national coordination with district programs, fund-raising, and Missionettes. The first publication offered by the department was the quarterly *Missionette Memos* in 1956, edited by Charlotte Schumitsch, which offered advice and program helps to local leaders of the Missionettes program for girls. Next, the department began to publish *WMC Slant* in 1957 (*Woman's Touch* after 1977), also a quarterly magazine. Edited initially by Mildred Smuland and later by Ann Ahlf, it provided suggestions for local chapter meetings, information about the missions enterprise and its personnel, and projects that could be undertaken by the women. These publications assisted in coordinating and promoting the national program, as well as inspiring loyalty to the department's objectives. Carefully written and edited, they provided valuable information for understanding the nature and history of women's ministries in the Assemblies of God and their influence on home and foreign missions.

The coordination of the program necessitated the close cooperation of district and local WMC chapters. The first national seminar for district WMC presidents took place in Cleveland, Ohio, in 1957. Beginning in 1959, it became an annual event. The seminars provided inspiration, workshops, and business sessions.[3]

The task of assisting home and foreign missionaries covered a wide field of projects. Our attention here will focus on aid to the overseas effort. The provision of "outfits" for departing missionaries required considerable attention. In an article published in the *Pentecostal Evangel* entitled "Necessity—The Mother of WMC," Mrs. Annie Walton, Oregon District WMC president, reported in 1961 that while her district WMCs had initially met a few of the most urgent needs, such as personal clothing, luggage, and sewing machines, the list continued to grow. Outfits came to include washing machines, camping equipment, pumps, refrigerators, stoves, kitchen utensils, beds, medical supplies, and food staples. Walton sent a list of needs to all 150 WMC groups in the state and suggested that larger churches supply the more expensive items and smaller churches contribute what they could. Obtaining these supplies, however, tells only part of the story. The women had to find temporary storage and then pack the smaller items into metal barrels for transport—a considerable task, requiring much planning and the selfless dedication of volunteer workers.[4]

After the missionaries arrived at their destinations, the Adoption Plan went into effect: Local chapters focused on sending their missionaries certain items they could not purchase abroad, such as supplementary clothing (in some cases), certain foods, games, and books.

WMC members also became known for making and sending thousands of patchwork quilts abroad for missionaries, as well as for orphans, lepers, and other needy people. Made from colorful scraps of material left from other sewing projects, the quilts featured designs that were distinctively Early American.[5]

The WMC chapters further helped the missionaries with their adjustments to homemaking in the United States after returning on furloughs. Some districts kept storage areas stacked with furniture and other household items for use when the missionary established residence. For example, when the Jimmie W. Davis family, missionaries to Japan, returned to Seattle on medical leave, they discovered that the Harmony Crafters WMC group (young homemakers) of Calvary Temple had arranged for their housing. In conjunction with other WMC chapters, "furniture in abundance, rugs, dishes, and linens came rolling in."[6] This example was typical of many instances of generosity and care provided by chapters of the WMC.

To subsidize their projects, WMC chapters engaged in various fund-raisers. On the local level, they often collected Betty Crocker coupons (to be exchanged for tableware for home and foreign missionaries); the national office received the tithe of coupons to assist in furnishing the homes provided for furloughed missionaries residing in Mission Village in Springfield, Missouri. Cancelled stamps were also collected and sold to dealers. In turn, they used the cash to purchase books for the libraries of overseas Bible institutes.

On the national level, the Etta Calhoun Fund was created by the District WMC Presidents' Seminar and approved by the Executive Presbytery in 1957. This annual offering is received by local groups on the Sunday nearest September 19, Calhoun's birthday. Forwarded to the national office, it provides indoor furnishings and equipment for home and foreign missionaries, as well as benevolence institutions that no one missionary is responsible for.[7] Originally, the national women's department hoped to receive a yearly contribution of 10 cents per WMC member and Missionette (which would have amounted to $6,000 at the time). Receiving an initial amount of $780 in 1957, the cumulative total exceeded $11,000 by 1966.

Local members collected pennies and dimes for the fund as well. Besides aiding other projects, their monies went toward a kitchen stove at the Bible school in Taipei, Taiwan; kitchen equipment and plastic dishes for the Bible school in Santiago, Chile; 20 steel cots for the school in Natitingou, Benin; and sewing machines for the women students at the Lowlands Bible Institute in Santa Cruz, Bolivia.[8] Later efforts included furnishings for the Christian Serviceman's Homes in Seoul, Korea, and Taipei, Taiwan, and the equipment for "a commodious five-unit motel-type missionary rest home" in Jos, Nigeria.[9] Total WMC giving doubled during the years of Global Conquest, from $1,266,292.20 in 1960 to $2,438,673.55 for 1967.[10]

Another important aspect of the work of the department was the Missionettes program founded in 1955 for girls 12 to 17 years of age to establish "a wonderful bond of fellowship . . . as the girls meet to work for missionaries, for the ill and the aged, and for their local church."[11] Charlotte Schumitsch was the first coordinator of the program. By 1967 there were 6,500 local clubs with 75,000 Missionettes. The achievement program, Stairway to the Stars, was divided into four steps and the requirements included reading the entire Bible through, memorizing Scripture verses relating to the doctrinal statements of the Assemblies of God, reading missionary books, completing handicraft projects, and involvement in other local activities to assist in the mission of the church.[12] For young adult women, 18 years and older, the Young Women's Missionary Council was launched in 1965 (later renamed Young Women's Auxiliary [Ys]).

The enthusiasm and example of the American WMCs soon caught on overseas, resulting in organizations among nationals, thus affording women in many countries an important outlet for ministry. By 1965 WMC programs were underway in 25 countries. In Nigeria, Stella Ezeigbo, national WMC director and wife of Matthew Ezeigbo, the general superintendent, reported that their activities included literacy training, systematic Bible study and spiritual nurture, sponsoring Bible schools for women, as well as instruction in cooking, hygiene, child care, washing and ironing, and the Christian home.[13] On a different field of activity, missionary Janie Faulkner recounted that Filipino WMCs in Cebu City mended used clothing and sewed small garments with remnants of new material they had purchased. In her words, "Every woman present could have used the cloth for her own family, for the Filipino ladies are very poor in this world's goods. However . . . they prepared for each national minister a parcel of clothing that will be a Christmas gift to his family."[14] Other notable WMC organizations could be found in Latin America and the West Indies.[15] In each instance, their ministries were tied closely to the development of the national church.

Although the number of ordained women in the Assemblies of God continued to decline and their status was unfortunately complicated by restrictions and hesitations, women did find creative roles of service in the Christian world mission through local, district, and national WMC organizations.[16] Their zeal in fund-raising, providing for the needs of missionaries, packing barrels for transport, and ministering to the needy and suffering, whether at home or abroad, established a clear identity for them in the denomination, although not in the ranks of the clergy. This grass-roots support for the missionary enterprise reflects the auxiliary contribution that women have historically made to the expansion of Christianity.[17]

Light-for-the-Lost

The origin of the Men's Fellowship Department, which sponsors the Light-for-the-Lost literature evangelism program, has been traced to the inspiration and work of Jack Epperson of Calvary Assembly of God in Inglewood, California, in 1947. After several years of planning and study, the General Council authorized the establishment of the department in 1951. J. Otis Harrell, manager of Gospel Publishing House, became the first national secretary the following year. The Men's Fellowship Department began the same year the widely influential Full Gospel Business Men's Fellowship, International, (FGBMFI) was founded by Oral Roberts and Demos Shakarian.[18] Although the department never matched the size and popularity of FGBMFI among denominational Pentecostals, its programs were more effective in supporting local church ministries and foreign missions.

The story of Light-for-the-Lost began later with a layman, Sam Cochran, a successful insurance broker who attended First Assembly of God in Santa Ana, California. While praying after a Sunday evening service at the church, Cochran recounted that he received a vision from the Lord:

> I saw a great multitude of people standing, looking up. A large hand out of heaven was holding a Bible toward the people. The people were all reaching up as far as they could, stretching out their hands to take the Bible. As the hand and Bible came down, a trap door opened beneath them, and flames and smoke shot into the air as the people dropped screaming into the pit.
>
> I knew at that moment what God's purpose was for my life . . . to send the Word of God to every soul on earth as long as He gave me breath.[19]

Sharing his vision with several men of the church, Cochran pledged to set aside a certain amount of money each week to purchase gospel literature for distribution; each man agreed to do the same. Among this group were members of a quartet that sang in churches in the surrounding area. Refusing to accept remuneration for their expenses, they requested that offerings be taken instead for literature evangelism. Before long, the monies were used to purchase Gospels of John for Mexico; later shipments went to Central America, Peru, Argentina, Brazil, Italy, and Ceylon. Eventually, the men realized the need for more organization and petitioned the Southern California District Council of the Assemblies of God for recognition. As a result, they created a board of directors and chose the name Missionary Gospel Society. Cochran served as chairman along with an elected vice-chairman and secretary-treasurer. By 1959 the program had become so popular that the General Council incorporated it into the Men's Fellowship Department and renamed it Light-for-the-Lost. Within the next 2 years, the endeavor sent more than 3 million gospel portions overseas. In 1962 its efforts were coordinated with the Global Conquest initiative of the Foreign Missions Department to supply literature for evangelistic crusades in large foreign cities.[20] In the following year the program contributed to 49 literature saturation campaigns.

Light-for-the-Lost has been based on three concepts of evangelism: (1) The power of the Word of God is able to convince men of their need of redemption, (2) literature is an effective means of evangelism, and (3) gospel literature distribution accompanied by personal witnessing reflects the pattern of the New Testament church.[21] Most of the funds for the program have been generated by areawide banquet meetings where participants are invited to make pledges. Shouldering the promotional responsibilities alongside the officers of the Men's Fellowship Department were 154 active members of the National Council of Light-for-the-Lost. At their own expense, these councilmen promoted the work in their own communities and sometimes other areas as well; all of the funds went for the purchase of literature.[22]

Light-for-the-Lost literature gradually became a key ingredient in overseas evangelism. In Calcutta, India, missionary Mark Buntain reported that the program subsidized the printing of 90,000 tracts per month and that 15,000 copies of *Who Is Jesus?* by Elton Hill had been translated into Bengali and Hindi for workers to give away to interested people.[23] In the 2 year period from 1965 to 1966, Assemblies of God men contributed more than $200,000 for Light-for-the-Lost literature used in 271 foreign city crusades in Africa, the Middle East, Latin America, Europe, and the Far East.[24]

Speed-the-Light

The financial support of the denomination's youth for home and foreign missions dates back to 1944, when Ralph W. Harris, national secretary of the Christ's Ambassadors (CA) Department, proposed

Speed-the-Light (STL). Catching the imagination of the denomination's postwar generation of youth, the fund-raising increased every year until by 1966 the total had surpassed $6 million. Giving for that year alone reached $653,333—having doubled since the decade began.[25] These funds were often generated by sponsoring car washes, bake sales, selling candy, auctioning "slaves" (youth who were willing to do household and outdoor chores for a few hours in return for an offering), team contests, king and queen contests, banquets, and other creative revenue-producing projects.

While the BGMC and Light-for-the-Lost provided literature for missionary use, STL provided vehicles, radio equipment, and printing equipment. Home missions endeavors also benefited from their funds. To illustrate the magnitude of what 1 year's revenues could produce for transportation, on March 12, 1967, with the help of several automobile dealerships, 188 vehicles were assembled in front of the headquarters on Boonville Avenue in Springfield, Missouri: 81 cars, 20 station wagons, 16 motorcycles, 6 buses, 12 trucks, 48 bicycles, 2 boats, 2 trailers, and 1 jeep. Six lanes of vehicles, bumper-to-bumper and curb-to-curb, filled the street for almost the entire block in front of the building. Also on hand for the occasion were 30 missionaries in national dress. After three speeches, the cavalcade moved about a quarter of a mile down the street, disbanding after three simultaneous blasts of all the horns.[26] The event, inspired and coordinated by STL representative Verne B. MacKinney, received local and national television coverage, showing that by the 1960s Assemblies of God missionaries were among the best equipped in the Protestant missionary force.

Jointly administered by the CA Department and the Foreign Missions Department, STL represented the type of interdepartmental relationship that many had hoped for. The missionaries, of course, gratefully received this vital means of assistance in defraying the costs of transportation; some limited assistance from STL has also been extended to national ministers, although on a much smaller scale. Stories abound in Assemblies of God publications of the help that the program has provided. In "Speed-the-Light on Four Wheels and Four Hoofs," an article printed in the *Pentecostal Evangel*, missionary John F. Hall shared his experiences of traveling to and from a remote site of ministry in Haiti, utilizing an STL Scout jeep and an STL horse. Reflecting on the experience, he stated, "What but Speed-the-Light could have provided us with such thrills and opportunities?"[27] This was a sentiment shared by many.

Unfortunately, the administration of this program produced many frustrations, particularly as the missionary force expanded. At times some missionaries became presumptuous with unrealistic expectations of what the funds could provide. Policies were increasingly developed to insure equity and cope with the increasing costs of vehicles, import duties, and taxes. Robert T. McGlasson, foreign missions secretary, reminded the missionary family that "no missionary need feel that he is receiving second-class treatment because he is asked to take over a car that has been used by another missionary. The important fact is: we are still able to provide wheels beneath the missionary to speed his work and to speed the light."[28] The benefits of the program for the overseas enterprise, however, have far surpassed the difficulties in managing the operation.

Boys and Girls Missionary Crusade

Missions education through the national Sunday School Department promoted the Boys and Girls Missionary Crusade (BGMC) and encouraged children under the age of 12 to contribute through the means of "Buddy Barrels," small wooden banks. The total of these funds amounted to $203,068.93 in 1966 and were used exclusively to translate and publish gospel literature, including Sunday school materials, tracts, gospel portions, and teacher training books. Local churches often enthusiastically supported the program. For example, the Grand Award in 1966 for BGMC giving went not to a large suburban superchurch but to Fair Ridge Pentecostal Assembly in Shade Gap, Pennsylvania. After winning recognition for 6 consecutive years, the church won the top award in the nation for 3 consecutive years. Having an average Sunday school attendance of 279, the church's children contributed $3,337.18, an increase of $1,215.56 over the preceding year.[29]

BGMC has provided valuable financial assistance to overseas literature production and distribution. Mrs. Harold S. Jones, a missionary to Burkina Faso, reported that BGMC funding made possible Sunday school literature for the first time in the Mossi language and significantly "with pictures of black figures, rather than white figures as before" (prepared by missionary-artist John Weidman).[30]

On the Latin American and West Indian scene, Melvin L. Hodges praised BGMC for contributing to the support of the Spanish Literature Division and assisting with children's work, Sunday school materials, opening new bookstores, tract distribution, and the work of colporteurs.[31] From 1949 to 1967, Assemblies of God children gave a total of $1,800,000, and $203,068.93 for 1966 alone, an increase of more than $10,000 over the previous year.[32]

In terms of fund-raising, Assemblies of God support agencies promoted world evangelization before every age level with considerable success. Ministries at home and abroad benefited from the monies they raised. The popular support, however, extended beyond financial assistance and participation in the work of local chapters of the WMC and Men's Fellowship. The national leadership gradually recognized that a vast reservoir of skilled lay people were interested in giving their time and energies to assisting the ministries of the church. This desire took concrete form in the development of the Mobilization and Placement Service (MAPS) and Ambassadors in Mission (AIM).

Mobilization and Placement Service

To study the needs of evangelism in the Assemblies of God, the General Presbytery approved the formation of a Committee on Evangelism in 1962. The committee was appointed in March of the following year and received two assignments: (1) to study the concerns behind the General Presbytery's resolution, the decline of evangelism in the churches, the decrease in the number of evangelists, and the necessary steps to improve the quality of evangelists, and (2) to review the work of the Department of Evangelism (established 1953) and its relationship to other departments in the denomination.[33] When the General Council met in August 1963 to hear the report and recommendations, the committee affirmed that "prior to any Pentecostal organization, God indicated that evangelism is the whole work of the whole church, and Holy-Ghost-filled people [are] the evangelistic agency of God. True spirituality and evangelism are inseparable."[34] The great achievement of the Day of Pentecost was not glossolalia, but the 3,000 people who became believers. Therefore, success must not be measured by financial gains or new buildings, but "success in the spiritual realm is determined by the souls set free from the power of Satan."[35] The Council thereupon resolved to make evangelism the top priority of every department and centered the responsibility for this in the office of the general superintendent, Thomas F. Zimmerman. In so doing, the Council also abolished the Department of Evangelism; in 1965 the Executive Presbytery replaced it with the Spiritual Life–Evangelism Commission. D. V. Hurst received appointment as the first coordinator of the commission and was succeeded by Charles W. Denton in 1966.[36]

Two initiatives launched by the Spiritual Life–Evangelism Commission, MAPS and AIM, have made especially important contributions to missions. Begun in 1964, MAPS was designed "to ascertain areas of need and opportunity in the United States for . . . individuals who can assist districts, churches and institutions on a short term, temporary or permanent basis" and "the need and opportunity overseas for short term (two years or less) Christian service. . . ."[37] This new door of ministry for laymen in the Assemblies of God afforded college students, retirees, business and professional people, teachers, technicians, office workers, and other adults opportunities to work in home missions (Indian missions, prison ministries, literature and media ministries, construction, etc.) and foreign missions (office work, media ministries, construction, printing, etc.) on short-term assignments. Specifically, the new program hoped to maximize the involvement of laity in spiritual ministry and evangelism, church planting, and strengthening existing congregations.[38]

Veteran missionary Normal L. Correll became the first MAPS field representative (December 1966–1967).[39] A year later, MAPS volunteers began work on the pilot project of constructing a new church on Grand Bahama Island in the West Indies. Under the supervision of missionary Robert E. Ferguson, "construction missionary" Gordon Weden, and Correll, Assemblies of God church members—working as carpenters, electricians, plumbers, painters, and laborers who paid their own expenses—began building a church structure. The second phase of the project commenced in 1968 and led to its completion.[40] In the same year, John V. Ohlin succeeded Correll as MAPS representative and remained in this position until 1974.

By 1969, the program had caught the excitement of the denomination's lay constituency and projects began to dot the globe. Even one independent Pentecostal congregation, the famed Garr Memorial Church in Charlotte, North Carolina, supported MAPS workers from its membership. [41] New undertakings included an additional building for the Bible school in San Jose, Costa Rica, the evangelistic center in Teheran, Iran, and the church in Nassau, Bahamas. [42]

Ambassadors in Mission

The leadership of the Assemblies of God hoped to tap another available human resource, namely the youth (16–24 years of age) of the movement. Several of its colleges had already developed successful summer internship programs (e.g., Southwestern Assemblies of God College in Waxahachie, Texas, and Central Bible College, Springfield, Missouri) and they were studied carefully. For a time, however, it appeared that the newly organized Youth With A Mission (YWAM), founded in 1961 by an Assemblies of God minister, Loren Cunningham, and approved by the Southern California District, might fill the need and be integrated into the Assemblies of God youth program. A study committee on YWAM was appointed in 1963 and included representatives of the denomination's Executive Presbytery, Southern California District, and YWAM. Impressed with the operation, the committee made five recommendations that the Executive Presbytery approved on December 5, 1963, thus setting the stage for amalgamation. [43] Cunningham was offered the post of national representative for the Spiritual Life–Evangelism Commission, including oversight of YWAM, but he declined because the new structure would function without the autonomy that his program enjoyed. In addition, his dream of large numbers of young people serving overseas was not shared at that time by the denomination's executive leadership. [44]

With this change of course, another appointed committee met to formulate a youth witnessing program compatible to the existing structure. Members came from several related departments at the headquarters, and the coordinators of the Spiritual Life–Evangelism Commission (Hurst and later Denton) chaired the sessions. From their study came the inauguration of "International Youth Witness" in 1966. On its first two pilot projects in the summer of that year, eight young people traveled to Jamaica with Mel Steward as field supervisor and four to British Honduras (later Belize) with Dick Eastman. While in these countries, they engaged in door-to-door evangelism. So successful were these ventures that several more were planned for 1967 with 10 teams going to several Central American and West Indian countries. These and later efforts were co-ordinated with the work of other auxiliary agencies. The WMCs provided funds to defray the expenses of housing and feeding the team members, and Light-for-the-Lost provided for the literature that was distributed.[45] The team members themselves covered most of their personal expenses (e.g., transportation).

When the teams returned home, they reported 1,610 conversions from their witnessing and the distribution of 325,800 pieces of literature, including 19,000 copies of the *Pentecostal Evangel.* As a result of this experience, one youth stated, "I received a definite call to foreign missions and surrendered to this call."[46] With the growing number of teams sent out every summer (European countries were added in 1970), testimonies such as this were repeated again and again. The program increasingly became an important recruiting ground for future missionaries. In January 1968, the name International Youth Witness was changed to Ambassadors In Mission.

While Global Conquest epitomized the forward thrust of the Foreign Missions Department in the 1960s, the older as well as the newly-established auxiliary agencies within the Assemblies of God exhibited remarkable vitality. This no doubt stemmed from the heartfelt piety of the constituency, its commitment to world evangelization, and the dynamism of the new leadership.

Philippine minister with bicycle provided by Speed-the-Light funds

Bolivian pastors crossing Andes Mountains in 1966 for a series of local campaigns in the lowlands jungle area. Transportation was provided by missionary Harold Carpenter and his Speed-the-Light truck.

To display the number of vehicles supplied to missionaries by Speed-the-Light funds in one year, Verne MacKinney organized this parade on Boonville Avenue in front of the Assemblies of God headquarters in 1967.

Children participate in BGMC Day at Central Assembly of God, Baytown, Texas, in 1967.

Verne MacKinney, Speed-the-Light representative, receives award on the 25th anniversary of the program in 1969 from Norman Correll, national youth secretary.

The inspiration for the Light-for-the-Lost literature program began with a vision Sam Cochran reported receiving, which vividly depicted the eternal plight of those who had not received the gospel message.

6

Missiology and
Fraternal Cooperation

More than ever before, far-reaching changes began to affect Assemblies of God missionaries in the 1960s. Rapid strides were made in the training of missionaries, representing the continuing development of a distinctively Pentecostal missiology that encompassed both theological and practical concerns. Changes also occurred in the missionary task itself, triggered by the dismantling of the colonial empires and the rise of nationalistic sentiments in many regions, the move from oversight of, to partnership with, national church organizations on many fields, strategic planning, and policy changes. During these years, the work of the Assemblies of God increasingly gained the attention of the larger church world because of the remarkable growth of its fraternally related churches overseas.

Missiology

Training

One of the most dramatic changes in the operation of the mission enterprise came with the increased demand for effective missionary training. In recognizing that the planting of indigenous New Testament churches carried the key to church growth, the leadership and many missionaries clearly saw the value of specialized instruction on subjects such as cross-cultural communication, building the indigenous church, programs and policies of the Assemblies of God, world trends affecting evangelism—subjects that extended beyond their Bible college education. J. Philip Hogan noted that "to travel and live abroad as Americans as well as ministers of the Lord Jesus Christ and not to offend in either category requires considerable wisdom."[1] Thus the School of Missions became an effective vehicle for such study.

The School of Missionary Orientation, first offered in the summer of 1959 on the campus of Central Bible Institute (CBI) became an annual event required of all furloughed missionaries and missionary candidates. In 1961 the name was changed to School of Missions since the subject matter addressed the needs of veteran missionaries as well as new recruits.[2]

The intensive 2-week period of training (the length has varied over the years) included a variety of speakers: officials of the Foreign Missions Department and the General Council, as well as evangelical leaders and specialists, such as Clyde W. Taylor, executive director of the Evangelical Foreign Missions Association; Frank C. Laubach, internationally acclaimed authority on literacy; Donald A. McGavran, father of the church growth movement and dean of the School of World Mission at Fuller Theological Seminary; Arthur F. Glasser, prominent missiologist and educator; Eugene A. Nida, secretary for translations for the American Bible Society; Henry R. Brandt, representative of the Inter-Mission Candidate Training Program; and Richard H. Cox, clinical psychologist. The program included daytime sessions on different subjects and Bible study, and evening church services for inspiration and prayer.

The School of Missions became an effective means of building communication between the department and the missionary personnel. It also assisted in preparing new missionaries for the challenges they would face abroad. Although children were not invited in the earlier years, this eventually changed as the missionaries and leadership recognized that the need of preparation faced the entire family.

As a program of continuing education, it helped the missionaries grapple with the increasing complexities and requirements for effectively implementing indigenous church principles and adjusting to their changed roles with new national church organizations. Never before had so much been demanded of Assemblies of God missionaries in how they ministered abroad. At the same time, the advancing church growth on many fields justified the increasing emphasis on missionary training. Paul Greisen, a missionary to Hong Kong, commented that it "helps the missionary retain his sense of balance after working in a difficult culture. . . . [I]t is easy to forget many important principles that are needful to foreign missions work."[3]

Another benefit of the School of Missions has been the welding of positive relationships between the missionaries and the department's leadership. Prior to this, contact with missionary colleagues had been generally limited to General Council meetings (that happened to coincide with their furloughs) or to field fellowship gatherings overseas. The School of Missions fostered a growing sense of family, or camaraderie, in the years that followed its inauguration.

Since 1944, when a fourth year of advanced courses for missionaries was added to the curriculum of CBI, members of the Foreign Missions Department recognized the value that such training could bring to the operation. As the department entered its fifth decade, more of its missionary personnel began to request time and assistance for graduate study in the United States. In 1962 the Foreign Missions Board, "in an effort to participate in the training of veteran missionaries to become directors of missions in our Bible schools," inaugurated a scholarship program. The first two missionaries to receive this aid were Hugh P. Jeter (Peru, Cuba, and Spain) and James G. King (Liberia and Nigeria). After years of service abroad, Jeter served as professor of missions at Southwestern Assemblies of God College, Waxahachie, Texas, and King at North Central Bible College, Minneapolis, Minnesota.[4] When Louise Jeter Walker, coordinator for Bible schools in Latin America, received a Master of Arts degree from Central Bible College in 1965, the department published her thesis, *A Faculty-Training Program for Overseas Bible Schools,* for other missionaries and teachers to study. Melvin Hodges commended her achievement by writing, "[W]e feel that a significant contribution has been made toward solving the problem of preparing national teachers and directors for our Bible schools abroad."[5] This trend in recognizing the values of higher education for the mission endeavor continued and laid the groundwork for the Assemblies of God Graduate School in 1973.

The department also continued to publish the *Missionary Forum* (a quarterly magazine) for the missionary personnel until 1967. Initially, it had been intended as a medium for exchanging ideas, which sometimes included constructive criticism and defining policy. Generally, however, it carried information about policies, indigenous church relationships, advice on problems germane to missionaries, and important news about personnel changes.

Theology

Although the School of Missions provided practical help with implementing indigenous church principles and handling various problems, the need for better articulation of a Pentecostal missiology became increasingly apparent. During this period, however, whenever it was addressed, the emphasis was usually top-heavy with practical suggestions, reflecting the fact that Pentecostals have excelled more as practitioners than theorists.

Traditionally, Pentecostal missions have been propelled by three goals. First, Christ commissioned the church to proclaim the good news of salvation to every person (Matthew 28:18–20; Mark 16:15–18). The need for everyone to have a "born-again" experience of conversion could not be negotiated without surrendering the integrity of New Testament evangelism. Second, the church, "the worldwide union of all Christian believers," must be established in every land. To Hodges "this mystical Church is the work of the Holy Spirit, and it is composed of the innumerable local churches in every clime. The Spirit operates through us not just to 'make disciples,' but to foster churches in which disciples can work and grow."[6] The building of these New Testament churches required them to be self-governing, self-supporting, and self-propagating to insure maturity, independent of foreign support. In turn, their New Testament credentials would be readily apparent by their own missionary vision, energized by the gifts and power of the Holy Spirit.[7] The third goal focused on hastening the return of Christ in the last days by preaching the gospel to every nation (Matthew 24:14). This event would then be followed (after a period of tribulation) by the establishment of Christ's millennial kingdom on earth.

Although the objectives of the mission enterprise were clear, the exposition of a biblical theology of mission developed slowly, initially reflecting the strong dispensational orientation of Assemblies of God theology. Because of the popularity of a modified dispensationalism encouraged by the writings of Ralph M. Riggs, Frank M. Boyd, Finis Jennings Dake, John G. Hall, D. V. Hurst, T. J. Jones, and Carl Brumback, the many New Testament references to the kingdom of God as a present reality in the hearts of the redeemed barely received notice; its future millennial appearance received extensive consideration.[8] With their hesitancy to forthrightly link the church to the spiritual presence of the kingdom (dispensationalists separate the church from the kingdom), they chose to ignore the deep implications of some passages of Scripture for their restorationist claims to apostolic power in the last days. These references include the following:

> Jesus went through all the towns and villages, teaching in their synagogues, preaching the good news of the kingdom and healing every disease and sickness (Matthew 9:35, NIV).

> And this gospel of the kingdom will be preached in the whole world as a testimony to all nations, and then the end will come (Matthew 24:14, NIV).

> But when they believed Philip as he preached the good news of the kingdom of God and the name of Jesus Christ, they were baptized, both men and women (Acts 8:12, NIV).

> For the kingdom of God is not a matter of talk but of power (1 Corinthians 4:20, NIV).

Some Assemblies of God theologians, such as Ernest S. Williams and Stanley M. Horton, did clearly identify the kingdom of God (briefly defined as the rule or reign of God) with the church, recognizing the vital connection to Pentecostal claims about the Spirit's contemporary activity in the church. Their treatments, though consistent with their premillennialism, were nevertheless limited, as evidenced by Horton's *Promise of His Coming* (1967).[9] Nevertheless, the startling emphasis on the contemporary presence of the kingdom in Appalachian District Superintendent W. Glenn West's sermon, "The Triumph of the King," at the 1967 General Council signalled growing interest in the subject.[10]

The postwar period witnessed renewed study in evangelical circles on the missiological implications of the kingdom of God.[11] Developments in the Assemblies of God paralleled those in the evangelical mainstream. Noel Perkin, executive director emeritus of the Foreign Missions Department, wrote in 1963 that "we enter Christ's Kingdom now through the revelation and acceptance of Him who is Lord and Saviour. . . . Our message to the world could be summarized in the words of Jesus when he said, 'The time is fulfilled, and the kingdom of God is at hand: repent ye, and believe the gospel' (Mark 1:15)."[12] However, in *Our World Witness: A Survey of Assemblies of God Foreign Missions,* published in the same year, Perkin and John Garlock failed to mention it when discussing the biblical basis of mission.[13]

As the premier Pentecostal missiologist, however, Melvin Hodges recognized the importance of the kingdom for understanding a New Testament theology of mission. Speaking at the Congress on the Church's Worldwide Mission at Wheaton College in April 1966, he declared the church to be "the present manifestation of the kingdom of God in the earth, or at least, the agency that prepares the way for the future manifestation of the kingdom. Its mission therefore is the extension of the Church throughout the world. . . . It is the Holy Spirit that gives life to the Church and imparts gifts and ministries as well as power for their performance."[14] In *Grow Toward Leadership,* he wrote, "[T]he success of the kingdom of God depends on the calling of chosen workmen, and on their growth and development, so that they will fulfill the purpose of God. Ministers are God's key men in the advancement of the kingdom."[15] Despite the brevity of these statements on the kingdom, they indicated an important trend in Pentecostal missiology, for their import was shared by many of Hodges' colleagues.[16] The connection between the "signs and wonders" of the advancing kingdom (power manifestations of the Spirit associated with the preaching of the gospel) awaited further exposition.

Closer cooperation with evangelicals through means of the Evangelical Foreign Missions Association provided an opportunity for Pentecostals, and Assemblies of God mission leaders in particular, to identify with the missiological concerns of theological conservatives. Assemblies of God representatives participated in the Congress on the Church's Worldwide Mission, which was designed to address the task of the church's universal mission in the world in light of the changing times. They readily endorsed "The Wheaton Declaration" with its commitment to the inspired Scriptures, a universal declaration of the gospel, a call for more indigenization overseas, a concern for social justice and racial equality, and an interest in evangelical unity. At the same time, the declaration expressed reservations about Roman Catholic theology in spite of the recent changes in the church and denounced syncretism with the world's religions, neo-universalism, and the current tendency of some churches and agencies to foster organizational unity at the expense of doctrine.[17] Although compatibility of their missiology with the evangelical community afforded the Assemblies of God encouragement, ironically the charismatic renewal in the Roman Catholic Church and the historic Protestant churches would soon challenge all Pentecostals to rethink both the level of divine activity outside evangelical auspices and the doctrine of the church.

History

Although the organization of the National Association of Evangelicals in 1942 opened the door for increased communication and cooperation between evangelicals and Pentecostals, the church growth of Pentecostals at home and abroad brought them a new prominence by the 1960s. Harold Lindsell, the associate editor of *Christianity Today,* wrote that Pentecostals had been viewed with suspicion because of their Pentecostal distinctives and their Arminian (Wesleyan-Arminian) theology, but were "markedly used of God in missionary endeavor."[18] The passing of time had drawn them closer to the broader evangelical community, finding there a common loyalty to the authority of the Bible, belief in the lostness of men, and their need for personal salvation.

The Congress at Wheaton, convened by the Interdenominational Foreign Missions Association (IFMA) and the Evangelical Foreign Missions Association (EFMA), was an important historic event: a significant step in communication and cooperation between the two agencies—and for Pentecostals, a level of recognition previously unknown. Arthur F. Glasser, later dean and senior professor at Fuller Theological Seminary's School of World Mission, stated that "the sheer vitality of such EFMA-member missions as those belonging to the Pentecostal wing of the worldwide church could no longer be either dismissed or discounted. They represented a way of preaching the gospel that differed significantly from the somewhat cerebral and modified Calvinist form that characterized many of the IFMA groups." In addition, they "unabashedly grappled with the complexity of the physical needs of those they sought to win for Christ" through prayer for the sick, and were willing "to tackle 'the dark side of the soul' and challenge the growing phenomenon of occultism, Satan worship, and demon possession."[19] Illustrative of their new found stature, Melvin L. Hodges presented one of the major study papers, entitled "Mission—and Church Growth."[20] When J. Philip Hogan reported on the conference to the Assemblies of God constituency, he wrote:

> The presence of an Assemblies of God missions leader on this program, especially handling this subject, is indicative, first, of the acceptance with which the missionary program of the Assemblies of God is received worldwide; and, secondly, it is indicative of the fact that we, by God's grace, have been able, particularly in Latin America, to achieve a degree of success in the vital area of planting the indigenous church and encouraging indigenous revival.[21]

Hodges had also previously contributed chapters, along with Donald A. McGavran, Robert Calvin Guy, and Eugene A. Nida, to an important book edited by McGavran entitled *Church Growth and Christian Mission,* published in 1965. This growing recognition and acceptance, however, remained limited because of lingering suspicions about the doctrinal distinctives of Pentecostals. At the World Congress on Evangelism in Berlin in 1966, the list of speakers representing the rapidly growing world Pentecostal movement amounted to only a token number.[22] And although noted evangelical mission leaders were invited to speak at the School of Missions in Springfield, Missouri, reciprocal invitations were rare, with the exception of EFMA meetings.

Nevertheless, the executives of the Foreign Missions Department and sympathetic evangelical leaders remained undaunted in their friendship and good will toward each other, their forbearance leading to many positive relationships. The spectacular reports on church growth overseas gave the Foreign Missions executives reason for confidence and pride in their efforts. Identification with evangelicals broadened their view of what God was doing in the world, without threatening their belief that they had been raised up at this final juncture in church history to evangelize the world in apostolic power. When the Assemblies of God celebrated its 50th anniversary in 1964, a special commemorative book likened the remarkable growth of the Assemblies of God to a river, referring positively to "[i]ts tributaries . . . from many branches of historic Christianity."[23] Fifty years earlier, the founding members of the denomination, considering their former churches spiritually cold or apostate, had left or been rejected by them. At long last, after having entered the evangelical church world in 1942, the Assemblies of God was experiencing the recognition it had long desired and gaining respect for its successful initiatives in church planting overseas.

Strategy and the Spirit

As never before, Assemblies of God mission leaders and missionaries engaged in planning for the future. J. Philip Hogan's pragmatic attitude toward new programs for accelerating evangelism and assisting fraternal church organizations created a conducive atmosphere for applying the creative suggestions of indigenous church advocates like Melvin Hodges and others within the department. However, this new forward thrust for world evangelization, symbolized by the theme of Global Conquest, required enormous commitment and teamwork. The coordination alone of the department's initiatives with those of the Women's Missionary Council, Light-for-the-Lost, BGMC, Speed-the-Light, and AIM required considerable attention. By 1963, the department had taken decisive steps to plan for the future: (1) Hogan called for a strategy meeting to discuss evangelism in Europe. (2) Melvin L. Hodges, field secretary for Latin America and the West Indies, appointed a committee to coordinate Sunday school outreach in that region. And (3) Wesley R. Hurst, secretary of promotions, called a committee of educators and missionaries to study more effective ways of communicating to the home churches.[24]

Such endeavors and the new programs they spawned were nevertheless resisted in some quarters. When a veteran missionary wrote to Hogan stating, "It is our glorious Pentecostal heritage to be free, to go where we please and develop our work as we individually see fit and are led," he responded by questioning whether such an attitude was "practical, successful, or Pentecostal."[25] The demonstrated benefits of teamwork and planning had convinced many that there could be no return to the earlier days of independence, when accountability for one's missionary work and expenditures hardly existed.

The records from this period indicate that the increase in strategizing was undergirded with Pentecostal spirituality. Hogan remarked: "In these days we must be strategic in all we do. God is moving and pouring out His Spirit in many parts of the world. We must move in the direction God is working, meeting needs as they arise and as He supplies."[26] Many others shared this sentiment. Planning and spirituality could proceed together when directed by the Holy Spirit and in harmony with His objectives. One without the other, however, could jeopardize the work of God. Hodges encouraged the missionary personnel by saying, "None of us is wise enough to chart the future course of missions. We don't have to be! The Holy Spirit will lead us on a better course than we could possibly plan. He is already doing so!"[27] For this reason, Assemblies of God growth concepts, particularly when compared with those of other church growth advocates, exhibit a certain tentativeness: They reflect a uniquely Pentecostal concern for the guidance of the Spirit, going well beyond what can be gained from the study of social structures.[28] So even though planning increased, concern for the guidance of the Holy Spirit remained an enduring cornerstone of Pentecostal thinking.

Cooperative Ventures

The Decline of Colonialism

Few could have foreseen at the end of the Second World War that within a short time the colonial empires of Great Britain, France, Belgium, the Netherlands, and Portugal would be largely dismantled and scores of new nations created.[29] The long-standing commitment of the Assemblies of God to the planting of indigenous churches helped it and the overseas constituencies to weather the storms of nationalism and move toward fraternal relationships. The expulsion of missionaries from Burma (including Assemblies of God personnel) in 1966 is a notable case in point; the national church subsequently continued to grow.[30]

With this important development on the world scene, the already shifting role of the missionary from that of overseer to consultant and partner quickened. Indeed, Maynard L. Ketcham, field secretary for the Far East, saw nationalism as a potential force for good and admonished the missionaries to take steps to obviate its negative effects. Reporting that he had "repeatedly seen a lack of consideration thoughtlessly manifested toward nationals by missionaries," Ketcham recommended corrective procedures for the future.[31] His advice joined that of numerous writers in the *Missionary Forum* and lecturers at the School of Missions who were attempting to help the missionaries adjust to the changed relationship.

The upsurge in nationalism forced most mission agencies and their personnel to reevaluate policies and procedures. Some Assemblies of God missionaries found the transition difficult; most of them, however, accommodated well to the new arrangements, reflecting their spirituality, recently improved training, and respect for the national churches they ministered among. The results of partnership quickly became obvious on some fields that had only recently set up their own national organizations. Vernon Metz, a missionary to Togo-Dahomey (later Togo and Benin), reported that on his field, "the work is stronger than it has ever been before. Our African brethren seem to have more stability and sense of direction."[32] The fraternal bonds also reinforced the mutually shared spiritual and personal relationships between missionaries and nationals. After having suffered intensely for 6 days with typhoid fever and experiencing the presence and prayers of Madame Poco, wife of the general superintendent of the Togolese Assemblies of God, missionary Colleen Tipton remarked that "during this time the color of skin was forgotten. The differences in our ways of life were forgotten. It was just one child of God interceding for the need of another. Needless to say, this woman is very dear to me as a sister in the Lord."[33] Although having been generally present for many years, respect increasingly flourished among the missionaries for the caliber of leaders and the intensity of Christian zeal produced by their churches. Notable leaders came to include Rudy Esperanza (Philippines), Matthew Ezeigbo (Nigeria), David Roychoudhury (India), Kiyoma Yumiyama (Japan), and Gustavo Galdamez (El Salvador).[34]

Unexpectedly, the promotional campaign of Global Conquest became a casualty of nationalism. While it had captured the enthusiasm of the American Assemblies of God at a time when the United States enjoyed unprecedented influence, its sponsors had unwittingly chosen a slogan that backfired in some regions of endeavor. Mounting

criticism of the theme's militaristic overtones and the requests by
some missionaries to actually stop sending copies of *Global Conquest*
magazine to their countries forced the Foreign Missions Department
as early as 1961 to modify the emblem. The rocket circling the globe
(originally designed to reflect preparedness—an American interpretation) was replaced by a man kneeling in prayer next to a globe,
with a large cross positioned nearby. The theme, however, remained
unchanged.[35] Six years later, the theme was discontinued and *Global
Conquest* magazine was renamed *Good News Crusades,* a more
positive title focusing on Christian witness. Significantly, Global
Conquest itself had already changed: Light-for-the-Lost taking over
the literature agenda and the Bible school endeavor already developing on its own. The goal of mass evangelism remained and was
incorporated into Good News Crusades, constituting "a complete
program to sponsor, organize, accomplish, and follow up large city-
wide crusades that can bring a solid, productive thrust with the
gospel into mission areas."[36]

Fraternal Cooperation

The dream of an international Assemblies of God fellowship took
shape at the 1957 General Council: the Foreign Missions Department received approval "to take such steps as may seem expedient
to develop plans for the establishing of an International Assemblies
of God Fellowship by which authorized representatives of national
Assemblies of God groups may meet at regular intervals for fellowship and conference in the interests of world evangelism by the
closer co-operation of national Assemblies of God groups."[37] Having
been proposed originally by Noel Perkin, the initiative was carried
into the next decade by Hogan, and particularly Thomas F. Zimmerman, the newly-elected general superintendent. Proposals for
the organization included a statement of faith, constitution and bylaws, and when requested, the possible transfer of credentialed
ministers between church bodies.[38]

The overture generally found a warm reception on continents
where the Assemblies of God (U.S.A.) had pioneered in evangelism,
church planting, and ministerial training. Regional conferences of
Assemblies of God constituencies and other fraternally related groups
began to convene early in the 1960s. The Central American Fel-

lowship was established in December 1960 by 40 delegates meeting at Matagalpa, Nicaragua; from this later emerged the Committee of Executives of the Assemblies of God, representing Central America and the northern republics of South America. In 1961, delegates from the southern republics of the continent met in Santiago, Chile, and formed the Committee of the Assemblies of God of South America.[39] A later development came with the formation of the Caribbean Fellowship of Assemblies of God Executives in 1968.

The first Pan-African Conference occurred September 2–9, 1964, in Nigeria, bringing together 200 missionaries and church officials from every country on the continent except the Congo (later Zaire). Hogan reported that "it highlighted our common purpose, brought our efforts into coordination, and above all provided new incentive for bringing every part of Africa the witness it desperately needs."[40] Far East representatives met for similar reasons in Hong Kong in 1960. Maynard Ketcham reported, "We were not Americans, Chinese, Japanese; we were all blood brothers, all members of the body of Christ through his shed blood. We slept in the same dormitory, ate at the same table, prayed together, and shared mutual experiences."[41] From this conference came determination to coordinate aspects of the work, form a Far East Fellowship and Advisory Committee, plan further conferences, and coordinate advanced theological education.

Subsequent events, however, proved that the venture was launched before its time. Fears of domination surfaced, particularly in Europe. Although a European Fellowship of the Assemblies of God came into existence in Rome in 1966, within a short time the members reorganized under the name European Pentecostal Fellowship, thus rebuffing the hopes of an international organization.[42] Having originated independently of the Assemblies of God (U.S.A.) and historically following a congregational form of church government, some of the Europeans were suspicious of the proposals.

Nationalistic sympathies could not be easily ignored. Even the words "International Headquarters" on the front of the new Assemblies of God headquarters building in Springfield, Missouri (dedicated March 2, 1962), generated negative reactions from visiting church officials of sister organizations abroad. Despite the fact that the editor of the *Pentecostal Evangel* depicted the structure as the "headquarters of the worldwide missionary program of the Assemblies of God," sensitivities have remained over the meaning of the phrase.[43]

By the late 1960s the expected international fellowship had failed to materialize. However, the formation of regional conferences afforded concrete achievements in understanding and cooperation. These agencies have endured, providing within a fraternal context important benefits to the supporting constituencies.

Fraternal cooperation on a one-to-one basis proved to be challenging at times for both the parent organization and the emerging national church. Even though the Foreign Missions Department conceded that missionaries should not impose a type of Western organizational structure and that no single pattern was suitable for every country, it still urged "an autonomous Assemblies of God organization composed of cooperating sovereign Assemblies." At the same time, "the fundamental principles of democratic representative government for which the Assemblies of God stands should be encouraged."[44] This ideal has remained despite the actual practice of national church bodies adapting church polity to their own cultural patterns of authority.

In at least one instance, separation resulted partly because of divergent polities. The South African Assemblies of God eventually came to be closely governed by "apostles," who also spearheaded evangelism and church planting. Nicholas B. H. Bhengu, a prominent evangelist known as the Billy Graham of Africa, was considered such an apostle and strongly defended their system of church government.[45] Having major reservations about this kind of ecclesiastical structure and aware of Bhengu's fund-raising activities in the United States and other countries to support it, the Assemblies of God (U.S.A.) severed its fraternal relationship in 1964 and launched the International Assemblies of God in South Africa (designed to be linked to the proposed International Assemblies of God Fellowship).[46] In recent years both organizations have fostered cordial relations with each other. Nevertheless, this experience caused the parent organization to temper its expectations about the nature of indigenous church structures.

Views From the Outside

The spectacular church growth of Pentecostals overseas, and Assemblies of God church organizations in particular, became so apparent in the 1960s that the larger church world began to take serious notice. Donald A. McGavran, noted church growth authority, stated in his book *How Churches Grow* (1959), "[T]he tremendous increase of the Assemblies of God can, in part, be explained [because] [t]hey believe that the gift of the Holy Spirit is necessary to full Christian life, and that theirs is the only church that makes it available."[47] In the later *Church Growth in Mexico* (1963), McGavran emphasized that "the principle of *spontaneous action under the control of the Spirit of Jesus as revealed in the Scriptures* lies at the heart of the Pentecostal faith."[48] Insightful comments came from other quarters as well. In an article entitled "What We Can Learn From the Pentecostal Churches," published in *Christianity Today* in 1967, J. S. Murray, the overseas missions secretary of the Presbyterian Church in New Zealand, noted that Pentecostals "witness to what is real in their experience, to what they know is the most important thing in the world. . . . The constraint comes from within them, from something that has happened to them and that they know they must share."[49] He concluded by challenging Christians to reconsider the place of the Holy Spirit in the life of the believer and by asserting that with the proclamation of the gospel, the promise of the gift of the Holy Spirit should accompany the call to repentance and faith (Acts 2:38).[50]

Church growth scholars took particular note of the expansion of Pentecostalism in Latin America. One observer said, "While we spend our time inventing tickets or labels, the Pentecostals preach in season or out of season. While we have made the Christian life into a theology, they have made a theology into life. . . ."[51] In reference to the work in El Salvador, a Southern Baptist missionary, James D. Crane, reported that Assemblies of God missionaries "seem to have been successful in leading their churches to take responsibility for their own programs. At least they have been conscious of the danger of trying to do for the national Christians what they can and should do for themselves."[52] Such statements reinforced the confidence of Assemblies of God leaders and missionaries that they were channeling their efforts in the right direction. Mission leaders began to visit the headquarters in Springfield, Missouri, to inquire about the dynamics behind Pentecostal church growth. In reflecting on this newfound attention, J. Philip Hogan nevertheless lamented that Pentecostal successes overseas paled when compared to the millions yet unreached.[53]

Missiologist Donald A. McGavran, the father of the church growth movement, observed the rapid growth of fraternally-related Assemblies of God churches overseas beginning in the 1950s.

Responding to criticisms about the militaristic overtones of the Global Conquest logo, the Foreign Missions Department attempted to soften it by replacing the rocket with a man kneeling in prayer for the world.

Melvin L. Hodges, the dean of Pentecostal missiologists, addressing the Congress on the Church's Worldwide Mission at Wheaton College, Wheaton Illinois, 1966

Aspects of Missionary Life

In 1963 when the Foreign Missions Department published a revision of the *Missionary Manual,* 817 missionaries were serving in 73 countries of the world.[1] Although many of them enjoyed a more comfortable life-style than their predecessors, they nevertheless represented a dedicated band of Christian workers facing enormous challenges: increased promotional duties, financial pressures, cultural adjustment, education for their children, hostility, and danger—to say nothing of their primary responsibility of preaching the gospel. In many respects, their task had become more complex with the passage of time and the growing maturity of the enterprise.

Qualifications

The *Missionary Manual* defined missionaries as ambassadors of Christ, sent as representatives of God to the unsaved. While their primary objectives focused on evangelism and church planting, the missionaries were to model servanthood and consider themselves partners in working with national ministers. Since the need to evangelize unreached peoples was never to be far from their thinking, responsibilities in any given country could not be considered permanent.[2]

Flexibility had gradually become a crucial qualification for missionary service. With the theoretical demise of paternalism in the ranks (easier to disclaim than to eliminate), missionaries had to facilitate the growth of the national churches without dominating them. Indeed, due to the nature of fraternal relationships, the wise missionary himself could learn from his fellow workers. After observing the ministry of Slatiel Zuze, an Assemblies of God minister in Malawi, missionary Morris Williams confessed, "We have need to be taught and often are taught by those who, in their simplicity of faith, are taught by the Holy Ghost."[3] Such genuine humility welded the fraternal bond with good will and laid important foundations for long-term relationships.

The process of becoming a missionary began with a call from God to overseas ministry and a letter of interest to the Foreign Missions Department. Reviewed by a field secretary for the necessary qualifications, it was forwarded to the candidate secretary, who contacted the person's district superintendent for an endorsement. After this, the candidate received an official application form, which would then be returned for evaluation by the Foreign Missions Committee before processing.

Applicants were expected to be no younger than 23 (the minimum age for ordination) and no older than 35; if married, the number of children was not to exceed two or, at the most, three. The committee also expected the candidate to be ordained, having served a minimum of 2 years in a pastorate. Bible college training was the preferred form of preparation. This, however, was not required, although the vast majority of missionaries had received this kind of training. A survey of the 24 newly appointed missionaries in 1962 indicates that most had attended or graduated from a Bible college: Central Bible College—four; Southeastern Bible College—four; Southwestern Assemblies of God College—three; Bethany Bible College—two; Northeast Bible College—two; Northwest Bible College—two; and Western Bible College [Winnipeg]—two. Two were graduates of nursing schools and two had received master's degrees (Lloyd Marsh and Joseph Vitello, both degrees earned at Central Bible College).[4]

In addition to the above qualifications, foreign-born persons could not expect regular appointment to the land of their birth. However, exceptions were sometimes made for specialized workers (such as nurses) or unusual circumstances. In the majority of cases, candidates who received regular appointment were sent to the fields of their choice.

The department also continued the policy of requiring a physical examination. While affirming belief in divine healing and encouraging trust in God for physical needs, the manual indicated, "experience has taught that persons with a constitutional weakness may be seriously handicapped in missionary service."[5] By 1969 missionary candidates were also required to undergo a battery of standardized psychological examinations and a counseling interview to determine their mental and emotional health, considered necessary "in the light of increasing stress in missionary work."[6] Other requirements included references, a home interview, and an interview with the Foreign Missions Committee. Since the entire process of missionary approval, preparation, and itinerating cost the General Council a considerable expenditure of time and money, the department increasingly scrutinized the long list of applicants for those best equipped to minister abroad.

After the candidate was recommended to and approved by the Foreign Missions Board, he was then asked to sign the following statement:

> I do hereby express my wholehearted agreement with the principles and doctrines of the General Council of the Assemblies of God as set forth in the Constitution and Bylaws of the organization and in "The Missionary Manual."
>
> I intend, by the help of the Lord, to work in harmony with other ministers and missionaries of the General Council and shall seek to discourage and avoid discord, consulting with proper officials of the Field Fellowship and the Foreign Missions Department concerning areas of misunderstanding.
>
> I am willing to cooperate with the recognized officials of the General Council, both at home and on the field. I am prepared to live a life of dependence upon God, receiving with appreciation whatever may be given me for outfit, transportation, and support; and to trust God with the Foreign Missions Department for all my needs whether they may be supplied through the Department or otherwise.
>
> When I am placed on a regular missionary budget, it will be agreeable with me for 50 percent of my tithes to be deducted for the Foreign Missions Department office expense.
>
> I am going to the field for the supreme purpose of glorifying Christ, to win souls for Him, and to hasten His coming.[7]

The approved candidate then began itinerating among supporting churches to raise his budget and attended the next School of Missions. Although the application forms, references, and examinations have become more detailed, the application process and qualifications themselves have generally remained the same through the years.[8]

Budget

Following appointment, the missionary received a proposed budget prepared by the field secretary for his particular area of ministry. It included support of the missionary, support and educational expenses for his children, fees for language study, rent, travel fares, emergency expenses, and monies for maintaining his work overseas. The entire amount had to be raised in signed pledges before the prospective missionary could be cleared for departure.[9]

For itinerating among the churches, the missionary was advised to notify the district missionary secretaries, key liaisons for arranging services with local pastors. All receipts from offerings were then forwarded to the Foreign Missions Department, which in turn took care of the missionary's traveling expenses. These financial transactions demanded careful bookkeeping procedures by the missionaries and the Foreign Missions Department, because of new regulations issued by the Internal Revenue Service.[10]

Missionaries returning home on furloughs were also expected to travel among the churches to maintain their support (or increase it when the cost of living overseas increased). This approach to generating mission funds required beginning and veteran missionaries to travel thousands of miles and preach in scores of churches to raise and renew their support. In reflecting on this arduous task, John Weidman, a veteran missionary to Burkina Faso, advised his colleagues, "Be dauntless in attitude and faith. Certainly there is that stipulated budget set by the Missions Department. . . . There are moments of despair and discouragement. The important thing is to realize that you're God's and He can and will help at the most unexpected time."[11] Fortunately for the returning missionary, the time needed for itinerating did not include vacation time (1 month annually).

Adjustments in Life-Style

Moving from one culture to another required a great deal of adaptability of missionary families. The welfare of children especially became a mounting concern, necessitating study and consideration. Closely related to the problems of adjustment were the terms of service abroad. They had ranged from 3 to 6 years for some time but were changed to 4-year terms in 1967. Following a term abroad, a family was then thrust back into the (changing) American scene for another cultural response.

In possibly the first article published (1960) on the subject in the *Missionary Forum,* missionary Margaret J. McComber observed that children had little trouble adjusting to changes in their physical environments, but "encounter greater obstacles to social adjustments in the two cultures of which they are a part."[12] While most children accommodated easily to the new cultures, she noted the potential for them "to have a high tendency to develop deep-seated emotional problems and enduring social maladjustments."[13] In her opinion, however, most children had made the adaptations quite well.

McComber further discussed the pros and cons of avenues available for their education (home schooling, local schools, boarding schools, remaining with relatives in the U.S.) and concluded that along with the difficulties came important compensations for the children and their parents in living abroad. The Foreign Missions Department made a limited exploration of these problems in the 1960s; concerns for the welfare of the entire family would receive more attention in the next decade.

Missionaries also had to accommodate frequent visitors, including American pastors and evangelists. For this reason, they were often encouraged to have a guest room in their homes. At the same time, such visits sometimes hindered their work, and the department has attempted to regulate the volume of the visits; it has met, however, with only limited success.

In some cultural settings, hospitality has been required: a significant gesture of friendship and acceptance. It has also offered one of the few opportunities for evangelism and in some circumstances meant refuge for those who have been rejected by their families because of their faith in Christ (e.g., former Hindus and Muslims). As missionaries to Spain, Roy and Adele Dalton opened their home to many persons, recognizing that "making friends is just the first link in that ever-lengthening chain that we constantly pray will eventually bind our acquaintances to God."[14] Although the demands could be quite taxing, Adele Dalton noted that their home was where "the principles we preach in our services are interpreted into everyday living. Here is where people can become acquainted with our own Christ-centered attitudes toward life in general."[15] The importance of missionary hospitality has remained a vital aspect of ministry through the years.

Opposition and Suffering

Missionary life has also carried certain hazards, some common in most societies. Missionary B. Eileen Edwards died from being struck by a car in Bombay, India; automobile accidents also claimed the lives of Elmer C. Niles (Nicaragua, Venezuela) and Virginia Turner (Ghana).[16] The Talmage F. Butlers and their son, Talmage Stephen, (Bahamas, Senegal) died from an airplane accident in the Bermuda Triangle.[17] A gasoline explosion and severe burns caused the death of Sidney Goodwin (a second generation missionary), after only 22 days in Ghana as an appointed missionary.[18]

Hostility to the gospel message has taken its own toll. Several assailants attacked the Speed-the-Light Volkswagen of Paul Hutsell and R. S. Stawinski, missionaries in predominantly Catholic Paraguay. Breaking the windshield with a club, the attackers also beat Hutsell when he tried to get out of the car; Stawinski suffered from bits of glass in his face.[19] In Colombia, Protestant missionaries and believers, including Pentecostals, suffered terribly in the "reign of terror" (1946–1956), but by the 1960s the situation had improved and the churches were growing. Nevertheless, persecution was still widespread and incidents of stonings continued to be reported.[20]

In Assemblies of God circles, perhaps the best-known example of martyrdom in contemporary times is missionary J. W. Tucker, killed as a hostage during the Congo uprising of 1964. After weeks of house arrest with his wife, Angeline, and their three children, Johnny (18), Carol Lynne (13), and Melvin Paul ("Cricket," 11), Tucker was finally taken into custody and held with a number of others in a Catholic mission in the city of Paulis. Fearing an attack by American and Belgian paratroopers, the rebels hardened their attitude toward their hostages. Angeline Tucker received the news of her husband's death when she called the mission and inquired about his welfare: "The Mother Superior, I suppose it was, said,

'Well, things are going along.' I said, 'How is my husband?' She answered in French, 'He is in heaven.' "[21] A short time later, the remaining members of the Tucker family and missionaries Lillian Hogan (no relation to J. Philip Hogan) and Gail Winters were rescued in a combined Belgian and American rescue operation.

In a eulogy in *Global Conquest* magazine entitled "Love's Summit Reached," J. Philip Hogan wrote, "[L]ove taken to its limits means a life outpoured. For some this becomes a total life span lived out day by day in giving, yielding, and sacrificing. For some it may mean a sudden final investment."[22] The brutal murder of this gentle veteran missionary rocked Assemblies of God churches in America as well as its missionary personnel around the world, reminding them that martyrdoms could still occur in the 20th century. His death, however, prompted the dedication and rededication of many to world evangelization.

Missionaries also told of remarkable deliverances. David Kensinger related how he and several other national Christians escaped death after being caught in a flash flood in Costa Rica.[23] Divine intervention was credited with the recovery of missionary Deborah Irwin (Egypt, Malawi): After learning that she was pregnant, Irwin came down with hepatitis and shortly afterward, a form of paralysis known as Bell's Palsy. When the hepatitis and paralysis worsened, the doctors informed her husband that she and her unborn child were terminal; nothing could be done to save their lives. At that critical juncture, she later recounted, "the Holy Spirit was speaking to my parents about me. My mother, who is a very practical person and not given to having visions, heard a voice calling to her in the middle of the night. 'Mother, Mother.' "[24] Her parents, residing in Kansas, then spent 36 hours in prayer until they felt that God had answered their prayers. Not knowing what had happened to their daughter, they sent David a telegram saying, "When you receive telegram, rejoice! Don't know what's wrong with Debbie, but have assurance complete victory on the way!"[25] In the succeeding days, her health gradually improved and after 6 weeks she was released from the hospital; later she gave birth to their third son, a healthy baby. This belief in the power of prayer and the work of the Holy Spirit is representative of many other accounts of miraculous intervention that have been reported, serving as an important foundation stone in Pentecostal spirituality.[26]

Conclusion

The Assemblies of God launched its most aggressive evangelistic thrust to date in the early 1960s. Although the Global Conquest theme eventually had to be discarded, its emphases on literature evangelism, training national leaders, and sponsoring evangelistic centers in major cities around the world paid rich dividends in the number of converts made and the building of strong national churches. These efforts, sparked by unprecedented promotional endeavors, easily won the support of church members in America, who contributed ever larger sums of money to the mission enterprise. Their enthusiasm also radiated through auxiliary programs such as the Women's Missionary Council, Speed-the-Light, and BGMC, and prompted new ventures like Light-for-the-Lost and Ambassadors in Mission.

The rapid growth abroad and success in applying indigenous church principles caught the attention of the larger church world. Assemblies of God officials gained new stature among evangelical mission executives. Melvin L. Hodges became the premier Pentecostal missiologist through his ever-increasing list of publications, always practical in orientation and faithful to his Pentecostal theology. At the same time, the administrative policies of J. Philip Hogan provided a warm climate in which creative ventures could be developed to advance the cause of world evangelization. As never before, the missionary leadership and personnel attempted to balance strategic planning with the leading of the Holy Spirit.

Parallel to the development of evangelical missiology after World War II, Assemblies of God missionaries began to look more closely at references to the kingdom of God in the New Testament. Rather than diminishing their Pentecostal commitment or premillennial stance, they increasingly discovered it to be a valuable foundation for understanding the role of signs and wonders in the proclamation of the gospel.

With the decline of the colonial empires and the sudden appearance of new nations, the missionaries had to adjust to their revised role of partnership. The School of Missions and the *Missionary Forum* provided valuable assistance on how to work with national churches without jeopardizing their autonomy. The missionaries faced new challenges, which would have been unfamiliar to their predecessors. The taxing responsibilities and dangers in ministry abroad, however, reminded the missionaries and the faithful at home that obeying the Great Commission still required selfless dedication.

Missionary Talmage Butler (with his wife) preaching from his plane to an audience on shore in the Bahamas

J. W. and wife Angeline Tucker with their three children, Carol Lynne, Melvin Paul ("Cricket"), and John

Missionary kids attending a Christ's Ambassadors service at Hillcrest, a boarding school in Jos, Nigeria

Missionary-Evangelist Morris Plotts itinerating for ministry in Tanzania

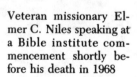

Veteran missionary Elmer C. Niles speaking at a Bible institute commencement shortly before his death in 1968

Part Three

Evangelism, Education, and Expansion (1968–1977)

8

A Forward Movement

Beginning with the Council on Evangelism in St. Louis, Missouri, in 1968, the Assemblies of God recommitted itself to the task of evangelizing America and the world before the return of Christ. In the years that followed, Good News Crusades dotted the globe as missionaries and national ministers held campaigns, often in large urban areas, to convert the unsaved and guide them into discipleship training.

On the home front, the Division of Foreign Missions (Foreign Missions Department until 1972) sponsored initiatives in missionary training: the Missionary-in-Residence program for Assemblies of God colleges and the founding in 1973 of the Assemblies of God Graduate School in Springfield, Missouri. Advances were made in Pentecostal missiology during these years as more missionaries entered graduate programs to enhance their expertise. The pen of Melvin L. Hodges continued to be productive as evidenced by the publication in 1977 of his significant *Theology of the Church and Its Mission.*

Closely related was the continued development of overseas training institutions to assist the maturation of national churches. At the same time, a new agency appeared on the scene, the International Correspondence Institute. Ministry to personnel in the armed forces also became an important endeavor. Popular support at home continued to generate more missionary personnel, funds, and volunteer service through Mobilization and Placement Service, which came to play an increasingly vital role in assisting the enterprise.

Council on Evangelism

The urgent concern within the Division of Foreign Missions to expedite the work of evangelization paralleled efforts at spiritual renewal and evangelism on the American scene. Discovering that the growth rate of converts, new churches, and ordinations had slowed in the 1950s and 1960s, church leaders called attention to the need for intensified spiritual vitality in the ranks. From this interest had come the Spiritual Life–Evangelism Commission (1965); *Advance* (1965–), a magazine for ministers containing promotional and program materials; and *Paraclete* (1967–), a journal of articles and book reviews focusing on the person and work of the Holy Spirit. The need, however, for an in-depth self-study of the Assemblies of God led the Executive Presbytery in 1967 to appoint a Committee on Advance to analyze reasons for the downturn in growth and develop a 5-Year Plan of Advance.[1]

As part of the denominational self-study, a specially-called Council on Evangelism was convened August 26–29, 1968, in St. Louis, Missouri. The gathering attracted some 7,000 ministers and lay-people who exhibited considerable enthusiasm for reviewing the purposes and objectives of the organization. In the keynote address, "The Mission of the Church," General Superintendent Thomas F. Zimmerman challenged them to fulfill the threefold task of the church: ministry to the Lord, to other believers, and to the world. The latter category placed particular emphasis on winning the lost to Christ. Although Zimmerman lauded the heritage of the Assemblies of God, he counseled, "[L]et us never get the idea that God has brought us to our present plateau to terminate progress—His command is, 'Go forward.' "[2]

At the conclusion of the meeting, the Council issued the "Declaration of St. Louis," which reflected the work of the Committee on Advance and expressed the resolve of the delegates. Emphasizing that the Assemblies of God was brought into being by the Spirit "as an instrument of divine purpose in these end times," it stated (1) God's purposes for man, (2) the triune mission of the church, and (3) the importance of strongly encouraging believers to be baptized in the Holy Spirit. Only this Baptism would enable them to evangelize accompanied by supernatural signs as in the Book of Acts, worship in the fullness of the Spirit, and respond to the "full working" of the Holy Spirit in the building of the body of Christ.[3]

This emphasis on the baptism in the Holy Spirit as empowerment for Christian witness, accompanied by glossolalia as initial evidence, has been the hallmark of Pentecostal theology and the main doctrinal divergence from evangelicalism, although belief in faith healing has been another important factor. To those in attendance, compromise on this point could only weaken spiritual energy; Spirit-baptism as an entry to the deeper work of the Spirit had to remain a cardinal teaching for revival and evangelization. In the words of Donald Gee, a prominent British Pentecostal who strongly influenced the American Assemblies of God: "To surrender it would be to surrender a sacred trust from the Most High and renounce a testimony of great value even to those who reject it. The Pentecostal revival performs its true function within the whole Body of Christ while it keeps unimpaired its own distinctive testimony. The Church *needs* a Pentecostal revival."[4] The Council, therefore, had faithfully returned to the church's theological heritage as the key to fulfilling its divine calling. This restorationist underpinning of Assemblies of God theology received further elaboration in David A. Womack's *Wellsprings of the Pentecostal Movement,* published in 1968 by Gospel Publishing House and introduced at the Council at the request of the Committee on Advance.

Following the Council, Zimmerman announced that the denomination had shifted from "a defensive holding action to a dynamic offensive outreach."[5] It was now time for the Committee on Advance to formulate a 5-year plan. The Division of Foreign Missions heartily welcomed the outcome: *Good News Crusades* magazine reported, "The Assemblies of God is determined that its people, its churches, and its leaders will not sleep through this crucial time of human history, but will bring to bear the full force of spiritual revival on our world."[6] The gathering had stirred representatives of the clergy and laity to move forward and highlighted the imperative of evangelism for the mission enterprise, a long-established priority that was already leading to spectacular church growth abroad.

Good News Crusades

Definition and Expenses

The change of promotional themes from Global Conquest to Good News Crusades proved to be wise, exchanging an unwanted militaristic implication for an emphasis on the evangelistic impulse of the missionaries and national churches. The new program comprised "a strategic and mobile ministry of worldwide evangelization . . . designed to assist Assemblies of God foreign missionaries with city-wide evangelistic crusades, rental of temporary halls or auditoriums, purchase of gospel tents, transportation of evangelists and workers for outreach projects, and sponsoring film, radio, and television ministries."[7] Promoted and publicized by *Good News Crusades* magazine, the crusades varied in cost. In 1977, for example, an evangelistic campaign in a small town or village might incur only a cost of one or two hundred dollars; one in a large city could require several thousand. In Bombay, India, for example, two Good News Crusades cost more than five thousand dollars.[8]

The Target

Although the efforts of the program did not exclude the rural areas of any given nation, its planners clearly looked to the cities for reaching the masses. The continuing migration to urban centers in many countries, accompanied by a breakdown of the traditional social and religious fabric, offered an unprecedented opportunity to make converts.[9] J. Philip Hogan lamented that in earlier years Assemblies of God missionaries had often concentrated their activities in remote areas, whose descriptions reinforced for American supporters the old stereotype of the missionary in pith helmet and bush jacket. Times had changed, however, and Hogan contended that "the mission field of greatest opportunity and challenge today is not the *bush*—it is the boulevard!"[10] Hogan recalled that in Roland Allen's *Missionary Methods—St. Paul's or Ours?* Allen had observed the Apostle Paul's strategic choice of cities for his evangelistic work.

Although Good News Crusades were planned and conducted in almost all of the 82 countries in which Assemblies of God missionaries worked in 1970, the Division of Foreign Missions targeted seven cities in particular for large-scale evangelistic thrusts: Djakarta, Indonesia; Mexico City, Mexico; Bahia Blanca, Argentina; Kinshasa, Congo (later Zaire); Teheran, Iran; Salisbury, Rhodesia (later Zimbabwe); and Noumea, New Caledonia. The Sunday of August 24, 1970, was designated Good News Crusades Day and Assemblies of God churches were invited to send offerings to underwrite the expenses of these campaigns. The program needed additional funding because so many crusades had been scheduled in the previous year that all of the monies had been depleted.[11]

Experience had taught the Division, however, that mass evangelistic efforts were ultimately successful only if long-range planning for follow-up contacts and discipleship training had been made. This required the close cooperation of the evangelist, missionaries, and national church leaders. The helpful Light-for-the-Lost literature program of the Men's Fellowship Department supplied a key ingredient for the success of these endeavors. In addition, individual American congregations sometimes gave direct financial assistance to particular campaigns. To underwrite a Good News Crusade led by missionary-evangelist Bernhard Johnson in Rio de Janiero, Brazil, in 1969, five churches gave $3,000 each (their pastors having opportunities to assist in the services).[12]

The Evangelists

Full-time missionary-evangelists, visiting American evangelists, missionaries, and national ministers conducted Good News Crusades. Bernhard Johnson stated that successful Pentecostal evangelists were gifts of Christ to His church (Ephesians 4:11), characterized by moral integrity, spiritual maturity, and zeal for soul-winning. Johnson elaborated on another mark of the evangelist, responsiveness to the leading of the Holy Spirit: He was to seek God for direction in his scheduling of campaigns, not automatically accepting every invitation or basing his response to invitations on financial considerations alone. Instead, wrote Johnson, he ought to be "sensitive to the areas where God is moving and where there is a harvesting of souls. He will be alert to God's visitation in certain countries and areas. . . . The Holy Spirit will lead him to meet the needs of men."[13]

Some of the most successful evangelists have come from the national churches themselves. J. Philip Hogan commented that although Americans have held many successful campaigns, "the most effective evangelists are those whom the national church produces. They minister to the people with a knowledge of the language and cultural mores unequalled by those not native-born."[14] This consistently positive attitude of Hogan and many missionaries toward national ministers has served to strengthen the bonds of fraternal relationships over the years. Not surprisingly, however, the crusades of American evangelists have received most of the publicity in the promotional literature of the Division of Foreign Missions and the *Pentecostal Evangel,* giving the supporting constituency information on the ministries of personalities they are familiar with. That national evangelists have not received more coverage is unfortunate, particularly in view of the concern for fraternal ties. Evangelists such as Julio Cesar Ruibal of Boliva and Daniel Munshi of Bangladesh, for example, have made significant contributions to evangelism and church growth.[15]

At times, the evangelists, whether American or national, have displayed considerable courage and perseverance. Verlin Stewart, a missionary to Colombia, recounted the story of one evangelist and church planter, Gonzalo Quintero. After conversion and Bible school training, Quintero and his family of six went to evangelize a jungle region of the country. Making this move on "faith" (without any pledged financial support), the Quinteros began their challenging ministry. Tragedy struck when their 4-year-old daughter Silvia died, apparently unable to make the climatic adjustment. Nevertheless, in the midst of their sorrow they rejoiced that a church of ten new baptized members had been started.[16] Similar stories could be heard on other fields of endeavor as well.

Evangelism With Signs and Wonders

Some Christians have argued that the apostolic miracles of the early Christian church have not been restored in the 20th century. Be that as it may, Pentecostal periodicals (e.g., *Global Conquest, Good News Crusades, Pentecostal Evangel*) have recorded thousands of healings, exorcisms, and deliverances from chemical addictions, often in association with evangelistic campaigns. Although Pentecostals have not adequately addressed the theological tension between the sovereignty of God and the frequency of signs and wonders in everyday church life or in evangelistic campaigns, they have forthrightly trusted in the promises of Christ (e.g., Mark 16:17, John 14:12) and the model of the apostles (e.g., Acts 2:43) as their pattern. As A. M. Cakau, general superintendent of the Assemblies of God of Fiji, stated in reference to preaching the gospel, "God has given us the enduement of power and the authority to declare it, to carry it, to demonstrate it."[17] This exuberant faith has led Pentecostals to confront evil forces, pray for the sick, and believe that God will deliver people from addictions and other forms of spiritual bondage by the power of the Holy Spirit. "We must start there, for that is Satan's stronghold," asserted David K. Irwin, foreign missions editor (and later professor at the Assemblies of God Graduate School). "Many times the spiritual breakthrough in a crusade comes at the exact moment that Satan's power is broken."[18] The recorded miracles from such campaigns have undoubtedly bolstered this confidence.

Responsiveness to the gospel message by the hearers has usually been considered a crucial factor in successful campaigns. For not all evangelistic crusades have witnessed miraculous happenings or resulted in large numbers of conversions. Occasional hostility from opposition groups has sometimes hampered such efforts. Publications have often emphasized the successful ventures to the exclusion of less productive ones. At the same time, the following are a sampling of Good News Crusades with their emphasis on evangelism accompanied by signs and wonders.

A particularly successful crusade in Africa was held at Gwanzura Stadium in Salisbury, Rhodesia, in 1971. It was carefully coordinated with the assistance of important branches of the national church: Women's Missionary Council, Men's Fellowship, and Christ's Ambassadors. Four hundred churches in America pledged to pray for the services. Roy Sapp, an Assemblies of God minister from the United States served as evangelist, assisted by musicians. At the conclusion of the first service, over 400 people responded to his invitation to receive Christ as Savior; great care was then taken to give doctrinal instruction and encouragement to the converts. Several persons testified to having been delivered from demons. Missionary Paul Wright wrote in the *Pentecostal Evangel* that "the most impressive incident to the people was the concluding ceremony when Alice [Ndhlove] and three others who had been delivered from demon power brought their paraphernalia of roots, bark and branches, skin and animal bones, bottles of foul-looking medicine, cloths, and beads. . . . While the Christians sang, 'There is power in the Blood,' the whole pile was set ablaze."[19] A total of 6,000 conversions were recorded at the end of the crusade.

In the stadium in Morogoro, Tanzania, national evangelist Immanuel Lazaro preached for 7 days to crowds of 20,000. People who had been deaf as well as people who had been blind were healed. On the final day, a man confined to a wheelchair stood up and walked to the platform, testifying that after prayer he was miraculously healed. From this campaign a new church was constructed in Morogoro; among those assisting was the man who had been in the wheelchair.[20]

Five thousand people attended the opening service of the Good News Crusade conducted by Evangelist William Caldwell near Ja-Ela, Sri Lanka, in 1973. On the second night the crowd doubled and the entire supply of 10,000 decision cards was exhausted; demand later exceeded another printing. At the conclusion of the campaign, the number of reported conversions exceeded the resources of the national church to properly follow-up with discipleship training. Caldwell reported, "It was glorious to see someone suddenly discover that God had done a miracle for him! The crowd was too great for all those who were healed to get to the platform to testify, but all over the audience the deaf heard, the dumb spoke, the blind saw, and cripples walked."[21] From this crusade emerged a new congregation in this largely Buddhist country.

Spectacular healings were reported in Evangelist Richard Vinyard's crusade in Taiwan in 1973; he later reported that "all over Taiwan, Pentecostal churches have been set aflame and we have seen a breakthrough among the heathen because our God is a God of miracles."[22] When missionary John Hurston conducted a campaign in Djakarta, Indonesia, 500 people were converted, 2 young men (mute from birth) received the baptism in the Holy Spirit and spoke in tongues, 1 of them having had a demon exorcised from him.[23]

Two of the most successful evangelists in Latin America have been Richard Jeffery and Bernhard Johnson. Jeffery lengthened the time of his crusades to nurture new converts and establish churches. Through effective radio advertising, he announced that prayer would be offered for the sick in his services. In one campaign in Chile, he reported that five cripples were healed in a single service. In San Salvador, El Salvador, Jeffery's crusade led to 33 new churches being started within the following year. Jeffery had a marked impact on the methods of two other influential evangelists and church planters, David Godwin and Doyle G. Jones.[24]

Over the years, missionary-evangelist Bernhard Johnson has become known as the Billy Graham of Brazil. In 1974, 50,000 people attended the closing service of his Good News Crusade in Porto Alegre. Feeling "a tremendous surge of God's power flowing throughout the stadium," Johnson sensed that something unusual would happen. When he requested prayer for the 10 invalids present, over 200 people testified to having seen the resurrected Christ walking above the crowd in the direction of the invalids. All 10 reported instant healings.[25] In a letter to Executive Director J. Philip Hogan, Johnson recounted that in the same year, 41,430 people had been converted in his meetings.[26]

Church Planting

Evangelistic crusades and church planting have been closely related in the history of Assemblies of God missions. It is not surprising, therefore, that the Division of Foreign Missions, its missionaries, and national ministers have sometimes refused to promote and identify themselves with evangelists and agencies whose use of funds, though well-meaning, has amounted to a shift back to paternalism. An example of this was the Division's refusal to cooperate with T. L. Osborn's Association for Native Evangelism.[27] In the view of the missionaries, the evangelization of the world could be achieved only through encouraging the development of strong indigenous church organizations; outside funds needed to be used judiciously or they could stifle proper growth. Reflecting the opinion of many, Morris O. Williams, a missionary to Africa, wrote, "I have yet to see a national worker who is on salary from the 'outside' get any sizable response from his congregation in the way of tithes and offerings."[28] Although missionaries were generous with their assistance, helping national workers build churches and secure transportation among other things, they steadfastly advocated that congregations become self-supporting and ministers maintain loyalty to their own national churches.

This strategy has proven to be far-sighted, promoting successful national church organizations over the years. In surveying the advance in the 1960s, the following statistics indicate decadel growth:

	1959	1969	%
National workers	12,657	15,537	23%
Organized churches and outstations	12,459	20,387	64%
Adult members and adherents	985,241	2,859,339	190%
Number baptized in the Holy Spirit	88,042	685,744	679%
Sunday school enrollment	255,753	1,075,301	320%
Bible schools	69	91	32%
Bible school enrollment	2,509	3,672	46%

Foreshadowing the trend of the next two decades, this statistical comparison from the 1960s demonstrates a remarkable growth rate.[29]

One popular means of promoting evangelism and subsequent church planting has been the use of tents. Although the healing campaigns of Jack Coe, Oral Roberts, and others had gained wide publicity in the 1950s through the use of large tents, which could accommodate thousands, in America their crowds diminished in the next decade and tent evangelism became another chapter in the history of American revivalism. Overseas, however, tent evangelism has continued to be effective and helpful for starting churches. Tents have been successfully used in many countries, from Korea to Latin America.[30] In Argentina, a Good News Crusade was planned for Bahia Blanca, one of the seven target cities for 1970. Beginning in a tent in a residential neighborhood, missionary Paul Brannan as well as national pastors and evangelists shared the preaching responsibilities. Eventually Good News Crusades funds helped the fledgling congregation that emerged from the campaign purchase property, and First Assembly of God, Waxahachie, Texas, contributed $1,000 for the purchase of a portable tabernacle to be used as a temporary church home. Finances for a permanent building came later through the assistance of the Argentina Assemblies of God; church members donated their labor in construction and raised money for furnishings.[31] The vital connection between tent evangelism and the provision of temporary shelter for a congregation has proven to be of strategic importance for fostering new churches.

Two of the best-known church planting endeavors experienced

rapid growth through establishing home cell groups or satellite congregations in the 1960s and 1970s. By 1969, the Seoul Evangelistic Center had grown to a membership of 7,500 and later built a sanctuary seating 10,000, constructed entirely with Korean funds. It eventually became known as the Yoido Full Gospel Church. After 10 years it was well on its way to becoming the largest congregation in the Pentecostal movement, and soon became the largest in the world.[32] Paul Yonggi Cho, the pastor, effectively utilized women in the congregation as assistant pastors and cell group leaders. Sensing the direction of the Lord for this new and revolutionary role of women in Korea, he concluded that "a woman could have a ministry as long as she was under the authority of the church. She just could not teach her own doctrine, but she could witness and minister my teaching."[33] This approach proved to be a major factor in the success of the church. Since its founding, the church has experienced phenomenal growth and Cho has become a leading figure in world Christianity and a widely recognized authority on church growth.[34]

The Evangelistic Center in San Salvador, El Salvador, has also experienced remarkable growth. Shortly after the founding of the center in 1960, missionary John Bueno and his wife, Lois, became its pastors. In 1970, Bueno began to study the New Testament patterns of Christian expansion. Focusing on the first seven chapters of the Book of Acts, he was struck by the implications of submission to the Lordship of Christ, particularly in Acts 2:36, "Therefore let all the house of Israel know assuredly, that God hath made that same Jesus whom ye have crucified, both Lord and Christ." His subsequent preaching on this theme led to a Friday night prayer meeting and a door-to-door witnessing program. With the resulting revival came a willingness of the congregation to sacrifice their time and resources for evangelism. Branch churches were started throughout the city. In 1970, 1,000 persons were attending Sunday school and the church had an adult membership of about 400. Six years later the mother church and 200 branch churches had grown to almost 13,000 people, a growth pattern that has continued to the present.[35]

Other notable church planting ventures included the building of the Teheran Evangelistic Center in Teheran, Iran (dedicated in 1971, it has remained open and the congregation has grown despite the Iranian Revolution of 1978–1979), and the Nairobi Christian

Center in Nairobi, Kenya (dedicated in 1974), both projects assisted by the fund-raising endeavors of famed missionary-evangelist and church planter Morris Plotts.[36] The crusades of missionary-evangelists Watson Argue and Paul Olson also made important contributions to church planting.[37] In addition, concern for unreached peoples mounted during these years.[38]

Missionaries continued to face hazards in their activities. In 1970, fighting in the city of Amman, Jordan, forced the Warren Flatterys and the Habib Iskanders to leave for safer places of ministry. The Kenneth Godbeys and Gerald Falleys narrowly escaped danger during the Nigerian civil war. An automobile accident not only injured Mark Bliss and his wife, missionaries to Iran, but also took the lives of their three children.[39]

Armed Forces Personnel

An unexpected resource for church planting came with the activities of American military personnel living abroad. Assemblies of God missionaries often cooperated with the programs of military chaplains and sometimes started churches close to military installations. The ministry to Armed Forces personnel has come under two umbrellas: Europe and the Far East. The first full-time representative for Europe, arriving in Germany in January 1963, was missionary Richard C. Fulmer, a former national secretary of the Christ's Ambassadors (Youth) Department of the Assemblies of God. In the Far East, missionary Jimmie Davis spearheaded the ministry among servicemen and women beginning in 1966 and was later assisted by Fulmer in developing the program. Although the methodologies of the two ministries have been different in the two regions, they both go by the name Berean Missionary Fellowship (BMF). Since military bases were scattered over wide regions in the Far East and post chapel facilities were booked, military personnel sought fellowship off post, encouraging the building of Assemblies of God churches.[40] On the European scene, military posts were closer together, facilitating access to post chapels. Thus, on-post sponsorship of denominational services were possible and productive. For example, BMF groups use military chapel facilities and Assemblies of God personnel are encouraged to participate in general Protestant chapel programs as Sunday school teachers, choir members, and in other helpful capacities.

The first annual servicemen's retreat in U.S. military facilities was held in Chiemsee, Germany, in 1957. A year later, it moved to the General Walker Hotel in Berchtesgaden, Germany. Planned under the auspices of the Berean Missionary Fellowship in Europe, these retreats—designed to provide Christian fellowship, recreation, and spiritual challenge—have been attended by hundreds of military personnel. Many have been converted to Christ, pursued ministerial training, and entered full-time Christian ministry as a result. [41]

To assist with evangelism and church planting in Europe, the Centurion Foundation was set up in 1965, supported by the donations of servicemen and American civilians stationed in Europe, including schoolteachers and missionaries. After 5 years their contributions to the foundation's revolving loan fund, designed to aid Assemblies of God churches and Bible institutes, totaled more than $34,000. Through the years, special offerings have also been received to help in various related projects. [42]

One of the key people in promoting and coordinating the work and programs of the Berean Missionary Fellowship in Europe was Helen Braxton, who served under Richard Fulmer from 1965 to 1984. As an appointed missionary, her duties included publishing the *BMF Newsletter,* assisting with planning the retreats at Berchtesgaden, and various other responsibilities. In spite of her taxing schedule, she said, "I loved it! I felt needed. And the program met spiritual needs. Many, many servicemen and families were brought into the Kingdom through BMF's outreaches." [43] Braxton's work indicates that women continued to fill important roles in Assemblies of God missions.

Asked by Swedish Pentecostal missionaries to help their efforts, the Division of Foreign Missions also sent missionaries to evangelize, train national workers, and develop a Teen Challenge ministry in South Vietnam during the final years of the conflict there. [44] Relief work and ministry to servicemen was included in this endeavor as well. Such work was cut short, however, by the communist takeover in 1975.

Bible Distribution

Over the years, Assemblies of God missionaries have been keenly interested in the distribution of Scripture portions and Bibles. The

Division of Foreign Missions has worked closely with the American Bible Society and solicited finances for translation and distribution, offering denominational World Ministries credit to churches for their contributions. In 1969, the Division pledged to raise $50,000 to underwrite the distribution of Bibles in Burma in the Burmese and major tribal languages.[45] It promised an equal amount for sponsoring a new translation of the Bible into Chinese at a time when American relations with China were beginning to improve.[46]

More directly, missionaries themselves were sometimes involved in important translation projects. In an article in the *Pentecostal Evangel*, "The Bible in Our Time," J. Philip Hogan particularly praised the labors of Eva Radanovsky, a missionary to Burkina Faso, West Africa, in revising the More Bible, a translation originally done by Assemblies of God missionaries many years before.[47] In late 1975, the Divison of Foreign Missions began to have more contact with Wycliffe Bible Translators, signalling the start of a positive relationship that has endured.[48]

Church Growth Studies

As Donald McGavran's writings on church growth increasingly caught the attention of Christians worldwide, farsighted practitioners of missions in the Assemblies of God began to explore the causes for growth as well. Melvin Hodges led the way through his many published articles and books (e.g., *A Guide to Church Planting* [1973]). His timely article, "A Pentecostal's View of Mission Strategy," in the *International Review of Mission* (1968) reached beyond evangelicalism to the churches associated with the ecumenical movement.[49]

Another prominent Assemblies of God missiologist was David A. Womack, a former missionary to Colombia and then home secretary for the Division of Foreign Missions. His popular *Breaking the Stained-Glass Barrier,* which articulated a Pentecostal strategy of mission, was published by Harper and Row in 1973. An excerpt from the book was published in *Christianity Today* under the title "The Only Hope for World Evangelization."[50] Four years later, Bethany Fellowship, Inc., published his *Pyramid Principle of Church Growth,* another study in church growth principles. The books and articles by Hodges and Womack not only served to articulate Pentecostal perspectives, but through occasionally publishing outside of denominational channels, they gained a broader exposure for Assemblies of God missions.

Perhaps the most startling review of the Assemblies of God mission enterprise came out of Dallas Theological Seminary, an institution not known for its Pentecostal sympathies. One of its leading missiologists, George W. Peters, a longtime friend of the Division of Foreign Missions and occasional speaker at its School of Missions, issued a 14-point evaluation:

1. They [the Assemblies of God] have achieved to a considerable degree a balance of faith and sound mind, strategy and structure, function and organization, human effort and spiritual dynamics;

2. They believe in the sufficiency and efficiency of the Holy Spirit, practice the Pentecostal presence of the Holy Spirit, believe in the miraculous, and anticipate miracles;

3. They are clearly focused in their ministries and know where they are going and what their plans and purposes are;

4. They are narrowly channeled—they are out to evangelize and plant evangelizing churches by a direct gospel preaching approach;

5. They are uniformly trained in basic missionary principles, practices, and relationships;

6. They are thoroughly integrated functionally—all have the same goal interpreted uniformly—with a great deal of latitude and flexibility structurally and methodologically. No one method is forced on all;

7. They are carefully programmed from a central office in Springfield by a secretariat that spends about half time in the field without, however, cramping or paralyzing personal initiative, responsibility, and genius;

8. They are well sustained financially, and the Lord's money is carefully guarded and wisely invested in projects that produce;

9. They are fraternally related to the churches in the fields of operation, and the missionary-church relationship is closely guarded on a Christian basis of mutuality and equality;

10. They are unashamedly Pentecostal in doctrine and practice and uncompromising in their uniquenesses and emphases;

11. They reinforce their regular missions ministries by campaigns known as Good News Crusades which serve to revive, mobilize, and expand the ministry of the churches;

12. They most effectively mobilize hundreds of young people for short term service and employ them widely in their programs of saturation evangelism which they carry from city to city around the world;

13. They have established large and effective evangelistic centers in numerous cities of the world;

14. They have uniquely succeeded in remaining an evangelism movement in missions rather than to petrify into a denominational structure of hierarchy.[51]

This sympathetic assessment brought cheer and encouragement to Assemblies of God missionaries and the members of the Foreign Missions Committee, since it praised their efforts and assured them that they were on the right course.

Various church growth studies also corroborated the effectiveness of the mission enterprise and its fraternally-related national churches in church planting. Among these were the monumental study by William R. Read, Victor M. Monterroso, and Harmon A. Johnson entitled *Latin American Church Growth* (1969), C. Peter Wagner's popular treatment, *Look Out! The Pentecostals Are Coming* (1973; later, *Spiritual Power and Church Growth: Lessons from the Amazing Growth of Pentecostal Churches in Latin America [1986]*), and Donald A. McGavran's "What Makes Pentecostal Churches Grow?" in *Church Growth Bulletin* (January 1977).

The increasing analyses of church growth in various countries revealed, however, that evangelism and church planting among Assemblies of God constituencies were not uniformly successful. For example, McGavran noted in one publication that the work of the Assemblies of God in Chile lagged far behind that of the Methodist Pentecostals, the latter having a greater appeal to the masses.[52] However, as a whole, Latin America represented the most fruitful area for church planting in the entire missions operation of the Assemblies of God, with the exception of South Korea. Leaders partially attributed the unevenness of growth from country to country to the sovereign moving of the Holy Spirit. Nevertheless, they viewed every country as having potential for revivalistic evangelism and church planting—and strategized accordingly.

Missionary Jimmie Davis had an influential role in ministering to military personnel in the Far East.

Ministering to military personnel in 1965 in Europe were Dick and Jean Fulmer, Helen Braxton, Ruth and Eddie Washington, and Jackie and Filian Hetzel.

During a Good News Crusade in Panama this woman praised
God for healing after prayer by evangelist Richard Jeffery.
She had traveled a great distance on crutches to attend.

Church officials praying a prayer of dedication over Light-for-the-
Lost literature in preparation for Good News Crusade with Evangelist
Paul Olson in Ghana

Missionary-evangelist Bernhard Johnson

Internationally known expert in church growth, Paul Yonggi Cho pastors the Yoido Full Gospel Church in Seoul, Korea.

As an evangelist and church planter, Daniel Munshi has made a significant contribution to the development of the Assemblies of God in Bangladesh. He currently serves as the chairman (general superintendent) of the organization.

General Superintendent Thomas F. Zimmerman became a well-known international leader among Pentecostals and evangelicals. During his tenure the Assemblies of God clarified its mission in the world.

Teheran Evangelistic Center in Teheran, Iran, 1972

The successor to *Global Conquest* magazine, *Good News Crusades* highlighted the overseas evangelistic efforts of the Assemblies of God and its fraternally-related churches without a militaristic connotation.

9

Missions Education and Missiology

The need for advanced theological and missiological training in the Assemblies of God became increasingly apparent in the decades of the 1960s and 1970s. The founding of the Assemblies of God Graduate School in 1973 as an institution specializing in theology and missions represented a milestone in the development of higher education within the denomination and in the level of missiological training available for personnel in the Division of Foreign Missions. Its opening occurred at a time of heightened interest in exploring and developing Pentecostal missiology for the promotion of world evangelization. Graduates of the school who had served overseas and other veteran missionaries began to enhance the undergraduate programs in missions offered by Assemblies of God colleges through another innovation, the Missionary-in-Residence program.

The Assemblies of God Graduate School

Steps Toward Postgraduate Training

The interest in advanced studies in missions became apparent as early as 1943 when the Foreign Missions Department under the leadership of Noel Perkin successfully urged the administration of Central Bible Institute (CBI, Central Bible College after 1965) to offer a special nondegree fourth year program of courses for people interested in missionary service.[1] Two years later, the General Council authorized adding an education department to the headquarters structure. In addition to the department's other responsibilities, it added this charge: "As progress and growth demands, the Educational Department may provide a Full Theological Seminary Course in addition to the Bible Institute course, and provide postgraduate work for graduates who seek special training for the ministry in the United States or foreign lands."[2] After the founding of the American Association of Bible Colleges in 1947, Assemblies of God Bible schools upgraded their programs to the collegiate level and began offering bachelor's degrees in various fields of ministry. Despite this significant improvement in ministerial training, the Council also went on record in 1949 as opposing the use of academic degrees as a requirement for ordination.[3]

Postgraduate work came 2 years later when CBI was authorized to offer a fifth-year degree, the bachelor of theology (Th.B.). The institution subsequently became known as Central Bible Institute and Seminary, a name (somewhat of a misnomer) it kept until 1957. At that time it began a graduate program leading to a master of arts in religion degree, which effectively discontinued its limited cultivation of a seminary program. The curriculum offered nine courses in missions, including apostolic patterns of evangelism, the indigenous church program, personal and social problems of the missionary, Roman Catholicism, and organization and administration of national Bible institutes.[4] Philip A. Crouch, a veteran missionary to Egypt and member of the faculty having an M.A. in Islamic Studies from the Hartford Seminary Foundation, taught many of these courses in addition to similar undergraduate courses. Although the graduate school had competent part-time faculty members, which it shared with the college, and a potentially bright future, the General Council did not fund or promote it, and the enrollment remained small. Nevertheless, several missionaries did complete the program, notably Louise Jeter Walker, whose thesis was published by the Foreign Missions Department. The graduate school was, however, discontinued in 1966.

Northwest Bible College (later, Northwest College of the Assemblies of God) in Seattle, Washington, also began to offer an M.A. in 1958. One contribution of this program was David A. Womack's thesis, which became the basis for his *Wellsprings of the Pentecostal Movement* (1968). The attempt was shortlived, however, and a year later the school reverted to a Th.B. program. The lack of adequate funding and support by the General Council and hesitations expressed by the American Association of Bible Colleges about the offering of master's degrees frustrated the efforts of both schools.

Consequently, Assemblies of God missionaries gravitated toward various evangelical schools for graduate education.

By the 1960s graduate and seminary education in the Pentecostal movement was becoming a reality. In 1963, evangelist Oral Roberts, then a minister in the Pentecostal Holiness Church, opened Oral Roberts University in Tulsa, Oklahoma. After 2 years, he added a graduate school of theology, which ceased operation after only 4 years. The Church of God in Christ began the Charles H. Mason Theological Seminary in Atlanta, Georgia, in 1970, becoming the first successful (and later fully accredited) Pentecostal seminary. Another graduate school appeared when the Melodyland Christian Center, a large independent charismatic church in Anaheim, California, sponsored the Melodyland School of Theology in 1973; it discontinued operation in 1981. Although these institutions produced some lasting results, none of them was noted for a focus on advanced training in missiology.

The Graduate School Established

The demands within the General Council continued to mount for starting a graduate school, broader in scope than what had been offered by Northwest College and Central Bible College, one with the component of a standard seminary curriculum. For their part, the missionary personnel keenly felt the pressure for additional training and master's degrees, not only for the improvement of skills, but because pressures to introduce collegiate programs in some overseas Bible schools (163 by 1977) increasingly required faculty members (often missionaries) to have graduate level training. This necessity reflected the growing desire in developing nations for the academic advancement of their own educational institutions, a concern voiced by maturing national churches as well. Thus, the Division of Foreign Missions had long recognized the urgency for such a program and directly requested that a graduate program be expedited.[5]

Although the General Council had authorized such a school in 1961, it did not materialize until 1973.[6] Because of anti-intellectual sentiments and suspicions about the possible negative spiritual impact of a seminary, the name Assemblies of God Graduate School of Theology and Missions (AGGS) was chosen. Among other objectives, the planners designed AGGS to help students acquire "the characteristics and skills which will prepare them for places of leadership, and teaching ministries in Bible colleges at home and abroad," in an atmosphere charged with a passion for missions and evangelism.[7] Since it opened, the school has been housed in the headquarters complex of the Assemblies of God in Springfield, Missouri. Thomas F. Zimmerman, the general superintendent and chairman of the Executive Presbytery (also the AGGS Board of Directors), received appointment as president of the school on a part-time basis, assisted by Assemblies of God educator Cordas C. Burnett as executive vice-president.[8]

The Missions Division

In its early years, the name "Assemblies of God Graduate School of Theology and Missions" served as an umbrella for what were virtually two distinct schools: the Theology Division and the Missions Division. Each had its own dean, faculty members, degree programs, and academic schedules. After its first year of operation, the school published six objectives for the Missions Division. They focused on helping veteran missionaries sharpen their skills, offering specialized studies and degrees, assisting missionaries in meeting increased immigration requirements (graduate education) for some foreign countries, training professors of missions for undergraduate programs in Assemblies of God colleges, and "to establish a focal point for the various levels of missionary education and training, thus producing a totally integrated concept of missionary preparation in the Assemblies of God."[9]

Delmer R. Guynes, the personnel secretary for the Division of Foreign Missions, became the first dean of the Missions Division by adding its portfolio to his already heavy responsibilities. Having spent two terms as a missionary in Malaysia, Guynes had also pastored, served as academic vice-president of Southwestern Assemblies of God College in Waxahachie, Texas, and was a doctoral candidate in counseling and personnel administration when the school opened.[10] After the death of Cordas Burnett (1975), Guynes was appointed to the post of executive vice-president (1976–1979); during his administration AGGS received its initial accreditation as a graduate institution from the North Central Association of Colleges and Schools.

The joint responsibilities of personnel secretary, dean of the Missions Division, and (part-time) professor reflected the close relationship between the Division of Foreign Missions and the school in its early years. From its inception, AGGS played a key role in the preparation of missionary candidates (the Candidate Graduate Training Program, CGTP) and the provision of continuing education for veteran missionaries. Although the school officially opened its doors on September 4, 1973, a special "pre-inauguration" summer session had already been held from June 25 to July 27 for 65 missionaries remaining in Springfield after the school of missions.[11] The next year J. Philip Hogan applauded the "well-defined goals" of the Missions Division, writing, "It is extremely exciting to know that the Assemblies of God stands in the forefront of the greatest spiritual movement the world has ever seen."[12]

The development of the missions curriculum and its degree programs directly related to the faculty members who staffed the Division, their educational backgrounds and missionary experiences. Each professor was selected on the basis of his academic background and actual missionary experience. Although largely self-taught and without an earned degree, the best-known faculty member was Melvin L. Hodges, who had recently retired from the office of field secretary for Latin America and the West Indies. In reference to Hodges' new avenue of ministry, Hogan remarked that "God has been preparing His servant for what may be the most influential and creative role he has yet known."[13] Indeed, the next 10 years of his instruction and writing continued to mold the course of the denomination's mission enterprise. Other instructors included Delbert H. Tarr, Jr., a missionary to Burkina Faso and doctoral candidate in communications at the University of Minnesota, and later, David K. Irwin, a missionary to Egypt and Malawi and foreign missions editor, who was pursuing graduate studies in anthropology at the University of Missouri–Columbia. By 1977, part-time instructors included Ronald A. Iwasko, a former missionary to Brazil and by then personnel secretary for the Division of Foreign Missions, and Monroe D. Grams and Hugh P. Jeter, both veteran missionaries to Latin America.

The Missions Division initially offered one master's degree, but by the second year a student could choose among concentrations in missions science, missions communication (later cross-cultural communications), and missions anthropology. The expansion continued and the 1975–1976 catalog announced three separate degree plans for the above areas.[14] The M.A. in missions science (missiology) addressed strategy, techniques, and relationships with national churches. The degree in cross-cultural communications was designed "to facilitate interpersonal relationships in divergent cultures" for effective preaching and teaching. And the program in anthropology focused on "the religious and societal factors in world cultures that affect receptivity to the gospel."[15] The mainstays of each degree were Hodges (missions science), Tarr (cross-cultural communications), and Irwin (cultural anthropology). It should be noted that Guynes also taught selected courses in each of these areas.

The Division of Foreign Missions had never insisted on any particular academic path in preparation for missionary service. Although it recommended Bible school education and required the School of Missions for candidates and furloughed missionaries, it accepted persons as qualified for overseas ministry if they had met district qualifications for ordination (which varied considerably), had a proven ministry, felt called to missions, and met several other criteria. Undoubtedly this ambiguity about formal training reflected the denomination's hesitancy about academic requirements for ministry.[16] Nevertheless, leaders in the mission enterprise had long encouraged the offering of specialized courses in the Bible colleges as valuable tools for preparation. After the establishment of AGGS, however, they confidently endorsed the offerings of the Missions Division, believing that the expertise of its faculty, in consultation with a representative of the Division of Foreign Missions, had accurately appraised the needs of the missionaries.[17] In this way the missions leaders hoped that the present and future demands of the enterprise would be met accordingly.

However, several flaws were soon found in the blueprint; although not hindering the enormously positive aspects of the program, they forecast problems. First, the operation of two schools under one umbrella proved to be ultimately unworkable. This became quickly apparent in the lack of integration of the degrees offered by the institution, a problem that began to receive attention during the initial self-study (1976–1977) for accreditation.[18]

Second, the educational directions of the two divisions began to diverge. Although the Theology Division quickly moved toward a standard seminary curriculum (a master of divinity degree was added in 1974), the Missions Division viewed itself as primarily a graduate school of missions, providing master of arts degrees. However, in tailoring itself to the needs of missionaries, none of its three degrees required more than an undergraduate major in Bible for admission, an awkward arrangement that could not be easily corrected.[19]

Third, the relationship was uncertain between the AGGS Missions Division as a graduate school and the Assemblies of God Bible colleges' undergraduate programs in missions. Specialized missions courses at the undergraduate level for basic missionary qualification called into question AGGS courses, which were sometimes repetitive. On the other hand, students in undergraduate institutions sometimes avoided missions majors, knowing that if they intended to serve overseas, such courses would be required in the AGGS Candidate Graduate Training Program.

Fourth, extended missionary furloughs became a problem when the number of veteran missionaries requesting graduate study increased: The months normally required for itineration among the churches for the maintenance of financial support were lengthened by time spent on academic work at the school. Gradually the strain on the availability of missionaries for their posts of ministry caused concern.

Fifth, although all candidate missionaries did not enroll in degree programs, they were required to take courses taught by Hodges, Tarr, Irwin, and Guynes as part of their prefield training (CGTP). Veteran missionaries often enrolled as well, although not always pursuing degrees. In some instances, criticisms surfaced from individuals who were not prepared for this level of work and/or did not possess undergraduate degrees.

Despite such problems and shortcomings, the work of the Missions Division represented the boldest thrust in missionary training that the Assemblies of God had ever formulated. The problems overseas and the need for higher qualifications had helped to trigger the founding of the Graduate School at a strategic point in the history of the mission enterprise. The keys to the success of the program can be traced to (1) the close relationship with the Division of Foreign Missions, (2) the generous financial assistance it provided, (3) the capable instruction of the professors, and (4) the general maturity and cross-cultural experiences of many of its students.

Missiological Contributions

Assemblies of God Graduate School

Both professors and students made important contributions to the promotion and understanding of Assemblies of God missions during these years. The most significant faculty publication was Melvin L. Hodges' *Theology of the Church and Its Mission: A Pentecostal Perspective* (1977). Recognizing that few books had been written by Pentecostal missiologists to explain the reasons behind the global expansion of the movement, Hodges aimed to rectify the situation by writing a theology of the Church and its mission to the world from a frankly Pentecostal perspective.[20] It was perhaps his most ambitious literary project.

Hodges' perspectives are strongly restorationist, viewing the New Testament as not merely an account of God's activities, but an indispensable pattern for contemporary evangelism. Time-honored philosophies and procedures in Christian missions must be examined accordingly if the world would be won for Christ. Using this framework, he asserted that the key to Pentecostal success has been the willingness "in preaching and experience to give the place to the Holy Spirit which the New Testament indicates should be given."[21] Simple obedience to the commands of Christ is not enough without divine empowerment. For this, one must turn to the spiritual dynamics in the Book of Acts, beginning with the baptism in the Holy Spirit. Herein lies the foremost cause for the swift Pentecostal advance in missions. Failure to seek the power of the Holy Spirit in his fullness will mean stagnation in church growth.

For Hodges, the Church (*ekklesia*) represents those who have been called out from the world. Their mission is threefold: worship, service, and witness. The true Church is found within the visible church on earth, although the latter at times may deteriorate into simply a human organization, devoid of the power of the Holy Spirit.[22] Although Hodges linked the church to the (spiritual) presence of the Kingdom of God, he failed to effectively tie this to the manifestation of signs and wonders in the ministries of Jesus and the apostles.[23] Nevertheless, this identification of the Church with the kingdom is an important interpretation (which Hodges had insisted on in earlier statements). Increasingly, others began to echo this perspective. David K. Irwin, for example, editorialized in *Good News Crusades* magazine that "the mission of the church is the actualization of the kingdom of Christ [synonymous with kingdom of God] in the world. . . . [T]he Church is literally an *interim* agency. We live and work 'between the times': that is, between our Lord's First Coming and His Second Coming. However, this . . . is no barren period of waiting. It is God's NOW—the time of the Spirit— the time of evangelism."[24] References to the kingdom also appeared more forthrightly in the denomination's Word of Life Sunday school curriculum.[25]

Hodges, reflecting the opinion of many evangelicals, focused on the conversion of the individual. This accounts for his denunciation of universalism, which was becoming increasingly evident in some quarters of Christendom.[26] He also sounded a word of caution about Donald A. McGavran's perspectives on "people movements" in church growth. Without condemning McGavran's views, Hodges nevertheless warned about the dangers of the potential entry of the unregenerate into the ranks of the church. This would only sap its spiritual vitality and lay a foundation for failure.[27] In addition, he spoke at length about the tension between evangelism and social concern, fearing the impact of humanism, liberation theology, and the positions held by some in the ecumenical movement. As long as evangelism has the first priority, relief and aid to the needy should be encouraged; the missionary, however, must always avoid political involvement.[28] In these and other respects, Hodges closely agrees with the pronouncements of the Wheaton Declaration (1966), Frankfurt Declaration (1970), and the Lausanne Covenant (1974), important evangelical statements on missiology from the period.

While Hodges addressed other important items (i.e., the nature of a New Testament church, indigenous church principles), he adroitly examined the problem of proselytism in missionary evangelism. Specifically, he asked, "What is the responsibility of evangelicals to members of a church who may now have experienced a spiritual new birth?"[29] This bore particular relevance for Pentecostal expansion in countries where Roman Catholicism is the dominant Christian faith. In his view, the unfortunate practice of infant baptism and belief in the sacramental system mitigated the possibility of one coming to a genuine faith in Christ. Ideally, an awakening of spiritual life within an existing church, whether Roman Catholic or Protestant, will "bring such people to the knowledge of experimental *[sic]* salvation and into the fellowship of the life in the Holy Spirit."[30] When this does not occur, however, they should be actively evangelized and nurtured even though this may mean a change in church affiliation. The "true church" cannot be harmed by the gospel witness in the power of the Holy Spirit.[31]

The contemporary worldwide emergence of the charismatic movement in the historic Protestant churches and particularly in the Roman Catholic Church created another vexing problem. Assemblies of God missionaries in Latin America, like their evangelical counterparts, had long viewed the Roman church as apostate and had no hesitations in urging their converts to leave it. The presence of charismatics, however, receiving the baptism in the Holy Spirit and experiencing unprecedented spiritual renewal touched the chords of Pentecostal pneumatology and ecclesiology, raising the issue of proselytism to a new level of sensitivity. Hodges did not offer easy answers, but significantly he recognized the charismatic movement as valid. Spirit-filled bishops, priests, and nuns could have a powerful spiritual impact if they remained in the Catholic church. Although he trembled over Catholic theological errors and their potential spiritual damage, he nevertheless stated, "we are not working for church affiliation but the kingdom of God," which is ruled by God in his sovereignty.[32] Charismatics should, therefore, receive spiritual encouragement in their progress in the kingdom and trust the Holy Spirit to guide them on the issue of church affiliation. This echoed the brief statement on the charismatic movement issued by the General Council at its specially-called Council on Spiritual Life on August 14–16, 1972, as well as the important papers presented by Joseph R. Flower and D. Leroy Sanders on that occasion.[33] In the following year, J. Philip Hogan observed that the charismatic movement represented "a new move of the Spirit . . . sweeping around the world and gathering momentum every day. It is accomplishing that which councils and budgets and human planning could never achieve."[34] This new development appeared to demonstrate the continuing need for responsiveness to where, and in what way, the Holy Spirit was active in the world.

The timing of Hodges' remarks significantly paralleled evangelical attempts to address the proper relationship to "gospel-minded Catholics," notably at the Consultation on Theology and Mission sponsored by Trinity Evangelical Divinity School, Deerfield, Illinois, in March 1976. At this conclave, well-known evangelical theologian David F. Wells remarked that "contemporary Catholics are recovering the personal, subjective dimension of faith which has been absent for so long. Faith is now more frequently defined as being open to the Spirit, or as encountering Christ, than it is believing what the church teaches."[35] This changing theological climate had set the stage for meaningful dialogue. Even so, the unity achieved in the Spirit between some Pentecostals and charismatics (including Roman Catholics), experienced in local contexts or in nondenominational conferences, has often surpassed evangelical aspirations for closer fellowship and cooperation with members of the historic churches.[36] Although the recommendations of Hodges have not received further official elaboration since the publication of his book, the attitude of Assemblies of God missionaries toward charismatics has generally ranged from the traditional hostility to fellowship and cooperation.[37]

Since the master's programs in the Missions Division carried research options, students also made lasting contributions through their writing. Among these works are James E. Richardson's "Study of the Leadership Training Programs of the Assemblies of God in Spanish America" (1974); James W. Jones' "Some Factors Contributing to Missionary Withdrawals in the Assemblies of God and Including a Comparative Study With Other Missions (1965–1974)" (1976); and Robert B. Carlson's "Bible School Evaluation With Emphasis on the Bible School Teacher" (1977).

Other Writers

The contributions of Assemblies of God missionaries who attended other graduate schools have also been significant. In the areas of church growth and education, Robert J. Bolton (Taiwan) and Richard B. Cunningham (Togo), among others, conducted valuable research. Bolton wrote "Treasure Island: Church Growth Among Taiwan's Urban Minnan Chinese," a 389 page M.A. thesis at Fuller Theological Seminary's School of World Mission and Institute of Church

Growth (1974). Focusing on ministerial education, Cunningham completed a doctor of education program at the University of Utah with a dissertation entitled "An Investigation of the Use of a Taxonomy of Education as an Evaluation Device for Assemblies of God Overseas Bible Schools" (1974). Outside of a classroom context, valuable insights came from the pen of David A. Womack, foreign missions editor and later home secretary, particularly through the publication of his *Breaking the Stained-Glass Barrier* (1973).

On occasion, national leaders enrolled for advanced training and completed insightful projects. One such inquiry was completed by Benjamin P. Shinde, a prominent Indian church leader, who wrote "The Contribution of the Assemblies of God to Church Growth in India," an M.A. thesis at Fuller Theological Seminary (1974). Shinde later completed a doctor of missiology degree there.

Missionaries sometimes made historical contributions as well. Jerry L. Sandidge concluded valuable research in his M.M.R.S. thesis at the Catholic University of Leuven, entitled "The Origin and Development of the Catholic Charismatic Movement in Belgium" (1976). George R. Stotts, 3 years before his missionary appointment to Europe, finished a significant Ph.D. dissertation at Texas Tech University, "The History of the Modern Pentecostal Movement in France" (1973). It was later published as *Le Pentecôtisme au pays de Voltaire* (1981).

Despite the importance of these and other research projects, few were published. Even with the major contributions of Melvin Hodges and David Womack, as late as 1977 the larger Christian world still pondered who these Assemblies of God Pentecostals were and why their missions program had become such an outstanding success.

Missionary-in-Residence Program

In 1976 a new dimension in missionary preparation on the undergraduate level emerged with the Missionary-in-Residence (MIR) program for Assemblies of God colleges in the U.S. The program was not designed to replace the permanent professor of missions on a campus; its intent was to supplement the program with a furloughed missionary's fresh insights from his or her field of ministry and "a forceful presentation of the work of the Holy Spirit in world evangelism today."[38] The expertise of the MIR would also broaden the scope of the available training, particularly if his overseas assignment was in a different part of the world than that of the regular professor. Hopefully, the missionary's impact would be felt throughout the institution by all majors. At the same time, the permanent professor would secure the long-range goals of the college's department of missions.

The MIR assignments have been given to furloughed missionaries for 1 year. In some cases, due to health factors or special family responsibilities, they have been allowed to teach for a maximum of 2 years. The Division of Foreign Missions has also looked at the academic qualifications of potential missionaries-in-residence to insure that they satisfied the requirements for teaching in colleges. In 1977, MIR's were serving in seven Assemblies of God ministerial training institutions: Bethany Bible College, Santa Cruz, California; Central Bible College, Springfield, Missouri; North Central Bible College, Minneapolis, Minnesota; Valley Forge Christian College, Phoenixville, Pennsylvania; Northwest College, Kirkland, Washington; Southwestern Assemblies of God College, Waxahachie, Texas; and Trinity Bible Institute, Ellendale, North Dakota.

In 1977, President D. V. Hurst of Northwest College noted that "the results have been an intensification of interest for missions on campus. . . . [W]e had 60 students apply for missionary internship for next summer. Only eight positions are available. . . . One of the contributing factors has been this program."[39] The timing for the introduction of this program reflected not only an interest in enhancing the quality of undergraduate offerings in missions, but the availability of a larger pool of academically-trained missionaries (many through AGGS).

Raised in an Assemblies of God orphanage, Benjamin P. Shinde became a prominent Indian church leader and educator.

David A. Womack, a former missionary to Colombia, served as foreign missions editor (1965–1970) and home secretary (1970–1978).

Missionary, editor, and educator David Kent Irwin founded the Center for Ministry to Muslims before his untimely death in 1984.

Missionary Delmer R. Guynes became the first personnel secretary of the Division of Foreign Missions in 1968 and later had a formative influence on the development of the Assemblies of God Graduate School.

Missionary to Africa and cross-cultural specialist Delbert H. Tarr, Jr. taught in the Missions Division of the Assemblies of God Graduate School.

Veteran missionary and missiologist Melvin L. Hodges teaching at the Assemblies of God Graduate School

THE GRADUATE SCHOOL OF RELIGION
Graduate School Faculty

Chairman, Donald Johns

Old Testament—Bible, theology, and languages . . . Stanley Horton, William MacDonald

New Testament—Bible, theology, and languages . . . Anthony Palma, Russell Spittler

Bible history and archaeologoy . . . Robert Cooley, William Menzies

Religious education . . . Donald Johns, David B. Drake, T. A. Kessel, T. F. Zimmerman, Jr.

Missions . . . Philip Crouch

Master of Arts in Religion

This program is designed to provide advanced but terminal training beyond the normal Bible college course for the mature student. The objective is to equip him to reach the lost more effectively for Christ in such ministries as pastor, teacher, missionary, and religious education director.

Admission and Matriculation Requirements

1. Possession of the standard B. A. degree from an accredited college, or its equivalent. Persons with less than a 2.0 average will be admitted on probation.

2. Prerequisite courses are those adopted by the American Association of Schools of Religious Education, December 28, 1949.

    a. English (composition, literature, speech, etc.) 12 hours.

    b. Humanities (philosophy, language, fine arts, history) 18 hours.

    c. Physical and biological sciences (physics, chemistry, botany, zoologoy, astronomy) 8 hours.

    d. Social sciences (economies, sociology, psychology, applied religion) 22 hours.

    e. A major in undergraduate work corresponding to the major emphasis in the graduate program.

3. Election to candidacy for the degree by the Graduate Committee upon successful completion of the comprehensive written examination at the close of the fall semester.

Note: Students who contemplate future graduate study in Bible, religion or theology are strongly urged to include Greek or Hebrew language in their undergraduate program.

80

Central Bible Institute began a graduate school of religion in 1957 leading to a master of arts degree. This is a page from the academic catalog for 1964–1965. The program was discontinued in 1966.

10

New Ventures in Education

Through the years, Assemblies of God missionaries have expended considerable energy on publishing religious magazines and curricular literature and promoting the training of national pastors, evangelists, and other church leaders. Indeed, this interest in writing and distributing materials for spiritual nurture has been one of the chief characteristics of the Pentecostal movement from the beginning, and the Assemblies of God in particular.[1] It has also been closely coupled with a keen interest in formal Bible instruction for those pursuing full-time ministry. Accordingly, the balanced Spirit-filled life requires the believer not only to be sensitive to the directives of the Holy Spirit, but to be learning the Word of God for the acquisition of proper Christian doctrine and for understanding the boundaries of spiritual experience. Bible study, therefore, brings maturity and prepares the individual for Christian service, whether as a layperson or as a minister. Naturally, this keenly felt imperative surfaced in missionary activities abroad. J. Philip Hogan observed that "wherever Assemblies of God missionaries have gone, they have established some kind of systematic training program almost immediately. . . . Versatility has been the hallmark."[2] In this, the Assemblies of God has led all other Protestant mission agencies for many years.

Regional Advanced Schools

With 163 overseas training schools in 1977—an increase of 72 over the 91 reported just 7 years before—the need for postgraduate training in many countries had finally become acute. To remedy the problem, the Division of Foreign Missions encouraged the founding of regional advanced schools. In some institutions, this came to mean the offering of baccalaureate degrees and for others, master of arts and master of divinity degrees. In the case of some institutions desiring college degree programs, vital assistance came with the founding of the International Correspondence Institute's collegiate division. Overseas training opportunities gradually paralleled educational developments in the Assemblies of God in the United States, reflecting the growing needs and sophistication of national churches and the widespread interest of younger nations in educational betterment.

Africa

The idea for the founding of the West Africa Advanced School of Theology (WAAST) emerged from a special conference of West African Bible school officials held in Monrovia, Liberia, in 1966. Property and buildings that had recently been erected for a Bible school in Lome, Togo, were offered as housing for the new advanced school. Richard B. Cunningham became the first president and Delbert H. Tarr, Jr., academic dean.[3]

Beginning with a 3-year program leading to an associate of theology degree, the school opened in 1971 as "a partnership venture of the Assemblies of God churches of West and Central Africa and the U.S.A."[4] Students, often mature ministers pastoring churches, enrolled from Burkina Faso, Ghana, Togo, Benin, Nigeria, and Zaire. While in school, they were supported by the tithes and offerings of their congregations. WAAST has produced some notable church leaders, including Richard Shaka, a general superintendent of the national church in Sierra Leone (1985–1987); Deme Bot, a district superintendent of the Nigeria Assemblies of God; and Mitre Djakouti, general superintendent of the Assemblies of God in Togo.[5] In 1979 the Board of Governors approved the introduction of a bachelor of arts in Bible and theology for the English-speaking program; a specialist diploma in Bible and theology was available to French-speaking students.

The growth of fraternally-related Assemblies of God constituencies in East and Central Africa prepared the way for the launching of the East Africa School of Theology (EAST). Initially, the concept of a regional school germinated on the campus of the Northern

Tanzania Assemblies of God Bible School in Arusha, Tanzania, in 1973.[6] In 1976, however, under the leadership of missionary Delmar C. Kingsriter (area representative for the Division of Foreign Missions), the school in Arusha was relocated in Nairobi, Kenya, to facilitate further growth; it was then renamed EAST. (The Tanzanian Assemblies of God later reopened a national Bible school at the same site in Arusha.) The government donated valuable property for the project and, before long, buildings were constructed, making the campus one of the most beautiful of all Assemblies of God training institutions overseas.

The school has offered a 3-year diploma in Bible and theology as well as a 4-year program leading to a bachelor of arts in the same fields. EAST has consequently provided "the pattern for curriculum and study materials for a number of affiliated and sister theological schools throughout East and Central Africa."[7] Notable curricular contributions have been made by Paul C. Wright, long-term missionary and former instructor at the school.

Students at EAST are afforded considerable opportunities in practical ministry. A committee organizes the student body into teams and they are subsequently assigned to minister in street meetings, churches, visitation of the needy and infirm, Sunday school teaching, witnessing, and other avenues of Christian service. As a result, its graduates have made significant contributions to the development of the national churches in the region.[8] Many students from independent Pentecostal congregations have attended the school, broadening the impact of the institution.

Eurasia

The Eurasia region of Assemblies of God missions represents one of the most complex in the enterprise, covering Europe, the Middle East, and Southern Asia. The oldest advanced school, Southern Asia Bible College (SABC) in Bangalore, India, traces its history to the establishment of Southern Asia Bible Institute, founded by missionary Alfred Cawston in 1951. Leaders of Assemblies of God constituencies for North India, South India, and Sri Lanka (formerly Ceylon) formed the board of directors. In its early years of operation, the school offered a 3-year certificate in theology; a 4-year graduate in theology program was inaugurated in 1958. In 1966 the name was changed to Southern Asia Bible College. The school added a bachelor of theology degree (Th.B.) 4 years later. The interest of university students in ministerial training led to the development of a bachelor of divinity program in 1974. SABC has enjoyed the highest level of academic recognition among the advanced schools of the Assemblies of God.[9]

Like other overseas training schools, SABC has attempted to balance the academic with the spiritual and practical dimensions of ministry. In 1977, students at the school ministered in 77 villages and visited over 21,000 homes in evangelism. They also conducted 114 meetings and distributed more than 45,000 gospels, books, and tracts. Converts totaled 203, mostly of Hindu background.[10]

Ministry on the European scene has been complicated over the years because the origins of Pentecostalism on the continent predate the organization of the American Assemblies of God (1914).[11] Many European Pentecostals have long held to a congregational form of church government and tied ministerial training to the instruction of candidate pastors in local churches. For example, the Assemblies of God in France has developed Le Stage ("The Apprenticeship"), an apprenticeship program under a pastor in preparation for ordination, lasting at least 5 years and potentially 12 to 15. Some Europeans, however, favored Bible institute education, often having received training themselves at the (independent) International Bible Training Institute (IBTI) in England founded by Frederick H. Squire in 1947.[12] An example of an influential leader who graduated from IBTI is Francesco Toppi, currently the general superintendent of the Assemblies of God in Italy.[13]

Recognizing the need for a degree-granting Bible college on the continent, Charles E. Greenaway, the successor to Victor G. Greisen as field secretary, strongly promoted the realization of such a school.[14] Since the Belgian Assemblies of God (with Greisen's assistance) had already set up Emmanuel Bible Institute in Andrimont, Belgium, in 1959, Greenaway concluded that this would be the logical institution for developing into an advanced school. With the cooperation of the Belgians, the name was changed in 1969 to Continental Bible College (CBC) and a bachelor of arts with a major in Bible was offered. An English language course of studies was added to the French program to attract a wider audience of students, a successful arrangement that has continued to the present. Recently, a Flemish language program was also added.

The school later moved to Brussels and then in 1977 to its present location in nearby St. Pieters Leeuw.[15] Although CBC continues to be governed by an American board of directors (the Foreign Missions Committee of the Division of Foreign Missions; an arrangement shared by the Far East Advanced School of Theology), European participation in the direction of the school has been encouraged: One of the key figures in the progress of the school, both in its earlier and later stages, has been the respected Belgian church leader and pastor Alfred F. Amitié. Further, an advisory council of Europeans has also been formed.

CBC has attracted students from a wide range of countries beyond Europe, including some from the Middle East and Africa. Notable graduates have included David Thomas, a later general superintendent of the Assemblies of God in Iran; Jacques Dernelle, currently general superintendent of the Belgian Assemblies of God and professor at CBC; and David Thevenet, pastor in Bordeaux, France, and professor at the Centre de Formation Biblique (Bible school of the Assemblies of God in France, founded in 1968).[16]

Far East

The call by the 1960 Far East Conference of Assemblies of God churches for advanced ministerial training culminated in the founding of the Far East Advanced School of Theology (FEAST) in the Philippines in 1964. With missionary Harold Kohl as the first president, it built on the 3-year Bible institute program common in many schools throughout Asia. Leading to either a bachelor of religious education or a bachelor of theology degree, courses were first taught on the campus of Bethel Bible Institute in Quezon City, Metro Manila.[17] The facilities there were later expanded.

The program received such an enthusiastic response that it began to offer on-site extension classes in three countries in 1973. By 1984, a bachelor's degree could be earned through FEAST in Korea, Japan, Hong Kong, Philippines, Fiji, Malaysia, Thailand, Singapore, and Indonesia. Three years later, extension sites were located in 11 countries. Additional academic programs included the inauguration of a bachelor of arts degree in 1973 and 4 years later, master of arts degrees in theology and Christian education. An M.A. in biblical studies was offered by extension in 1982 and a master of divinity degree through the resident campus in the Philippines. To staff the resident campus and the extension sites, FEAST has utilized missionaries, national ministers, and visiting professors from Assemblies of God colleges and the Assemblies of God Theological Seminary in the United States at their own expense. This sharing of adjunct instructors, characteristic of other overseas schools as well, has greatly enhanced the availability and quality of courses, in addition to the mission awareness of those participating.[18] New resident facilities were dedicated in Baguio City, the Philippines, in 1987.[19]

FEAST has had a considerable impact on the national churches in the Far East. Two outstanding graduates of the program are Dora Moses, director of Evangel Bible College in Rangoon, Burma, and Suwandoko Roslim, general secretary of the Assemblies of God in Indonesia.[20]

Latin America and the West Indies

The need for standardization of Bible school programs brought into being the Study Committee on Bible Institutes in Latin America and the West Indies in 1960 (Spanish acronym, CEIBAL). The members included Melvin L. Hodges, chairman, Ralph D. Williams (Central America), Elsie F. Blattner (Venezuela), Verne A. Warner (Dominican Republic), and Floyd Woodworth (Cuba). The committee made important recommendations on curriculum, administration, student activities, national church relationships, faculty, library holdings, and Bible school seminars for implementation, becoming known as the CEIBAL Plan.[21] This served as a model for the various schools across Latin America to follow in their growth and development. Veteran missionary Louise Jeter Walker was appointed coordinator for Latin American Bible institutes, the highest ranking position accorded to a woman in the Division of Foreign Missions.

The implementation of the CEIBAL Plan became known as PACE, the Program for Advanced Christian Education, giving further guidelines for standardized Bible institute education.[22] Recognizing that "the indigenous church principle has worked well in Latin America, but it does have the drawback of tending to produce churches and preachers at a faster rate than it produces the prepared leaders to guide a national church," the Advanced Ministerial Training Institute (AMTI) was added to provide postgraduate instruction.[23] The Foreign Missions Board selected missionary Verne Warner in 1967 to serve as the first director. AMTI began by providing month-long seminars in Buenos Aires, Argentina, and San Salvador, El Salvador. National superintendents, assistant superintendents, secretaries, treasurers, presbyters, Bible school directors, teachers, and sometimes missionaries attended the sessions, which lasted from 6:30 A.M. to 10 P.M. Correspondence work, guided research, and additional seminars followed for those interested in the program. Additional extension sites were added as AMTI grew.[24] Although not offering a degree, AMTI had the long-range goal of offering the equivalent of a fourth year of instruction given by an American Bible college.

By 1983, PACE was changed to Christian Training Network (CTN) to more accurately express that it "links arms with the Latin American church to train leaders at all levels—from the local church to Sunday school teachers to executives and Bible school professors."[25] CTN's postgraduate Bible institute program was then divided into two separate schools. AMTI would continue serving English-speaking Caribbean leaders and ISUM (Spanish for "Institute of Ministerial Excellence") would serve the Spanish-speaking countries. The name Latin American Advanced School of Theology (LAAST) was then chosen as the best English translation for ISUM. LAAST is a nontraditional program that offers Bible school training in the seven regions of Latin America and the West Indies, leading to a certificate, diploma, or licenciatura (highest award). Since some Bible institutes in Latin America had begun to offer collegiate programs and the licenciatura offered by LAAST is the equivalent of a degree, the school has also developed a master of arts program with extension sites in Argentina, Costa Rica, and Peru. Faculty members have included qualified national ministers, missionaries, and some professors from U.S. schools. This extensive project of nontraditional ministerial education, known by various acronyms, has trained hundreds of ministers in Latin America and the West Indies and made a profound impact on the advance of Pentecostalism.[26]

International Correspondence Institute

Origin

For many years, Assemblies of God missionaries had developed and promoted correspondence courses for nurturing believers in the faith.[27] Stateside, the General Council launched the Berean School of the Bible under the direction of Frank M. Boyd in 1947 to provide Bible and ministerial training for interested adults and potential candidates for ministry. An international correspondence school tailored for the use of overseas churches and training institutions, however, had not yet appeared.

The vision for what became the International Correspondence Institute (ICI) originated with George M. Flattery, the son of Assemblies of God missionaries to Burkina Faso, West Africa. His interest in nontraditional education dated back to his boyhood enrollment in correspondence courses to receive his educational training.[28] Sometime after graduation from Central Bible College (B.A., 1956), he became the director of Christian education at Oak Cliff Assembly of God in Dallas and later pioneered a new church in Richardson, Texas. He continued his academic training at Southwestern Baptist Theological Seminary in Fort Worth (M.R.E., 1958; Ed.D., 1966) and Southern Methodist University (B.A., 1959). His course work and doctoral dissertation ("A Comparative Analysis of Herman Harrell Horne's Idealistic Philosophy of Education and the Philosophy of Religious Education Reflected in the Adult Curriculum of the Assemblies of God, 1959–1964") amply equipped him as a specialist in religious instruction for adults.

Needing to fulfill a 6-month's vocational requirement to complete his doctorate, Flattery moved to Springfield, Missouri, in 1966 at the invitation of J. Philip Hogan. He was then assigned to assist in conducting research on overseas Bible institutes. Part of his work entailed traveling to Europe and the Middle East to survey the schools there and report his findings to the Division of Foreign Missions. Having a clearer picture of the overseas training programs of the Assemblies of God and its fraternally-related churches, he then began to research the potential for correspondence study.[29] The timing of his work significantly coincided with efforts in other mission circles to promote Theological Education by Extension.

Flattery's investigation also occurred at a time when officers of the Division of Foreign Missions and the missionary personnel exhibited growing interest in further exploration of nontraditional education. During the spring of 1967, Flattery presented some initial ideas to Hogan about the formation of an Assemblies of God home study school. Two alternatives were suggested: Such a school could be the extension arm of accredited colleges in the United States with separate divisions serving home and foreign constituencies or it could be an exclusively foreign missions school. At Hogan's request, Flattery then discussed these alternatives with Thomas F. Zimmerman.

With the aid of Flattery's research, Charles E. Greenaway gave a presentation on correspondence schools at the 1967 school of missions, a much-requested topic for study. Following the school of missions, while in conversation with Flattery, Hogan recommended by memo to the Foreign Missions Board that Flattery continue his survey work and that $5000 be set aside from BGMC funds for this purpose. This recommendation was approved on July 12, 1967.

Subsequently, Flattery submitted a full proposal to Hogan, recommending that the Division of Foreign Missions develop an international correspondence school. This received Hogan's immediate and enthusiastic endorsement. He passed the proposal on to the Foreign Missions Committee, which gave its approval on August 10, 1967, and George Flattery became president of the new school. Although nontraditional programs had been utilized in the mission enterprise for some time, this event signaled the beginning of a new and unprecedented march forward in theological education by extension.[30] Significantly, the pragmatic openness of Hogan and other members of the foreign missions committee to new ventures in evangelism and training had produced a friendly environment for this initiative.

After 2 additional years of research and travel, Flattery opened the International Correspondence Institute in 1969 with several Christian Life courses and a course on evangelism called "The Great Questions of Life." The first home office for ICI was located in Mission Village, adjacent to the campus of Central Bible College in Springfield, Missouri. In cramped quarters, Flattery was initially assisted by two veteren missionaries: Carl Malz (academic dean) and Louise Jeter Walker (assistant to the dean).[31] In the first promotional brochure, Flattery stated that the goal of ICI was "to harness the vast potential of correspondence courses for evangelism and instruction. . . . Our vision is to enroll *one million* new students."[32]

By July 1972, the main offices of ICI had been relocated in Brussels, Belgium, to avoid a "Made in America" label and to expedite the increasing volume of work. In the postwar era, Brussels had emerged as an important international center because the headquarters for the European Common Market, the North Atlantic Treaty Organization, and the Supreme Headquarters Allied Powers of Europe had located there. Shortly after arriving, the staff conducted its first writer's workshop in borrowed facilities at Continental Bible College. Professors Hugh P. Jeter (Southwestern Assemblies of God College), Anthony D. Palma (Evangel College), and John P. Phillips (North Central Bible College) were in attendance and began preparing the first Bible college courses.[33]

ICI later moved to larger accommodations and eventually considered designs for a permanent structure, the first bid carrying a price tag in excess of $1 million. The revenues began to come from a variety of sources. The Division of Foreign Missions sold valuable property in Jerusalem, representing an initial gift of $150,000. Another donation in the same amount came from the estate of an elderly man in southern California who had willed property to the Division. Smaller donations were raised as well. When the services of another architect resulted in a lower building cost, construction began and the new building was completed in 1975.[34]

Missiological Perspectives

The missiological foundation of the International Correspondence Institute has been labeled "cooperative multinationalism."[35] Acknowledging the contributions of indigenous church principles (the "three selfs") for global evangelization, Flattery, nevertheless, observes their potential for certain weaknesses: a failure to recognize commonalities in cultures, inadequate realization of the universality of the gospel or of the true church, the potential for self-centeredness, disinterest in working with others to achieve common goals, failure to come to grips with internationalism, and calling for the withdrawal of missionaries.[36]

Even so, Flattery built his missiology on the groundwork of indigenous church principles, including the interpretations of Melvin L. Hodges. Because of the advent of internationalism in the 20th century, Flattery proposed three cooperatives. The first is cooperative autonomy, whereby the national churches, retaining their internal independence, seek to work with other national churches "in building the kingdom of God which knows no national boundaries."[37] Thus, the role of nationals and missionaries serving abroad would continue, but always in fraternal capacities. Since the missionaries and national churches would practice voluntary submission with each other, issues between the two could be resolved by negotiation.

The second principle is cooperative ministry, the sharing of ministers and ministries with church bodies in other nations. Given the universal scope of the gospel and the high level of cross-culturalization taking place in this century, "people of every country need to be exposed to the ministries of foreigners. New insights and perspectives, and interpretations of the Word are to be gained from this. Any nation that rejects the ministries of foreigners can only be impoverished by their isolationism."[38] Such sharing, therefore, can occur without threatening the autonomy of each group.

The third point is cooperative funding whereby national churches will have as their ideal the sharing of expenses for evangelizing, teaching, and training in countries. Cooperative funding can be accomplished as each nation supports its ministries in other lands or as they join in support of a given ministry. He adds that the latter type of funding is already underway as evidenced by the support several West African church organizations give to the West Africa Advanced School of Theology in Lome, Togo. In this context of cooperation, ICI, under the authority of the Division of Foreign Missions, sets up regional offices and national offices to coordinate efforts with national churches for expediting its international programs of evangelism, spiritual nurture of believers, and ministerial training. The objectives of the agency are accordingly summed up in the following statement:

> ICI is a school and service agency with four spiritual goals: (1) evangelism, (2) spiritual life development, (3) lay workers training, and (4) ministerial training. All levels of evangelism and Christian education are included. As these goals are pursued, the body of Christ (the Church) is enlarged and edified.

> With regard to methods, ICI's purpose is to utilize every available means to take our message to people where they are. Among the methods used are independent study courses, audio and video materials, learning centers, and seminars.

> Today, ministers from many nations are being sent by *home* churches to *foreign* soil. If Jesus tarries, the goal of tomorrow's churches will be to send ministers *from all nations to all nations.* As a multicultural platform, ICI anticipates this goal. Through its facilities, ministers from many nations will speak to the world.[39]

In view of these missiological perspectives, it is clear that Flattery's foresight and careful planning had set the stage for another important advance in evangelism and training, building on the earlier foundations of the mission enterprise.

Programs

For academic recognition, the International Correspondence Institute sought and received accreditation through the National Home Study Council in 1977. Through the avenue of the mails, it has developed a worldwide student body, many in countries hostile to the gospel and closed to missionary activities, and has enrolled 22 persons per hour in its programs since its inception. The methods include independent study courses, learning centers, cassette group study, Bible clubs, audio and video presentations, and seminars.[40] ICI courses, as well as audio and visual presentations, are sometimes translated into several languages (e.g., twenty courses had been translated by 1987 into Arabic), and every effort is taken to make them transcultural.

Through its Evangelism Division, ICI offers noncollege credit courses such as "The Great Questions of Life" and "Highlights in the Life of Christ." The Christian Education Division presents two programs, Christian Life and Christian Service, with noncredit courses that include "Your New Life," "When You Pray," "Spiritual Gifts," "Sharing the Good News," and "The Kingdom, the Power, and the Glory." An example of the effectiveness of these programs was the conversion of three American and three Australian prisoners in Tahiti. Karen Johnson, the ICI director in Tahiti, reported that the prisoners had studied "The Great Questions of Life" in English, Spanish, and Tahitian. Prison officials were carefully monitoring the results so that "if the tests are successful, they want all 200 of their prisoners to take this course."[41] Even more startling is the fact that, according to Flattery, involvement in ICI courses has actually contributed to the establishment of five racially mixed congregations in Southern Africa.

In the ICI College Division, two courses of study are available for ministerial training: leading to a diploma in Bible and Christian ministry or a bachelor of arts in Bible, theology, missions, religious education, or church administration. There are 44 courses available to choose from for the diploma and 88 for the degree programs. All courses were prepared by officers at ICI as well as by pastors and college and seminary professors. Studies on the synoptic Gospels, the Holy Spirit, evangelism, health and hygiene, and principles of leadership are among the courses offered. The first degree, a B.A. in Bible, was awarded to Paul O. Ajah, a student from West Africa, on August 31, 1979.

It is through standardized degree programs that ICI has made the greatest contribution to theological education abroad. Because of its accreditation through the National Home Study Council, the ICI bachelor of arts is an American degree offered through the international office in Brussels. Since many schools have not had the resources or academic personnel to offer more than Bible institute education, the ICI degree has met a vital need for many developing schools. Institutions that have depended on the ICI degree for their fourth year programs include Nigeria Advanced School of Theology; East Africa School of Theology in Kenya; Southern Africa School of Theology, Republic of South Africa; and Evangel Bible College in Burma. By 1985, ICI had enrolled its 10,000th student in the College Division and 170 degrees had been granted.[42]

Through the years, the program has been heavily dependent on Mobilization and Placement Service (MAPS) volunteers to assist in the skilled capacities of printing, accounting, writing, editing, graphic arts, photography, audiovisual technology, and secretarial skills. George Flattery reported in 1986 that "it would cost more than $5 million to hire local people to do the work MAPS volunteers have done in a 5-year period."[43] The close relationship of ICI to the MAPS program of the Assemblies of God continues to reflect the level of lay interest and enthusiasm in the mission enterprise.

In keeping with its name, the International Correspondence Institute has provided valuable services beyond the confines of the Assemblies of God. It has worked in cooperation with other Pentecostal organizations as well. For example, it assists the Te Nikau

Bible Training Centre in New Zealand, a school sponsored by the Apostolic Church (New Zealand Council) in that country.[44] Relationships also exist with the Church of God (Cleveland, Tennessee), Elim Bible College in England (Elim Pentecostal Church), Eastern Pentecostal Bible College in Canada (Pentecostal Assemblies of Canada), as well as with Bible institutes in Kenya, the Netherlands, Norway, Scotland, Zimbabwe, and other countries.

ICI activities have been highlighted in the bimonthly magazine *ICI Datelines* and promoted on television through *World Alive,* hosted by George and Esther Flattery. Pastors and other interested supporters of the agency's endeavors are encouraged to become ICI Associates, requiring a minimum monthly donation of $15, and attend the biennial (since 1986) World Missions Congress held in Brussels. In 1987, offices and directors of the International Correspondence Institute could be found in more than 100 countries.[45]

A graduate of Continental Bible College in Belgium, David Thevenet serves as a pastor in Bordeaux, France, and teaches at the Centre de Formation Biblique (Bible school of the Assemblies of God in France).

Missionary Verne Warner was a key figure in the development of PACE (Program for Advanced Christian Education) in Latin America.

Alfred Amitié, former general superintendent of the Belgian Assemblies of God, has had a formative influence on the development of Continental Bible College in Brussels.

Campus of Southern Asia Bible College, Bangalore, India

Students of Far East Advanced School of Theology, Manila, Philippines, preparing to travel in ministry, 1966. Harold Kohl, president of the school (left), and missionary Derrick Hillary (right).

A graduate of the Far East Advanced School of Theology, Dora Moses directs the Evangel Bible College in Rangoon, Burma.

ICI Christian Life and Christian Service courses have become a major aid to evangelism and discipleship training.

Two Asian men studying ICI courses in their village

Two writers for ICI collegiate level materials, Massyoshi Safu (left) and Hobart E. Grazier (right), at the ICI headquarters in Brussels, Belgium

George M. Flattery, president of ICI, at his office in Mission Village (adjacent to the campus of Central Bible College), Springfield, Missouri. ca. 1969

11

Expanding Ministries

By 1977 the Assemblies of God Division of Foreign Missions ranked as one of the major and most successful contemporary Protestant mission agencies. Although important changes occurred in the membership of the Foreign Missions Committee, the strong oversight of J. Philip Hogan provided stability and maintained consistency with the ideals of the enterprise. Along with specialized training (see chapter 9), greater care for the missionary family and instructions on interpersonal relationships received more attention during these years.

Long-standing agencies within the Division flourished as evidenced by the work of Life Publishers International (formerly the Spanish Literature Division and known in many countries as Editorial Vida). Overseas initiatives included campus evangelism and Teen Challenge. Financial contributions from the American constituency increased (though a corresponding lack of enthusiasm for underwriting administrative costs of the operation still hampered efficiency). Lay involvement climbed as more and more adults volunteered their professional expertise through Mobilization and Placement Service (MAPS) and sacrificed vacation times for church construction projects overseas.

Personnel

Officers

The recurring re-elections of J. Philip Hogan (always on the nominating ballot) to the post of executive director at the biennial General Council gatherings reflected the confidence the constituency of the Assemblies of God had in his leadership. Hogan's long-term leadership won recognition from his peers in evangelical missions circles as well. For three non-consecutive terms he served as president of the Evangelical Foreign Missions Association (EFMA; 1968–1970, 1976–1978, 1983–1985), the second Pentecostal leader to hold this office and the only one to be honored by re-election. Except for his participation in EFMA meetings, by the mid-1980s Hogan began to exhibit a certain disenchantment about what he considered an unnecessary multiplication of consultations and gatherings of mission executives. His concern about following the leading of the Holy Spirit for strategic planning, over that of merely theorizing about Christian missions, has been reflected in his activism in fulfilling the task of evangelization.[1]

The shift of other officers in the Division, nevertheless, represented a crucial changing of the guard, opening leadership posts to younger men—equally committed to the distinctives of Pentecostal theology and indigenous church principles, but carrying new insights and skills. In the day-by-day office management, the retirement of Robert T. McGlasson as foreign missions secretary in 1977, after a long and distinguished career in missions administration, signaled an important turn. McGlasson's tenure had made him one of the most knowledgeable sources of information about the agency.[2] He was succeeded by Joseph W. Kilpatrick. Holding a master's degree in business administration, Kilpatrick had served as finance secretary for the Division and then as a missionary assigned to the International Correspondence Institute (ICI) in Brussels, Belgium.[3] (The title of foreign missions secretary was subsequently changed to administrative assistant to the executive director in January 1978.)

The retirements of field secretaries Maynard L. Ketcham, Melvin L. Hodges, and Everett L. Phillips, however, had far more consequence for the overseas operation. Ketcham had served as a field secretary variously for Southern Asia and the Far East since 1952.[4] In this responsibility, he was replaced in 1970 by Wesley R. Hurst, who had been secretary of promotions since 1960 (the title was later changed to home secretary).[5] In the same year, Everett L. Phillips, praised for his "magnanimous spirit," announced his retirement as field secretary for Africa.[6] His successor, Morris O. Williams, had worked for many years as a missionary in Southern Africa and had become a well-known advocate for strong fraternal relationships with national churches.[7] Williams took office on January 1, 1971.

Apart from Hogan, the best-known officer of the Division of Foreign Missions was Melvin L. Hodges, field secretary for Latin America and the West Indies. Although retiring from that office in 1973, in becoming professor of missions science at the Assemblies of God Graduate School he gave another decade of service to the cause of missions. Loren Triplett, having served 12 years as a missionary to Nicaragua and then 7 years as general manager of Editorial Vida in Miami, Florida, followed Hodges.[8]

During these years, the regions of Europe, the Middle East, and Southern Asia were forged together as a new field under the term "Eurasia." Activities in Southern Asia (India, Pakistan, Bangladesh, Sri Lanka) had been variously under the guidance of separate administrators; the government-imposed exodus of many missionaries (particularly from India) made amalgamation advisable. Victor G. Greisen had served as field secretary over Europe, the Middle East, and Southern Asia from 1959 to 1963. After he retired, his post was given to two men with parallel responsibilities: Charles E. Greenaway (resident field secretary in Europe; 1963–1966) and Elton G. Hill (field secretary for Southern Asia and the Middle East; 1963–1966). Hill, who had previously served as a successful missionary-evangelist, resigned in 1966 to become pastor of Bethel Temple Assembly of God in Dayton, Ohio.

With this new development, the Division of Foreign Missions reorganized the field under Greenaway's oversight. During his years as field secretary (1966–1983), Greenaway, a well-known promoter of missions in the Assemblies of God, successfully drew attention to Europe as a mission field, a region that some viewed as having been evangelized centuries before and therefore without the priority of those areas having no Christian heritage. He also encouraged increasing numbers of missionaries to settle there and pragmatically favored the development of new ministries (e.g., campus ministries and Teen Challenge). The impact of his campaigning among the American constituency for increased evangelism in Europe, as well as his ardor for ministry to Muslims in the Middle East and the continued endeavors in Southern Asia, cannot be overestimated.[9]

Other important changes came with the establishment of the Personnel Division in 1968 and the appointment of Delmer R. Guynes to direct it. When Guynes vacated the position to become vice-president of the Assemblies of God Graduate School in 1976, it was filled by Ronald A. Iwasko, a missionary to Brazil and graduate of Trinity Evangelical Divinity School. Iwasko was the first seminary graduate and academically-trained missiologist to work on the Foreign Missions Committee.

Overseeing publications, David A. Womack continued to serve as foreign missions editor (1965–1970) until he succeeded Wesley R. Hurst as home secretary in charge of promotions, fund-raising, missionary itineration, and candidate processing. He remained in this capacity until 1978, when he left the Division of Foreign Missions and began pastoring Calvary Christian Center (A/G) in Alameda, California.[10] Closely associated with planning missionary itineration and writing promotional materials for many years was Christine Carmichael, who retired from the Division in 1973.

David K. Irwin followed Womack as the foreign missions editor and served in this office for 5 years before joining the faculty of the Assemblies of God Graduate School as a full-time professor. Joyce Wells Booze, a senior editorial assistant, replaced him as foreign missions editor and as editor of *Good News Crusades.* Booze later made an important contribution to Assemblies of God missions history through the publication of *Into All the World: A History of Assemblies of God Foreign Missions* (1980). Financial officers during this period were Clyde Hawkins, Joseph W. Kilpatrick, F. Jesse Hannah, and Paul D. Sherman.

Missionaries

The continuing number of applicants fed a steady stream of approved new recruits for ministry abroad. Most were Bible college graduates (recipients of diplomas or degrees) and a growing percentage had also completed some graduate work.[11] Although the Assemblies of God had never experienced a shortage of missionary candidates, there were growing concerns about the turnover in personnel and the quality of family life.

In 1976, missionary James W. Jones conducted an extensive demographic study of withdrawals among Assemblies of God missionaries. He noted that within a 10-year period (1965–1975), 1,351 missionaries had been appointed, but 265 (19.6 percent) of the total missionary force had withdrawn. This meant an annual withdrawal rate of almost 2 percent (actually quite low when compared with other agencies).[12] High on the list of reasons for leaving were (1) problems of a personal nature (43.2 percent): commitment/motivation, physical health, mental health, emotional immaturity, indiscreet/immoral behavior, etc.; (2) reasons related to the nature of the work (24.9 percent): decision to enter homeland ministry, dissatisfaction with work assignment, disagreement with policies of the Division of Foreign Missions, etc.; (3) reasons related to social or outside factors (31.9 percent): incompatibility with other missionaries, marital tension/conflict, family problems in the homeland, education of MKs (missionary kids), and incompatibility with national ministers, among others.[13] Jones discovered that young missionaries especially could become discouraged due to factors related to learning a new language, physical problems, compatibility with other missionaries, mental health, and emotional maturity. He further discovered that almost a third of all withdrawals occurred after the first term of service.[14] Although the figures for the study do not show a dramatic defection, nevertheless, the nearly 2 percent annual rate did pose questions about longevity of service, the character of prefield training, the commitment expected of missionaries, and the caliber of younger missionaries. James noted the "significant relationship between missionary withdrawals and the inadequate training and preparation of missionaries prior to their arrival on the field."[15] Although progress had been made in the training of missionaries, further improvement was essential. This was later addressed through the Candidate Graduate Training Program (CGTP). In addition, proper stewardship of resources, both personnel and finances, mandated that further consideration be given to preventing turnover, since every missionary prematurely leaving the field represented a disruption in the work abroad and the loss of thousands of dollars in training, equipping, and supporting him.

For these reasons, as well as others (such as care of the family of the missionary), the agency set up the Personnel Division in 1968 with Delmer R. Guynes as secretary (director). J. Philip Hogan reported to the church constituency that "one of the principal functions of this division is that it offers counseling aid in whatever category is necessary to the whole missionary family, but especially to the children, still here in the United States."[16] As part of his portfolio, Guynes served as dean of the annual School of Missions held in Springfield, Missouri, later improving its agenda by implementing more specialized training through the CGTP.

Since furloughed missionaries were required to attend the school before returning overseas, the school's program was made to deal with problems of missionary adjustment: physical and emotional health, interpersonal relationships, education of children, and other issues related to living overseas. Consequently, a Christian psychologist was often invited to speak to the missionaries. These topics complemented the traditional concerns of the school (spiritual renewal, missionary strategy, promotions and fund-raising for overseas ministries, etc.). Guynes reported that such in-service training "provides redirection, stimulates motivation, renews vision and burden, makes available new means of reaching missionary goals, and provides the supportive influences tired missionaries need." However, the single most important contribution lay in bringing missionaries together "in the presence of the Captain of the Lord's hosts [Jesus Christ] to receive from Him the orders of global gospel conquest. He who conditioned the promise of His abiding presence with the command to 'go' (Matthew 28:19, 20) has never and will never fail to meet those who take His commission seriously."[17]

Missionary life witnessed several significant changes after 1968. Regard for the welfare of retired missionaries led the Division of Foreign Missions to add the program of the Ministers Benefit Association (MBA) to its older pension coverage with Christian Fidelity Life Insurance Company of Waxahachie, Texas. MBA is the authorized benefit and retirement program for Assemblies of God ministers.[18] Hospitalization coverage had been handled through the resources of the Division itself with the Missionary Health Pool Fund. Rising costs and increased needs demonstrated the inefficiency of this approach, culminating in outside coverage, most recently with Christian Fidelity Life.[19]

Housing arrangements for missionaries on furlough, traditionally centered in apartments at Mission Village in Springfield, Missouri, also changed, for many preferred to purchase homes as a long-term investment (renting them out while living overseas) or to live in another part of the country. The Mission Village apartments had originally been army barracks, moved from the old O'Reilly General Hospital in Springfield; having no insulation, they ultimately required an annual subsidy of $10,000 for maintenance and utilities. Besides offering only cramped quarters for families, their Springfield location was geographically inconvenient for missionaries itinerating in parts of the country outside the Midwest. In 1976, the Division sold the Mission Village property to the adjoining Central Bible College.[20]

Structure and Finances

Administration

The governance of the mission enterprise was measurably helped by the establishment of the Foreign Missions Board in 1955 and the Laymen's Advisory Committee 2 years later. Representation on the board includes the executive director, two executive presbyters, the administrative assistant (formerly the foreign missions secretary), the four field secretaries, and six (later eight) pastors representing geographical regions of the United States. Their task has been to evaluate missions policies and disciplinary procedures, set standards of conduct for the program, review the applications of candidates, and serve as a board of appeal. The board also nominates four missionaries from each major region of endeavor (Africa, Eurasia, Far East, Latin America and the West Indies); the rest of the missionary personnel from each region vote for two of the four to represent them on the General Presbytery of the denomination (the field secretaries serve as well).[21] The eight members (originally six) of the Laymen's Advisory Committee also represent the geographical regions of the U.S. and "work in cooperation with the Foreign Missions Board in the promotion of World Missions."[22]

The general administrative work has been conducted by the Foreign Missions Committee, consisting of the executive director (chairman), administrative assistant (co-chairman and recorder), field secretaries (later directors), and other executive officers within the Division. From 1960 until 1971, J. Philip Hogan held the title of assistant general superintendent, a title shared by five other Council executives as well. His position differed, however, in that it carried the portfolio of executive director of foreign missions, giving him a unique status and authority over this area of ministry.

Growing out of the work of the Committee on Advance and the

Organizational Structure Study Committee, major constitutional changes were approved by the General Council at its meeting in Kansas City, Missouri, in 1971. The five assistant superintendents were replaced by one assistant general superintendent and their responsibilities for administering various departments at headquarters were transferred to national directors. Although an attempt was made to change the status of the executive director to that of a national director, thus placing him beneath the oversight of the general superintendent, the Council simply dropped the appellation of assistant general superintendent and gave Hogan the title of executive director of foreign missions.[23] Two years later the Council regrouped the departments at the headquarters under the heading "divisions." Hence in 1973, the Foreign Missions Department became the Division of Foreign Missions, a title it has retained.[24] With this new arrangement, the title of foreign missions secretary was also changed to administrative assistant to the executive director.

The most significant change in structure within the Division came through the addition in 1974 of a new administrative level between the field secretaries and the missionaries, that of area representative. From 1919, when the Division was begun, to 1942, when the first field secretary was appointed, the foreign missions director carried the bulk of administrative responsibility. Delegation of authority began with the coming of field secretaries, who devoted part of their time to office work in Springfield and the rest of their time to work overseas; this trend accelerated under Hogan's administration. It took years, however, for the responsibilities of the new office to be defined.

In the meantime, the overseas operation continued to expand. And whereas by 1974 the post of field secretary had become well defined, its work load had grown insurmountable. Following a 3-year study, the foreign missions board approved the installation of area representatives to represent the field secretaries to the field fellowships (missionaries) and the national churches. Their portfolio included the analysis of programs and problems, writing of job descriptions for missionaries, evaluating job performance, placement of personnel, pastoral oversight, and coordinating efforts with international ministries (e.g., ICI).[25] The first two appointments were Donald R. Corbin, missionary to Senegal, as area representative for West Africa, and John Bueno, missionary to El Salvador, for Central

America. Similar to the development of the office of field secretary, the position of area representative has varied in scope since its inception.

Finances

For many years the Division of Foreign Missions has operated on one of the lowest budgets for administrative expenses among mission agencies. In the earlier years of the Assemblies of God, the General Council promised that every dollar designated for missionaries would be sent without being tapped for administrative costs.

Although the sentiment behind this reflected paramount concerns for evangelism and integrity, it was a continuing hindrance to those trying to manage the operation, since monies had to be spent for office space, equipment, utilities, postage, and salaries. In previous years the budget of the Division had been underwritten by earnings of Gospel Publishing House, an arrangement that had ceased long before the spectacular expansion of the program and the necessary increase in office personnel. The 1955 General Council adopted the World Missions Plan as a program for local churches to contribute undesignated funds to support home and foreign endeavors. Accordingly, these offerings would be divided: foreign missions, 70 percent; foreign missions office expense, 5 percent; national home missions, 5 percent; district home missions, 20 percent.[26] Since many churches did not choose to follow this plan and continued sending monies directly to the Division of Foreign Missions, the 1957 General Council authorized that 10 percent of undesignated offerings could be used to cover administrative costs.[27] By 1961 no funds were available to cover emergency expenses and the General Council, praising the fiscal policies of the Division, voted to set up the Emergency Missionary Fund (later General Emergency Fund) by allowing 2 percent of all missionary funds (with the exception of special designations) to be placed in this account.[28]

This new policy, however, proved to be inadequate in the face of rising expenses. In 1960, undesignated giving represented 5.4 percent of all contributions, but by 1971 this had dropped to 2.2 percent. The leaders of the Division of Foreign Missions attributed this decline and the increase of designated gifts to Assemblies of God church members' growing awareness of the ministries of particular missionaries and projects.[29] When the General Council met in Kansas City, Missouri, in 1971, it recognized that with the steady decrease in undesignated funds the Division was "caught in a perpetual squeeze." Thereupon it approved the appropriation of 5 percent of all missionary funds (with certain exceptions) for transfer to the General Emergency Fund for office expense.[30] At the same time, to demonstrate its integrity, the Division could boast that administrative costs had been consistently kept under 6 percent of the total giving to foreign missions, a remarkable and rare accomplishment.[31]

Further complicating the situation, however, was the declining value of the American dollar, affecting both the missionary's budget and his itinerary to meet it.[32] Equally unsettling were the inflationary rates in some countries. In 1 year, for example, the cost of living jumped 91 percent in Brazil. J. Philip Hogan admonished the faithful to understand and be patient with these factors. In addition, he assured them,

> We do not say that for a given amount spent, a given number of souls will be saved. We totally reject this computer approach to evangelism and spiritual growth; but we can tell you that for every dollar invested, the most judicious administration possible will be taken and that funds will be sent where there are more reachable, winnable people than there have ever been.[33]

Although the fringe benefits for missionaries had risen in recent years, the personal allowances, by stateside standards, remained modest. For this reason, the foreign missions committee made a study of the entire financial operation and submitted recommendations to the foreign missions board in 1970. The "New Missionary Allowance Program" was accepted and implemented on January 1, 1971, relieving some disgruntlement in the ranks.[34]

Despite the frustrations in covering administrative costs and the inflationary problems, total missions giving rose to $11,132,617 in 1971, an increase over the previous year of more than 16 percent.[35] In addition, the Revolving Loan Fund for overseas ministries had reached $600,000.[36] By 1976, the contributions to the Division had grown to almost $20 million. Additional incomes from BGMC, Light-for-the-Lost, Speed-the-Light, and Women's Ministries Department added another $3.5 million.[37]

Expanding Ministries

In 1946, Henry C. Ball, field secretary for Latin America and the West Indies, founded the Spanish Publications Division to provide Christian literature in the Spanish language. Originally based in Springfield, Missouri, the operation moved to Miami, Florida, 20 years later because of its growing Spanish-speaking population and culture and its advantages of shipping, postage, and customs.[38] Considered an "international ministry" of the Assemblies of God, along with ICI, Editorial Vida, or Life Publishers International (as it was called in the United States after 1980), has produced tons of literature annually. Its publications include *Poder* ("Power"), a magazine on Christian living distributed throughout Latin America, Bibles, books, hymnals, tracts, and Sunday school literature (material now partially handled by Gospel Publishing House in Springfield, Missouri).

As its operation expanded, Life Publishers began to supply gospel literature in Portuguese and French as well. In 1976 alone, it published over 750 million pages of literature, a 328 percent growth within just 5 years.[39]

New ministries during these years included the extension of Teen Challenge and campus ministries to other parts of the world. The remarkable expansion of the Teen Challenge ministry in the United States had been triggered by the ministry of David Wilkerson among gangs of youths in New York City, beginning in 1958.[40] Of great importance was the publication of Wilkerson's *Cross and the Switchblade* (1963), recounting his ministry and emphasizing the power of the Holy Spirit to deliver from sin; it sold in the millions and was translated into more than 30 languages. It was only a matter of time before new recruits and veteran missionaries eagerly asked to evangelize young people in major population centers outside of the U.S. One notable example was Howard Foltz, director of the Teen Challenge Center in Dallas/Fort Worth, Texas, who felt called to develop a program in Europe in 1969.[41] Eurasia Teen Challenge quickly expanded into France, Austria, the Netherlands, West Germany, and the city of West Berlin. Three years later, teams of Teen Challenge staff members and other workers were contracted by the U.S. Department of Defense to minister to servicemen in Vietnam, assisting with drug abuse programs.[42]

Among the pioneers of campus evangelism overseas were Jerry and Pat Sandidge. Starting their ministry at the University of Brussels (Belgium) in 1972, they eventually moved to Louvain, where the Catholic University of Louvain had a student body of 33,000. There, University Action began as a ministry utilizing outdoor concerts, student evangelism teams from nearby Continental Bible College, ICI evangelism materials, worship services, and a bookstore.[43] Similar ministries were later organized in other countries.

Popular Support

The enthusiasm for practical support of the enterprise increased dramatically from 1968 to 1977. Churches and pastors were exhorted to give to missions because such concern would naturally enhance the spirituality, outreach, and generosity of local congregations. Missions conventions, always encouraged by the Division of Foreign Missions, focused on the Great Commission, heightening awareness for ministry to the community and the world. Examples of newfound growth and vitality were reported in the *Pentecostal Evangel* and *Advance* magazines (the latter being sent to ministers exclusively).[44] The emphasis on missions education through the years, whether through conventions, BGMC, Missionettes, Speed-the-Light, or Ambassadors-in-Mission, paid rich dividends as young people grew to accept responsibility for supporting and participating in world evangelization. Louise Jeter Walker, missionary and later curriculum specialist for the International Correspondence Institute, noted the long-term objectives for this emphasis in the local church:

> We want a missions-minded church—one whose members are concerned about others; who go, give, and pray for world evangelism. We want parents, Sunday school teachers, pastors, and church leaders who will teach missions. And we want a great army of young people who will dedicate their lives to God's service both at home and abroad. To have this kind of church tomorrow, we are sowing the seed today.[45]

Illustrating the concern for involving everyone, the annual BGMC

Day in Assemblies of God churches has been an occasion for highlighting for children the world mission of the church and providing them an opportunity to give. The offering goal for BGMC Day in 1972 was $85,000, earmarked for ICI. Monthly giving for the previous year had totaled $300,000. BGMC efforts, however, far transcended fund-raising by a strong emphasis on discipleship.[46]

The women of the Assemblies of God continued their essential support as well. With improved communications, housing, and the availability of more products overseas, the need for purchasing and shipping equipment declined; freight costs and importation tariffs were now exceeding, in some cases, the purchase price of the item. In view of these developments, the Division of Foreign Missions recommended that the Women's Missionary Council shift its emphasis to providing money for missionaries to purchase their supplies on the field. This would mean a considerable savings to the missionaries. In this way the women could still help in outfitting missionary homes abroad.[47] In 1975 the department was renamed the Women's Ministries Department. J. Philip Hogan, reviewing the work of the WMs, observed, "The gifts of material things that the WMs supply for missionaries have indeed made missionary life easier and better. But the greatest contribution . . . has been their responsiveness to pray as the Spirit directed."[48]

But individual ardor for missions sometimes exceeded organizationally-sponsored programs for the laity. For example, an Assemblies of God church member, Marian Munch, became concerned about her excess weight. Recognizing the need for better stewardship of her body and concerned about the problem of hunger overseas, she asked her husband to give her one dollar for every pound she lost. She then gave the money to missions. In an article entitled "I Gave My Fat to Missions," published in the Pentecostal Evangel, Munch wrote, "When I gave the Lord my 'fat offering,' I felt so good. I thought of the hungry Christians in other lands, and I said to myself, 'I'm losing; they're gaining.' "[49] She then recommended that others suffering with obesity follow her example.

The most spectacular lay involvement, however, has come through the popular Mobilization and Placement Service (MAPS) begun in 1964. The year 1976 proved to be pivotal in its development. When the country of Guatemala was shaken by a disastrous earthquake on February 4, 1976, over 100 Assemblies of God churches and parsonages were destroyed. There was an immediate outpouring of love and assistance to the congregations there. American Assemblies of God churches donated thousands of dollars in addition to the time given by more than 400 laymen who paid their own expenses for the opportunity to help in reconstruction. Robert C. Cunningham, editor of the *Pentecostal Evangel,* surveyed the work and reported that "MAPS workers went to Guatemala in crews of 10 to 20 at a time. Each work crew stayed [1] or [2] weeks—long enough to build the walls and roof of one or more churches. The Guatemalan brethren worked alongside them, and after the Americans left, they finished the building themselves."[50] In an article entitled " 'MAPS' Builds Walls of Love," Cunningham quoted one grateful pastor, Roberto Estrada: "These American brethren have shown us true Christian love. They have sacrificed by coming to live and work with us. They have slept with the fleas, and eaten off the dirt, so we could have a lovely church building."[51] Well into 1977 teams of men were being sent to complete the task, demonstrating the willingness of Assemblies of God church members to share their "time, talents, and treasure" for missions. Tragedy turned to triumph as Guatemalan church members joined with the MAPS workers in rebuilding their churches. The Guatemalans were thus inspired to evangelize, gaining an increase of 5,000 in Sunday school attendance, 2,500 in church membership, and opening 104 new churches.[52]

Replacing H. H. "Spud" DeMent as MAPS representative in January 1976, L. Lamar Headley, a former pastor and district youth director in Alabama, arrived in the office just shortly before the earthquake. He then faced the major task of coordinating the construction effort. Before long, it became apparent that the impact of the Guatemala experience had far transcended the work of rebuilding there. It had spiritually revitalized stateside congregations that had participated and generated an impulse to give additional practical assistance. In the years that followed, more and more Assemblies of God churches applied for construction projects in various countries, often sending teams long distances. By 1983 the number of churches sending construction teams had grown so much that Headley needed administrative assistance for coordinating them. Consequently, Bill Strickland, a missionary to Honduras, was appointed that year as the first MAPS construction field representative. Four years later, over 400 churches reported involvement in overseas projects, which embraced almost 4,000 workers, both men and women. Donated building funds for that year, when added to the expenses of the teams, totaled well over $2 million, thus representing a continuing and significant level of lay involvement.[53]

Through the years, MAPS has sent doctors, nurses, construction workers, teachers, secretaries, bookkeepers, electronic engineers, printers, and artists to work on the home and foreign fronts. At the same time, MAPS workers have provided vitally needed behind-the-scenes assistance in direct evangelism efforts. In Latin America, for example, they have erected and taken down tents used for crusades.[54] They have also handled the office work for follow-up communications with new converts after such meetings conclude. Currently the task force of MAPS volunteers overseas in any given year runs from 400 to 500 people. Their status ranges from retirees to career people to college students. Raising their own support, many devote an entire year or two to their assignments.[55]

A summer MAPS program sends approximately 500 workers (often college students) to churches and other sites at home and abroad. To publicize the program and current opportunities, the national office publishes the quarterly *MAPS News*. Many participants have later become career missionaries (both home and foreign). Without the vital assistance of MAPS workers, comprising all categories of involvement, the rapid expansion of Assemblies of God missions would have been measurably restricted and certain ministries (e.g., ICI) seriously impaired.

Conclusion

National churches, fraternally-related to the Assemblies of God overseas, witnessed extraordinary growth from 1967 to 1977. Good News Crusades circled the globe with American missionaries and evangelists, as well as national evangelists, conducting campaigns (often using tents) and expecting "signs and wonders" to follow the preaching of the gospel. Thousands of healings, deliverances, and exorcisms were reported, playing a key role in the spectacular church growth that occurred in many countries. This development paralleled efforts at home to stir the churches once again to pursue their evangelistic mission. Outside observers noted the unique distinctives of Pentecostal evangelism and expansion.

The longtime commitment to fostering strong national churches had prompted Assemblies of God missionaries to found an unprecedented number of Bible schools for ministerial training, ranging from elementary to collegiate levels. This worldwide effort met with such success that church leaders earnestly requested advanced training, reflecting the desire in many developing nations for educational betterment. From this interest came creative ventures, notably the regional advanced schools, Christian Training Network, and ICI. It is noteworthy that the development of ministerial training abroad has roughly paralleled that of the American Assemblies of God.

Ironically, this regard for postgraduate training accelerated the demand that missionaries, particularly those who served as faculty members, secure graduate level training and advanced degrees. This was a surprising development, for the denomination as a whole remained largely ambivalent about graduate education.

The establishment of the Assemblies of God Graduate School in 1973, with its offerings in missions science, communications, and anthropology, subsequently constituted the most significant attempt ever made by the Division of Foreign Missions or any other Pentecostal mission agency to furnish advanced training for its personnel. The benefits of the school could also be found in the provision of specialized training for new recruits through the Candidate Graduate Training Program and the availability of advanced degrees for furloughed missionaries teaching on American campuses through the newly-created Missionary-in-Residence program.

For some time, the pragmatic advantages of specialized training in missions, education, and other related fields had been obvious. The educational qualifications of George M. Flattery corroborated the belief that advanced training could contribute to evangelism and discipleship training. However, both denominational leaders and missionaries keenly realized that ultimate success required the indispensable spiritual vitality sustained by the baptism in the Holy Spirit and belief in the restoration of apostolic signs and wonders in evangelism. Educational training would best serve as the handmaiden of spiritual fervor.

Missionaries attending AGGS, as well as those attending other evangelical schools, made important missiological contributions through their research and writing. Even so, the paramount achievement was Melvin L. Hodges' *Theology of the Church and Its Mis-*

sion: A Pentecostal Perspective. This best reflects the development of Assemblies of God missiology by 1977, the influences of contemporary evangelical missiologists, the distinctives of Hodges' Pentecostal theology, his readiness to address the issue of proselytizing, and his good will toward the charismatic movement. The success of both Hodges and David A. Womack in publishing outside of denominational publications denoted some progress in apprising the larger church world of the theology and methods of Pentecostal missions.

The long tenure of J. Philip Hogan as executive director of foreign missions insured stability and faithfulness to the original objectives of Assemblies of God missions. Hogan's pragmatic openness to creative initiatives generated an atmosphere conducive to change. Strong and younger men came to important leadership posts, bringing new skills and insights. Through successful promotions (periodicals, missions conventions, etc.), the Division of Foreign Missions successfully highlighted the world mission of the church to its supporting constituency. A steady stream of new missionaries and the continuing growth of denominational support agencies reflected not only successful promotions, but growing spiritual vitality in the churches. The thriving enthusiasm for volunteer service via the Mobilization and Placement Service demonstrated the intense level of spiritual zeal and compassion found in many local churches. Few attending the Council on Evangelism in 1968 could have envisioned the level of grass roots mobilization for missions that would occur by 1977. The marriage of professional ministries with supporting lay ministries has been one of the outstanding accomplishments of the Assemblies of God.

In addition to serving as field director for Eurasia, Charles E. Greenaway became known for his promotion of missions in the Assemblies of God. Preaching to Bible college students, he strikes a characteristic pose: Bible in one hand and handkerchief in the other.

Wesley R. Hurst served as field director for the Far East before his death in 1987. Here he inspects the construction site for the new campus of FEAST in Baguio City, Philippines.

Morris Williams, field director for Africa, and his wife, Macey, ministering in a village in Malawi

Author and educator Joyce Wells Booze served as foreign missions editor from 1975 to 1981, returning to the post in 1989 after teaching at Central Bible College.

Beverly Graham served as foreign missions editor (1982–1986) before receiving missionary appointment to Africa.

Teen Challenge Center in Weisbaden, West Germany

MAPS volunteer Nadine Jones works as a computer operator at the headquarters of the International Correspondence Institute in Brussels, Belgium.

Laymen from Northwest Assembly of God in Ardmore, Oklahoma (Larry Pyle, pastor), who built three churches in earthquake-devastated Guatemala. At left is Rev. Lamar Headley, coordinator of the building projects. At right, Rev. Walter Haydus, Assemblies of God field chairman for Guatemala.

MAPS workers from Seattle's Shoreline Community Church installing curbing near the Charles E. Greenaway chapel-classroom building at Continental Bible College in Belgium

Part IV

Into the 80s
(1978–1989)

Partnership in Mission

After beginning obscurely, modern Pentecostalism reached worldwide proportions by the 1980s. As important components of this expansion, the Assemblies of God and the fraternally-related national churches gradually achieved exposure and recognition. Advances were also made in developing and publishing Pentecostal perspectives on missiology. Influenced by the growing attention in evangelical circles on evangelizing Muslims and other "unreached peoples," Assemblies of God missionaries moved in these directions, evidenced by the inauguration of the Center for Ministry to Muslims.

Changes also occurred in the area of missions education and promotion. The Division of Foreign Missions shifted its relationship to the Assemblies of God Theological Seminary (Assemblies of God Graduate School until 1984) by altering the nature of candidate training. At the same time, the promotion of the world mission of the church among local congregations continued unabated. Replacing *Good News Crusades* in 1979, *Mountain Movers* magazine became a highly successful vehicle for communication to the faithful.

Worldwide Pentecostalism

By the 1980s, outside observers were counting Pentecostals across the world in the tens of millions.[1] Four streams of Pentecostals (in the broadest sense) could be found: (1) classical Pentecostal denominations (and their mission churches), (2) charismatic renewal movements in the historic churches (and their mission churches), (3) independent congregations resulting from schisms in mission churches, and (4) indigenous nonwhite churches. Classical Pentecostals alone reportedly accounted for the largest family of Protestant Christians in the world by 1980, enjoying their newfound status as one of the fastest growing and most aggressive evangelistic forces in modern Christianity.[3]

Although fundamentalists and evangelicals had ridiculed and denounced Pentecostalism early in the century, by the 1980s its remarkable church growth won the respect and even awe of evangelicals. As evidence of the new climate, well-known evangelical church historian Earle E. Cairns argued that "when revival in the twentieth century is discussed, most people think of the Welsh revival under Evan Roberts. Actually, the Pentecostal revival which began in 1900 should have the priority. This movement became worldwide." This positive inclusion of the Pentecostal movement in his *Endless Line of Splendor,* a historical survey of Protestant revivals, represented a major turn in opinion.[4] Although skepticism about certain distinctives of Pentecostal theology has remained, the movement's contributions to Christianity have been widely acclaimed. In an editorial in *Christianity Today,* a magazine reflecting views within the mainstream of American evangelicalism, executive editor Terry Muck, noting contributions in evangelism and church life, stated, "[W]e owe the Pentecostal church an immense debt of gratitude. It has reminded us that the Holy Spirit makes worship come alive, that the Holy Spirit is not the power stored in unused batteries, but a live current running through our every action."[5]

Another significant indicator appeared in the January 1986 issue of the *International Review of Mission,* published by the World Council of Churches: All the articles focused on the Pentecostal movement. Observers from a variety of Christian traditions have joined a growing chorus heralding Pentecostalism's international achievements. W. Richie Hogg, an eminent historian of the ecumenical movement, contended in 1976 that "within the world Christian community the most explosive movement may be Pentecostalism."[6] A Lutheran historian, Milton T. Rudnick, observes that "perhaps few Christians of the modern era can match the evangelistic activity and effectiveness of the Pentecostals."[7] Trinity Evangelical Divinity School missiologist David J. Hesselgrave concludes that Pentecostalism "has usually produced a deep-seated missionary motivation, and it is this motivation that has propelled it to its present role as perhaps the most missionary-minded segment of world Christianity."[8] In view of this development, the American Society of Missiology chose "The Holy Spirit and Mission" for the theme of its annual conference in 1988.[9]

During the time that the missionary efforts of the counciliar denominations (members of the World Council of Churches and the National Council of Churches [U.S.A.]) declined in the post-World War II era, the limelight of church growth increasingly focused on evangelical and Pentecostal efforts, both parties realizing considerable success in their overseas endeavors.[10] This was momentously augmented after 1960 by the expansion in many countries of charismatic renewal in the historic Protestant churches (including evangelical circles), the Roman Catholic Church, and the Eastern Orthodox churches. Not surprisingly, the April 1986 issue of the *International Review of Mission* concentrated on the charismatic movement.

Charismatic perspectives on the work of the Holy Spirit in evangelism, however, have not occurred without some theological conflict. The controversy over the popular "Signs and Wonders" course offered by the School of World Mission at Fuller Theological Seminary illustrates the tension. Disagreements about the format of the course and some of the theological views that were presented led to a restructuring of the course and the appointment of a faculty task force to examine the role of the miraculous in ministry.[11]

Both Pentecostals and charismatics, nevertheless, have considered the future bright for evangelistic efforts empowered by apostolic signs and wonders. Church of God (Cleveland, Tennessee) missiologist L. Grant McClung, Jr., in an article entitled "Why I Am Optimistic About the Future of Pentecostal Missions," stated, "Under the leadership of the Holy Spirit, the Pentecostal missions movement is already moving into new areas of ministry which will set the course into the next decade."[12] At the 1987 New Orleans Congress on the Holy Spirit and World Evangelization, attended by approximately 35,000 Pentecostals and charismatics, historian Vinson Synan challenged his listeners by saying,

> As chairman of the North American Congress on World Evangelization, I have been asked many times what I will be doing between now and the year 2000. I plan to be in the harvest fields evangelizing for the rest of my life. It is probable

that most Spirit-filled ministers and priests will also spend the rest of their lives in this enterprise. . . .

With all the vision, resources and anointing that is represented in the New Orleans congresses, the Lord could well be preparing the greatest army of evangelizers ever seen in the 20 centuries since Pentecost.

This could be the finest hour in the history of the church. . . .[13]

Statistical speculations abound over the actual size and growth rate of worldwide Pentecostal and charismatic populations, often bearing a whiff of triumphalism. In reference to Assemblies of God achievements, however, J. Philip Hogan has cautioned, "[W]e must continually remind ourselves that, in spite of our successes, half the world does not yet have an adequate witness of Jesus. We can hardly stop to rest on our laurels."[14] At the same time, the emergence of the Pentecostal and charismatic movements has significantly altered the future course of Christianity.[15] In this march toward global evangelization, the Assemblies of God, with its fraternally-related churches doubling in size every 5 years by the 1980s, has played a key role.[16]

Missiology

Motives for Mission

Reflecting on the task of Christian mission in 1944, Missionary Secretary Noel Perkin observed,

No one who has truly received Christ into his heart can be indifferent to missions since the overflow experience of Pentecost results in 'you shall be witnesses . . . unto the uttermost parts of the earth.' Christ has not changed, so that while there are yet souls outside of the kingdom His heart still yearns that they may be brought in. Since our salvation is 'Christ within you,' that same yearning, burning within the soul of the redeemed is a normal reaction whenever the need of the unreached millions is presented. . . . The Christ within us responds to the world's need for Christ.[17]

These underlying purposes for the world mission of the Assemblies of God have remained constant through its history, although ministries of compassion have gained notable exposure and encouragement in recent years (see chapter 13). The 1980 foreign missions theme, "Jesus—No Other Name," encapsulated the core motivation for mission.[18] Steering away from the neo-universalism advocated by some Christians and the priority of social justice championed by others, Assemblies of God missionaries have been motivated primarily by four factors: (1) love for Christ ("For Christ's love compels us, because we are convinced that one died for all"—2 Corinthians 5:14, NIV); (2) obedience to the Great Commission (Matthew 28:19–20; Mark 16:15–18); (3) saving men and women from hell ("plucking brands from the burning"); and (4) compassion for the suffering who need some form of aid assistance or institutional care. Reflecting these objectives, the Division of Foreign Missions has stated: "The missions strategy of the Division of Foreign Missions is the widest possible evangelization of the spiritually lost through every available means, the establishment of indigenous churches after the New Testament pattern, the training of national believers to proclaim the gospel to their own people and to other nations, and the showing of compassion for suffering peoples in a manner representing the love of Jesus Christ."[19]

At the 1983 General Council meeting, General Superintendent Thomas F. Zimmerman exhorted the delegates by saying, "The only salvation man will ever need is the one provided by Jesus Christ. . . . This salvation will never deteriorate. This salvation can never be improved. It is perfect!"[20] However, in a recent issue of *Mountain Movers,* missionary-evangelist David Godwin cautioned that "we are not interested merely in getting the gospel to men. . . . Until the converts become participants in the body of Christ, our mission is not complete."[21] This concern for evangelism followed by intense discipleship training has resulted in the herculean efforts of missionaries to establish Sunday schools and Bible institutes, write curricular materials and training books, create correspondence programs, and utilize media communications. It has also made them wary of cooperating in evangelistic efforts that have been ambivalent or negligent about follow-up programs for new converts. The African evangelistic campaigns of German Pentecostal evangelist Reinhard Bonnke, although focusing on signs and wonders accompanying gospel proclamation, are a case in point.[22]

Underpinning the concern to win souls to Christ has been the anticipation of His imminent return. However, the intensity of this expectation has declined from previous years and been necessarily tempered by strategic planning. At the same time, J. Philip Hogan has warned, "We must continually believe and say that the terminus of history will be the return of the Lord Jesus Christ. We must hold Matthew 24:14 ever before us, remembering that this gospel of the Kingdom shall be preached to all nations—and then shall the end come. . . . As these challenges spur us on, we gain hope that the end of world evangelization and therefore the end of history may be near."[23] The contemporary periodical literature of the denomination affords ample evidence that the early Pentecostal linkage of premillennialism with evangelistic fervor, empowered by the Holy Spirit, has remained firmly intact.[24]

Prayer has been viewed as the key element energizing Pentecostal spirituality and evangelistic activities. Since the nature of the church's mission is spiritual, the believer's prayerful intercession is imperative for receiving the Spirit's empowerment. David Irwin, a missionary to Africa and later director of the Center for Ministry to Muslims, wrote:

> If we will identify with the lost, the sick, and the hopeless, if we will agonize over their condition, and if we will die to ourselves, there will come an authority in our prayer life that we have never known before. . . . Prayers also can reach around the world and touch a lost soul, a depressed national pastor, or a struggling missionary by the Spirit of God. Let yourself become the golden pipes through which the oil of the Spirit can flow.[25]

In an article in *Mountain Movers* entitled "How to Pray for Missionaries," missionary Jerry Sandidge (Europe) called his readers to prayer because "experience has repeatedly shown that . . . one humble intercessor can bring about a revival on the field and result in thousands turning to Christ."[26] This means of grace also equips missionaries and national workers for confrontation with evil powers. With their bedrock confidence in the Spirit's enablement and guidance, Pentecostals have refused to compromise their stance on the baptism in the Holy Spirit and the present-day manifestations of His gifts. Their restorationist interpretation of the Book of Acts, coupled with subsequent experiences of the Spirit's power in daily living and ministry, has undergirded their approaches to evangelism.[27]

Partnership

Moving into the 1980s, Assemblies of God missionaries continued to strive for building strong indigenous churches. The relationships, however, had changed considerably. Mature national churches were now celebrating 50th anniversaries. The times called for an end to paternalism where it still existed and the recognition that the sending agency and the national churches were "partners" in mission. Paternalism, however, has persisted—obvious in some quarters, subtle in others. Lamenting this inconsistency, missionary Jim Grams (Africa) remarked in 1979 that "mission leaders talk about our indigenous principles; beautiful goals are set before us; candidate missionaries are carefully indoctrinated; but out in the trenches the 'White Fathers' and 'Bwanas' still continue to surface. Personal kingdoms still are being built. National brethren still are being offended and becoming disillusioned."[28] The existence of such problems hardly surprised the officers of the Division of Foreign Missions, and they could take comfort in the fact that such practices had been officially condemned, that the enterprise as a whole had been unequivocally moving in the direction of indigenous churches for some time, and that the continuing education of veteran missionaries and improvements in candidate training would further stem such activities.

To address the character of fraternal relationships, a bonding long hoped for by indigenous advocates, the dean of Pentecostal missiologists, Melvin L. Hodges, penned *The Indigenous Church and the Missionary* in 1978, his last book. Reviewers hailed the book's practical benefits for contemporary missionary practice.[29] Others shared his concerns for addressing indigenous church relationships as well.

One of the most outspoken proponents of partnership has been Morris O. Williams, a missionary to southern Africa (1946–1971) who later served as field director for Africa (1971–1985).[30] Through his lectures at the School of Missions, articles in the *Pentecostal Evangel* and *Mountain Movers,* and the publication of his *Partnership in Mission: A Study of Theology and Method in Mission,* he has addressed some of the thorniest issues confronting rapport and cooperation with national ministers and church organizations. According to Williams, partnership does not mean the demise of Western missionaries, but signals a different role. "Given the right attitude and understanding, there is no reason why there cannot be a continued and effective ministry for the missionary. But his relationship to the national church will have to be clear. He will no longer be in control. He will cooperate fully with the national leadership. He will in no way be a threat to it, but rather strengthen it."[31] The foundations for this new arrangement are love, communication, and definition of role. Since the ultimate goal is the establishment of indigenous ("New Testament") churches, it logically follows that relationships will reflect the fruit of the Spirit's indwelling presence.[32] Few have argued as passionately and eloquently for humility and love in dealing with national leaders and ministers as Morris Williams.[33]

Theology of Mission

In the years following the publication of Melvin Hodges' *Theology of the Church and Its Mission* (1977), a growing number of missionaries approached vital issues related to the mission of the church. The towering shadow of Hodges, however, virtually guaranteed that this new generation of missiologists would wrestle with his perspectives when further exploring Pentecostal contributions to the field. In many cases, they have been academically-trained in biblical theology and missiology or trained in other areas relevant to their ministries overseas. Although the number of theses and dissertations has grown, indicating unabated interest in missiological studies, the number of published academic works in the field, articles as well as books, has remained small.

Interestingly enough, *Mountain Movers* magazine, though popularly written and centering on prayer support and promotion, has recently published two important series of articles on missiology. Harold R. Carpenter, a former missionary and later associate professor of missions at Central Bible College having a doctorate in missiology from Trinity Evangelical Divinity School, contributed 12 lessons on "The Biblical Basis of Missions" in 1986. Tracing the basis for missions through the Bible, he remarks, "The idea of missions derives from the eternal purposes of God for man."[34] Consequently, in regard to the uniqueness of Christianity, he adds, "If man can find salvation without a knowledge of Christ, through any other religion, then Christ died unnecessarily."[35] Carpenter also examines the requisite motives for Christian mission.

Reflecting the trend of studying the kingdom of God from a Pentecostal standpoint, former missionary Ruth A. Breusch notably approached the implications in a later series of 10 articles under the theme "The Kingdom, the Power, and the Glory." The articles by Breusch, a graduate (M.A.) of the Hartford Seminary Foundation and professor emeritus of missions at Southeastern College of the Assemblies of God, reflect serious interpretation of the New Testament and valuable familiarity with missiological literature. She defines the kingdom as the rule of God encompassing "the Church as the realm of God's blessings into which His people have entered. The Church is comprised of those who are rescued from the kingdom of darkness and brought into the kingdom of God's Son." Accordingly, "this Church is the *New Israel,* the people of God, under the new covenant. 'New' because Gentile believers are now included."[36] By God's choice, the church is the vehicle for the extension of His kingdom throughout the earth. To Breusch, the advent of the Spirit reflects His redemptive nature by dynamically empowering the church for the evangelization of the world.[37] She thereby concentrates on the aspect of the kingdom's contemporary presence, without diminishing its future millennial character. In so doing, her exposition adds significantly to Hodges' brief connection of the kingdom to the church.

Other writers have hailed the importance of the kingdom for building a biblical theology of mission that gives adequate place to the work of the Holy Spirit. One of the most influential is Dr. Peter Kuzmič, a national minister and director of the Biblical Theological Institute in Osijek, Yugoslavia. Kuzmič, a Pentecostal theologian who works closely with the Assemblies of God, has made significant contributions on a more academic level. In a recent publication, he notes,

> Pentecostals and charismatics are convinced . . . that "the kingdom of God is not a matter of talk but of power" (1 Corinthians 4:20), and expect that the preaching of the Word of God be accompanied by mighty acts of the Holy Spirit. . . .

> For the followers of Jesus who believe the "whole/full gospel,"
> the commission to preach the good news of the kingdom of
> God is linked with the equipping power of the Holy Spirit to
> overcome the forces of evil. . . .
>
> . . . In the age of rationalism, theological liberalism, reli-
> gious pluralism, Pentecostals and charismatics believe that ev-
> idential supernatural activity of the Holy Spirit validates the
> Christian witness. As in the apostolic days, the Holy Spirit is
> the very life of the church and its mission, not replacing but
> always exalting Christ the Lord. This is the Spirit's primary
> mission and the way in which the kingdom of God is actualized
> in the believing community. Christ rules where the Spirit
> moves![38]

Consistent with his biblical exegesis, Kuzmič also forthrightly speaks
to the implications of the kingdom for social ethics.[39]

This theological direction, signaling important exposition of Pentecostal theology, has produced numerous articles by other writers
in denominational publications, a remarkable occurrence when compared with earlier years.[40] Recent official pronouncements have also
mirrored the emphasis. Deliberating on methods in evangelism, the
Total Church Evangelism Strategy Committee of the Assemblies of
God reported to the General Presbytery in 1987 that "as strategy
is formed, it will project what we are willing to believe God to help
us do in building His Kingdom, and specifically, in reaching the
world with the gospel of Jesus Christ."[41] Of more direct importance
for the Division of Foreign Missions was the adoption of a "Statement of Basic Values" in 1988, which briefly correlated the present
and future aspects of the kingdom of God with the mission of the
church.[42]

Undoubtedly, the most serious missiological treatise to surface
among Pentecostals since Melvin Hodges' *Theology of the Church
and Its Mission* is the highly-acclaimed book *The Third Force in
Missions*, by Paul A. Pomerville, a former Assemblies of God missionary.[43] Published in 1985, it is an outgrowth of the author's doctoral dissertation at Fuller Theological Seminary School of World
Mission.[44] Pomerville's book marks a milestone in the elucidation
of the Pentecostal contribution to contemporary mission theology,
specifically addressing the "inordinate 'silence on the Holy Spirit' "
in the heritage of Protestant missions.[45] His exegetical and theolog-

ical analysis, familiarity with contemporary missiological perspectives, as well as original insights, offer the reader several challenging perspectives.

Pomerville believes that Pentecostalism should not be traced exclusively to the Azusa Street Revival, sometimes called "the American Jerusalem," simply because of its impact on the spread of the movement.[46] He points out that Pentecostal revivals occurred in other parts of the world without the tutelage of Azusa Street. Although evidence on them is limited, they nevertheless demonstrate the broader theological significance of the movement. Pomerville, however, goes beyond the traditional list of formative Pentecostal revivals by including various streams of the African Independent Church Movements.[47] Despite his positive assessment, most Assemblies of God missionaries have been wary of some of their theologies and practices.

More importantly, Pomerville decries the historic lack of emphasis in evangelical missions on the work of the Holy Spirit. He traces this to the rationalistic impact of post-Reformation Protestant scholasticism through the over-identification of the Spirit with the written Word and abhorrence of personal "experience" as a factor in spiritual authority. Accordingly, he states that "as a renewal movement, emphasizing a neglected dimension of the Holy Spirit's ministry, Pentecostalism sets the subtle influence of post-Reformation scholasticism in bold relief. It is at this point that Pentecostalism functions as a 'corrective' in contemporary missions."[48] Pomerville sharply clarifies the uniqueness of Pentecostal pneumatology from the common theological heritage shared with evangelicalism.

Another contribution is the author's "Pentecostal" focus on the kingdom of God. The New Testament theology of the kingdom lays the groundwork for properly understanding the outpouring of the Spirit both then and now. The proclamation of the gospel, coupled with the dynamic work of the Spirit, should characterize the extension of the kingdom of God before the return of Christ. Viewing the kingdom as the heart of a Pentecostal missiology, he observes that

> after Pentecost the redemptive activity of God is mediated primarily through the preaching of the gospel and the manifest power of the Holy Spirit in Jesus' name. The church empow-

ered by the Spirit demonstrates the Kingdom's presence by the preaching of the gospel, which is confirmed by signs and wonders (Mark 16:15–17, 20). It is in this saving activity of God the Holy Spirit, through the agency of the church, that the priority of mission is found. The priority of proclaiming the gospel . . . dominates the church's mission in the Book of Acts. Scripture does put emphasis on the evangelistic mandate, God's "special" mission.[49]

Although Pomerville praises the insights of the late evangelical New Testament scholar George Eldon Ladd on the kingdom of God (*The Presence of the Future,* 1974), he faults him for not emphasizing the apostolic work of the Spirit that must accompany gospel proclamation.

Pomerville accurately pinpoints the influence of post-Reformation scholasticism and its attendant prejudice against personal spiritual "experience" (an evangelical understanding versus an existential one) in some segments of American evangelicalism; however, he unfairly generalizes that all evangelicals have failed to emphasize the experiential dimension of the Spirit's ministry. In so doing, he ignores the pneumatological perspectives of the 18th century German Pietists and the Wesleys, as well as 19th century Holiness advocates and revivalists who have impacted evangelicalism and Pentecostalism in this century.[50] Nevertheless, by plowing new ground, Pomerville has made important contributions that continue to merit serious analysis.[51] Even so, further exegesis, theological reflection, and historical research must be done before a definitive Pentecostal missiology appears.

Recently, however, certain Pentecostals and charismatics have advocated "Kingdom Now" theology, which in some instances represents a departure from the traditional pretribulational rapture view and/or premillennial interpretation of the Bible. Focusing on "Christianizing" society now and minimizing or dismissing the teaching on the rapture of the church (though not necessarily the second coming of Christ), this teaching has generated serious controversy. Responding to the charge that "premillenarians are irresponsible on social concerns or that implicit in a premillenarian worldview one [must] embrace 'escapism,'" a Christian Leadership Summit Conference convened in Springfield, Missouri, in early December 1986.[52] Attending the gathering were several Assemblies of God ministers and church leaders. Although the relationship between the kingdom and the church in the conference's final declaration lacks clarity, it nevertheless affirms the present and future aspects of the kingdom and asserts that "many premillenarians, along with other Christians, have been at the forefront of social reformation both within the church and in society" (a judgment disputed by historians).[53]

Denominational concern that Kingdom Now theology could adversely affect the missionary enterprise by diminishing the priority of personal conversions with the reform of society, Dr. George O. Wood, a prominent California pastor and district official, was asked to discuss the dangers in the June 1988 issue of *Mountain Movers.* Wood, apparently perceiving Kingdom Now advocates as representing a monolithic theological perspective, condemns the teaching as heretical for reasons that include highlighting the present aspect of the kingdom to the obscurity of its future nature and importance.[54] Much of his analysis, however, particularly of the more radical positions, is accurate. The mere fact that the movement has emerged may demonstrate the concerns of contemporary Pentecostals to further explore their role as Christians in the world. The Kingdom Now remedies, however, illustrate the urgent need for further biblical and theological reflection on a wholistic view of the church's mission in the world.

Related Contributions

In recent years, Assemblies of God missionaries have produced several books dealing with an assortment of topics related to the mission of the church. In 1984 Hugh P. Jeter prepared a manual for missions emphasis in the local church entitled *The Local Church and World Evangelization.*[55] During the same year, missionary-evangelist David E. Godwin described his procedures in conducting overseas crusades and starting churches in *Church Planting Methods.*[56] In 1986 Delmer R. and Eleanor R. Guynes published a theology of mission, *The Apostolic Nature of the Church,* focusing attention on the mission of the church as empowered by the resurrected Christ.[57]

Reflecting the growing stature of the Assemblies of God within the Evangelical Foreign Missions Association, Personnel Secretary

Ronald A. Iwasko has presented papers at the organization's annual conference on several occasions. They include "Married Women in Missions: Attitudes and Opportunities" (1980) and "The Missionary Family: Coping With Change" (1982). In 1978, he presented "Making the First-Term Missionary Effective" at a meeting of the NAE.

In the field of historical research, Everett A. Wilson, academic dean and professor of history at Bethany Bible College, Santa Cruz, California, traced the growth of Pentecostalism in El Salvador, contributing "Sanguine Saints: Pentecostalism in El Salvador" to the journal *Church History*.[58] He surveyed the American scene in "Hispanic Pentecostalism," an article he wrote for the *Dictionary of Pentecostal and Charismatic Movements* (1988). Victor De Leon, Jr., assistant superintendent of the Pacific Latin American District of the Assemblies of God, authored *The Silent Pentecostals* (1979), a biographical history of the Pentecostal movement among Hispanics that focuses on its development in the United States, but discusses connections with Latin America as well.

Missionaries and national ministers continued to enroll in graduate programs in missiology. Indian church leaders Benjamin P. Shinde and Chelliah Zechariah completed doctor of missiology degrees in the School of World Mission at Fuller Theological Seminary. Shinde's dissertation addressed animism in popular Hinduism, and Zechariah developed a missiological strategy for the Assemblies of God in Tamil Nadu.[59] Included among such efforts are the dissertations of both missionaries and former missionaries: Koichi Kitano on ecumenicity between Catholics and Protestants in the charismatic movement (Centro Escolar University in the Philippines); Ronald A. Iwasko on training for missionary candidates (Trinity Evangelical Divinity School); Delbert H. Tarr, Jr., on cross-cultural communications (University of Minnesota); Dwayne E. Turner on teaching competencies of faculty members in Assemblies of God Bible institutes in the Philippines (Denver Conservative Baptist Seminary); and Harold R. Carpenter on Bible college training for future missionaries (Trinity Evangelical Divinity School).[60] This last dissertation was recently privately published as *Mandate and Mission: The Theory and Practice of Assemblies of God Missions* (1988) and is currently used as a textbook in several Assemblies of God Bible colleges. In the area of theological education by extension, George

M. Flattery penned the booklet *Current Frontiers in Theological Education: A Missions Strategy* in 1986.[61]

Students attending the Assemblies of God Theological Seminary also engaged in important research as well through the early 1980s. Two studies in particular merit attention: "Bibles for Berbers: Communicating the Good News to the Berber Minorities of North Africa," by Derek Eaton, and "Ethnomusicology: A Study of the Music in the South India Assemblies of God Churches," by missionary Beth Grant.[62]

Missionary Training

The relationship of the Division of Foreign Missions with the Assemblies of God Theological Seminary changed dramatically in 1982. Since the founding of the school, the relationship had been warm, illustrated by the willingness of the Division to contribute to the salaries of the missions professors (the missions personnel, Guynes, Tarr, Hodges, and Irwin had been seconded for service in the school) and to allow them to conduct the Candidate Graduate Training Program (CGTP) in association with the annual School of Missions. Eventually, a general subsidy of $40,000 per year from the Division replaced the monies designated for salaries to simplify bookkeeping procedures. During these years important strides were made in missiological study and training, perhaps exemplified by the attempt to establish the Noel Perkin Chair of World Missions in 1980; Melvin L. Hodges received appointment to the post.[63]

By 1982, however, the connection began to change, having two major results: the withdrawal of the subsidy and the gradual termination of CGTP. A complex of developments contributed to the reshaping of the relationship. First, the Division of Foreign Missions began to experience a tightening of its financial resources in the early 1980s.[64] Second, the tenure of Dr. Ronald E. Cottle as executive vice-president (1979–1982) witnessed considerable internal unrest among students and faculty members (and specifically the professors of missions), stemming from administrative policies and priorities.[65] Third, while endorsing the value of graduate education and generously supporting the seminary, the Foreign Missions Committee eventually questioned the need and expense of CGTP for *all* candidates as well as the practical orientation of the program.

The committee also became alarmed at the growing problem of new missionaries who had been filtered through the program, but dropped out after one term on the field (the reasons for this remain unclear). Fourth, uncertainties surfaced about the ever-increasing number of veteran missionaries seeking advanced schooling, which required 2-year furloughs for both study and itineration. In some cases, missionaries were unable to raise their support within the stipulated period, thus creating problems for the ongoing efforts overseas.[66] Finally, differences of opinion between the general superintendent's office and the Division of Foreign Missions figured into the events that transpired.

The changed role of the seminary did not, however, preclude missionaries from enrolling in the school, although it lost most of its missions faculty and student enrollment in missions degree programs subsequently plummeted. The Noel Perkin Chair, though briefly occupied by Melvin Hodges, also foundered for lack of funds. Nevertheless, the seminary has lately exhibited considerable growth and stability, maintaining its regional accreditation and gaining increased recognition from the Association of Theological Schools. Faculty replacements in missions studies (James E. Richardson and Morris O. Williams) have also consolidated the course offerings into one degree program: the master of arts in missiology. Significantly, the Division of Foreign Missions has continued to recommend the school for graduate training and made it possible for missionaries to attend. It recently funded specialized training at the seminary for missionaries preparing to evangelize Muslims, an indication that joint cooperation will continue but under a revised format.[67] When circumstances have warranted, missionaries have also been encouraged and assisted in studying at other institutions (e.g., Fuller Theological Seminary, Trinity Evangelical Divinity School) for advanced degrees. In retrospect, the redirection of candidate training away from the seminary's auspices (CGTP) reflects the agency's pragmatic search for adequate missionary preparation.

In place of CGTP, the Division of Foreign Missions developed an intensive training program for candidates known as Pre-Field Orientation.[68] This 2- to 3-week session occurs annually just prior to the School of Missions. Intensely practical, it stresses the value of teamwork in missionary endeavor. Studies include cultural adjustment, contemporary issues in missions, patterns of interpersonal communications, parenting, stress management, and indigenous church principles. Closely related are emphases on the nature of Christian discipleship and the necessary preparation for spiritual warfare in ministry. In 1987, the Division of Foreign Missions appointed a strategic planning committee to study the basic values of the mission of the church and the work of the agency so missionary candidates could be trained more effectively. The outcome of this study, the "Statement of Basic Values," is used to formulate and monitor the Pre-Field Orientation program.

The Missionary-in-Training (MIT) program launched in 1983 represents another innovation. Originally proposed by Ronald Iwasko, personnel secretary for the Division, this plan provides practical on-the-field training for prospective missionaries under the close supervision of veterans. Reasons for the program include (1) the ability of people in their 20s to learn foreign languages, (2) their generally more flexible attitude toward cultural changes, and (3) the difficulties that some have in obtaining sufficient ministerial experience before applying for foreign missionary service. As a result, the Division began to cautiously approve MITs who met the stringent qualifications. Without replacing the standard program requiring ordination and 2 years of pastoral experience, "the MIT proposal," Iwasko noted, "appears to offer the possibility of making a significant contribution toward getting the right people in the right place at the right time."[69] By advancing this new program, the Division has hoped it will serve as one more effective channel of qualified replacements for retiring personnel. Since its inception, the program has proven to be successful, several trainees having received regular missionary appointment.

Unreached Peoples

The Unfinished Task

Pentecostals have always been interested in reaching "the uttermost part of the earth" (Acts 1:8), since worldwide evangelization was mandated by Jesus before His ascension. They easily tied this commission with the eschatological urgency of living in "the last days." Hence, the words of Jesus, recorded in Matthew 24:14, succinctly dictated the task of the church in evangelism: "This gospel of the kingdom shall be preached in all the world for a witness unto all nations; and then shall the end come."

As Assemblies of God missionaries attempted to fulfill this objective over the years, certain forces hindered its progress. First, the lack of strategy among some missionaries led to their clustering in metropolitan areas and neglecting outreach to isolated peoples. Second, the founding and maintenance of charitable institutions abroad mitigated frontline evangelism on particular fields (in some instances, however, such institutions offered the only effective means of spreading the Christian witness and, not surprisingly, produced effective church leaders). Third, the implementation of indigenous church principles consumed the energies of missionaries, who increasingly taught in Bible institutes, directed ICI programs, worked in missionary administration, and served in other auxiliary capacities. These personnel occasionally found themselves far from direct involvement in evangelism. Fourth, missionaries and national churches have sometimes avoided certain sectors of population due to their hostility toward Christian witness; this avoidance has been especially true regarding Muslims. According to G. Edward Nelson, secretary of foreign missions relations in the U.S. for the Division of Foreign Missions (1979–1988), the ambivalence of some Christians toward non-Christians can be explained in several ways: (1) misunderstanding of the sovereignty of God and the doctrine of election, (2) naive belief in the universal salvation of all peoples, (3) a reinterpretation of the mission of the church that dilutes the imperative of evangelism, (4) spiritual self-satisfaction that lacks a concern for the unsaved, (5) substitution of skills in the behavioral sciences for the gifts of the Holy Spirit in evangelism, (6) lack of vision for the unreached, and (7) failure—due to cultural and racial prejudices—to see needy people around us who need the gospel. To Nelson, "the crying issue of God's prophets today is not the injustices of economic and political systems, but the injustice of the 'gospel rich' hearing the message many times while 3 billion souls languish in spiritual poverty, unreached."[70]

A heightened awareness among evangelicals and Pentecostals occurred following the 1974 International Congress on World Evangelization held at Lausanne, Switzerland. Missiologist Ralph D. Winter's paper, "The Highest Priority: Cross-Cultural Evangelism," stirred the delegates to reach the large blocks of non-Christians and unreached people groups with the gospel.[71] The Assemblies of God formally approved "The Lausanne Covenant," thus endorsing the work of the conference. Since that time it has continued to cooperate with the ongoing Lausanne Committee for World Evangelization.

"Unreached peoples" (a people group without an indigenous community of believing Christians who have the numbers and/or resources to properly evangelize them) quickly received more emphasis in the Division of Foreign Missions. Foreign Missions editor Beverly Graham challenged the readers of *Mountain Movers* by saying, "We thank God for the victories and successes He has given in our missions work around the world. But even as we number the growing Assemblies of God churches in 109 countries, we must also offer ourselves to be used by the Master in reaching the rest of the world that is lost. We dare not measure our success against anything but the unfinished task."[72] Indicative of this interest, the January 1983 issue of *Mountain Movers* was devoted exclusively to "New Frontier Evangelism." Articles by other writers have emphasized the challenge as well.[73] Closely related to this concern, George M. Flattery, president of ICI, called attention to the illiterate making up half of the world's population and the need to evangelize them.[74]

Center for Ministry to Muslims

One notable outgrowth of the concern for unreached peoples came with the inauguration of the Center for Ministry to Muslims (CMM) in 1982. David K. Irwin, well-known in Assemblies of God circles as a missionary (Egypt, Malawi), editor, and educator, spearheaded the new venture. Irwin was confident that if Pentecostals relied on the power and demonstration of the Holy Spirit, Muslims would be challenged to hear the gospel. In his words, "We will stress a Pentecostal methodology based on the Biblical teaching that the Holy Spirit was given to us as dynamite, thrusting us out to evangelize the world. Pentecost offers a viable, experiential alternative not offered by intellectualism or ritual."[75]

CMM faced several important tasks. The initial plan called for information gathering on the number of missionaries, churches, national ministers and evangelists, and Bible schools located in Muslim areas. Analysis could then be done on receptivity to the gospel and current efforts at evangelism. One of the findings from this study indicated that some missionaries were ill-equipped to evangelize Muslims and that certain national churches ignored them altogether.

Another task involved preparing research materials and conducting seminars for training missionaries, national pastors, and Bible school instructors to provide them an accurate understanding of the Islamic faith and methods to competently reach its adherents with the gospel. Irwin also envisioned evangelizing them in America through both pastors and lay people. Although planning and strategy were key components of his perspective, the backbone of the center's productiveness would be intercessory prayer.[76]

Irwin's untimely death on July 8, 1984,[77] in an automobile accident shocked his friends and colleagues but did not diminish the growing concern to evangelize Muslims. His stellar commitment to missions had a far-reaching effect on other missionaries, students at the Assemblies of God Theological Seminary, and many young people in the denomination. To replace Irwin as coordinator of CMM, the following year the Division of Foreign Missions selected veteran missionary Delmar Kingsriter (Africa). Under his leadership, the center moved its offices from Springfield, Missouri, to Minneapolis, Minnesota.

Since Kingsriter's appointment, CMM has intensified its promotion of Muslim awareness. It has effectively presented the need before the Assemblies of God constituency and recruited additional missionaries intent on ministering in countries having Muslim populations. Booklets on Islam and the possible methods of evangelism, the newsletter *Intercede,* tapes and videos, as well as membership in the Jumaa Prayer Fellowship,[78] have caught the attention of many within the denomination and heightened their interest in this large block of unreached people. Since 1987, the center has also worked closely with area representatives Douglas Clark (Middle East and North Africa) and Ronald Peck (Southern Asia, later assistant director of CMM), and the Assemblies of God Theological Seminary in offering specialized studies in Muslim evangelism oriented toward candidate missionaries and those moving into this field of evangelism. The initial course offerings were provided through the assistance of faculty members from the Zwemer Institute, an agency affiliated with the U.S. Center for World Mission in Pasadena, California.

Muslim Evangelism

Since the earliest years of the Pentecostal movement, Assemblies of God missionaries have been active in the Middle East (especially Palestine and Egypt) and Southern Asia (Pakistan, India, and Bangladesh). Some, traveling abroad as independent missionaries, later joined the fledgling organization after 1914. Even though they successfully evangelized among non-Muslim Christian populations (e.g., the Copts in Egypt), they realized little success among Muslims. In many instances, missionaries have been ill-equipped to face them with the gospel. Since the establishment of the Center for Ministry to Muslims and the availability of specialized training, an increasing number of missionaries have accepted the challenge.

Muslim evangelism has taken several forms. On one level, the task is approached through the use of ICI materials. Literature evangelism has penetrated barriers that prevent normal missionary activity. Missionary Mark Bliss reported Muslim conversions in Iran through ICI courses as early as 1971.[79] Another correspondence program, Allah-u Akbar, offered by the Center for Education in Malaga, Spain, aims specifically at Muslims. This program, directed by Egyptian-born Dr. Sobhi Malek and based on his doctoral dissertation at Fuller Theological Seminary, has also met with success. One convert wrote, "Before I believed in Jesus, my life was filled with uncertainty. Now, it is filled with light." Another reported, "The police have been to my house and have taken my Bible and it seems that they are checking all the mail that I send out of the country. So, could you send me another Bible and the other literature you told me about? May all the blessing of the Saviour be with you."[80] Malek's lessons are culturally adapted to Muslim audiences. In 1986 over 16,000 copies were distributed and more than a third were completed and returned. The number of conversions that have resulted, however, is difficult to determine for a number of reasons, one of which is the censorship of mails in some Muslim countries.[81]

The Center for Ministry to Muslims and the Assemblies of God Division of Foreign Missions, however, do not rely on any single strategy for evangelizing Muslims; rather, they utilize a variety of avenues, correspondence courses being but one of them. In countries where Muslims are in a minority (e.g., Israel), direct efforts at evangelism are feasible. However, where Islam is the dominant faith, laws against conversion are usually enforced and missionary activities must take a different tack. In some Middle Eastern and South Asian nations, Assemblies of God missionaries engage in low-key efforts at winning Muslims to Christ. Evangelism, therefore, is charged with dangers for both missionary and convert and must be approached with great caution.[82] (The mere mention of certain missionaries and converts in this book could potentially result in intense persecution and in some instances death.)

"Success" in this instance is considerably different from that of regions like Latin America, where converts can be numbered in the millions. Rather, a convert per year may represent great progress. However, Kingsriter observes that "wherever a godly witness of the gospel and its power has gone, Muslims are turning to the Lord in ever-increasing numbers."[83] This growing emphasis on reaching Muslims and other unreached peoples demonstrates the ongoing commitment of the Assemblies of God to world evangelization and a consistency with its undergirding theological motivations.

Missionary Byron Niles, area representative for Central America, presenting a diploma to a graduate at a commencement service. Niles had a formative influence on the development of the Christian Training Network before his untimely death in 1986.

G. Edward Nelson served as secretary of foreign missions relations in the U.S. from 1978 to 1988.

Francesco Toppi, general superintendent of the Assemblies of God in Italy, preaching at the 1988 Annual Youth Conference held in Rome

The Yoido Full Gospel Church in Seoul, Korea, pastored by Paul Yonggi Cho, is the largest congregation in the world. It has supported an extensive network of its own missionaries.

Missionary Delmar C. Kingsriter, director of the Center for Ministry to Muslims, with a Muslim religious leader

Herman N. van Amerom serves as the general superintendent of the Brotherhood of Pentecostal Assemblies in the Netherlands, formed in 1952. The Assemblies of God (U.S.) has a fraternal working relationship with this organization. Like other European Pentecostal churches, its Pentecostal heritage predates the founding of the Assemblies of God.

Mountain Movers magazine focuses on prayer support for Assemblies of God missions (Matthew 17:20).

Commissioning service for newly-appointed missionaries during the annual School of Missions. The service is held at the end of the school, which meets on the campus of Central Bible College, Springfield, Missouri.

Far East Conference of missionaries and Asian church leaders in
Seoul, Korea, 1978

Personnel Secretary Ronald A. Iwasko (left) conferring
with missionary Robert Abbott at a session of Pre-Field
Orientation

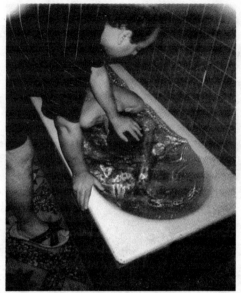

A Muslim convert to Christianity is se-
cretly baptized in North Africa.

Delegation of church leaders at the West Africa Assemblies of God Conference in 1988 at Lome, Togo, chosen to visit the president of the republic. Left to right: Bernard Hascoet (representative of the French A/G), Nanami Natani (general secretary, Togo A/G), Mitre Djakouti (general superintendent, Togo A/G), Bila Pasgo (retired general superintendent of Togo A/G), James Bryant (area representative for West Africa), Donald Corbin (field director for Africa), Franklin Ukomah (assistant general superintendent, Nigeria A/G), Jean-Baptist Sawadogo (conference chairman; general treasurer, Burkina Faso A/G), and Willard Teague (Togo Missionary Fellowship chairman).

13

The Undiminished Priority

As the Assemblies of God approached its 75th Anniversary in 1989, its missionaries continued to focus on evangelization and the fostering of strong indigenous "New Testament" churches capable of aggressive evangelism themselves. Although benefiting from advanced technology, better means of travel, and the improvement of living conditions in many countries, the missionary, in meeting the task, required extensive fund-raising and itineration in the United States when home on furlough, flexibility in cultural adjustment, and humility when dealing with national church leaders. Such responsiblities also generated unique stresses on their families. Despite these pressures, the number of veteran missionaries increased and the missionary roster swelled with new candidates every year, reaching nearly 1600 by the end of 1988. The missionaries usually found their labors to be rewarding and the attendant problems outweighed by the sense of divine mission.

Evangelistic efforts continued unabated into the 1980s, Good News Crusades finding marked success. New ventures also emerged, such as STAR Communications (Spanish Television and Radio) and International Media Ministries, both based on fraternal cooperation with national churches. Retaining firm ties to the American Bible Society, the Division of Foreign Missions also developed a working relationship with Wycliffe Bible Translators. Important developments occurred as well in the area of charitable ministries with the founding of a new agency, HealthCare Ministries.

Achievements, however, were tempered by growing pains. The activities of unethical people on some mission fields triggered serious problems. The moral failures of televangelists Jim Bakker, and particularly that of Jimmy Swaggart, caused acute embarrassment and challenged the ethical and spiritual resolve of the Assemblies of God.

Missionaries

As the mission program matured and expanded, qualifications for missionary service increased. New categories appeared (regular appointed [general missionaries and specialists], approved ministers abroad, missionary-evangelists, short-term evangelists, persons on special assignments, and candidate missionaries), demonstrating the complexity of opportunities and responsibilities abroad. At the same time, the spiritual burden for evangelizing the unsaved remained the undiminished guiding priority of the operation.[1] In an article entitled "Our Mission for the 90s," General Superintendent G. Raymond Carlson (elected in 1985) challenged the membership of the denomination by saying, "We must feel within our spirits the lostness of mankind—feel it so deeply that we will do our part to complete this great mandate."[2]

Although second and third generation missionaries had by now appeared on the scene, the risks of ministry abroad remained considerable on particular fields.[3] With the instability of governments, antimissionary campaigns of certain organizations, threats of terrorism, cash flow shortages, and unrelenting inflation in some countries, missionaries continued to face vexing problems. Despite medical advances, for example, perils from tropical illnesses and polluted water supplies have remained. When Donald R. Corbin (Senegal; later field director for Africa) came down with cholera, he reported that the day of his sudden recovery coincided with the prayers of friends in Texas, one of whom wrote to him saying, "Several months ago, . . . the Lord impressed me to pray for you because you had a physical need. I called my mother and the two of us prayed for you every day for five days. On the fifth morning we both felt that the Lord had done the work and we could stop praying."[4] Stories of such divine intervention are not uncommon within the ranks and denote ardent confidence in the provision of signs and wonders for the advancement of the kingdom of God; even so, missionaries have occasionally died prematurely from various ailments. But despite the sometimes high price tag for ministry abroad, the imperative of world evangelization has continued to capture the imagination and resolve of both supporters and missionaries.

Evangelism

Statistics and Reflection

The 1988 statistical report indicates considerable progress in fund-raising, evangelism, and training: a budget estimated at better than $82 million (total giving), ministry in 120 countries, 329 Bible schools, 32,628 students, 94,706 national ministers, 117,450 churches, and 16,269,817 members and adherents (conservatively estimated).[5] Undeniably, the last 30 years have depicted an exploding rate of growth—up from 13,975 churches and 627,443 national church constituents in 1959. It is important, however, to identify these statistics as those of the fraternally-related national churches. The Assemblies of God (U.S.) does not include them in its own roster of churches or membership and can claim only partial credit for their successes.

Even with these triumphs, the challenge of world evangelization looms larger than ever due to the high birth rate in many countries. Consequently, the Assemblies of God has resolved to accelerate its endeavors. Focusing on the spiritual foundations of the denomination, G. Raymond Carlson recently wrote, "We can talk about plans and programs. We can cite statistics and quote reports. We can laud past accomplishments, but any efforts on our part are destined to fall far short unless the Holy Spirit anoints and directs. Without the touch of God we are spiritually barren."[6] This concern for spiritual vigor best explains the dynamic behind the financial support of the American constituency (without discounting a very effective promotions department), the continuing supply of missionary recruits, the concern to foster New Testament churches abroad, and the growth of the national churches.

Good News Crusades

Over the years, Assemblies of God missionaries have become especially adept at evangelism and training national leaders. One effective medium has been the continued utilization of Good News Crusades. Whether held in large auditoriums or in tents, they concentrate on winning converts for the planting of local churches, followed by discipleship training to insure each congregation's mature development. In Africa, for example, teams have erected tents in cities and augmented the evening evangelistic services with daytime Bible classes. Sometimes, according to the degree of interest, the crusades last several months. The evangelist, often a national minister, stays to pastor the new church, which continues meeting in the tent until permanent facilities are arranged.[7]

Missionaries and national ministers, although engaging in extensive planning for such crusades, consistently credit their accomplishments to the proclamation of the gospel, expectancy of miraculous healings, and confrontation with evil powers. Missionary-evangelist Ben Tipton recounted that when he prayed for a man who was demon-possessed, the man's chest swelled and he went into a trance. After coming to consciousness, the man experienced severe pain in his legs. When the exoricism was accomplished, "this man, who had just received Christ into his life and who had no knowledge about the Holy Spirit and speaking in other tongues, began to overflow with a new language as the Spirit came upon him." Looking back on his ministry in Africa, Tipton observed, "This is only one of the many miracles I have witnessed in which demon-possessed people have been set free by Jesus Christ. Through Christ, we *can* take dominion over Satan. . . ."[8] In describing spiritual warfare, Loren O. Triplett, field director for Latin America and the West Indies, cited the confrontation with atheistic ideologies, which seek to control nations, as one of the characteristics of revival in Latin America. Furthermore, "the more we pray, the more the devil trembles. . . . In country after country, we see the urgent need of identifying the devil's territory and coming against it in the name of the Lord."[9] Whether through Teen Challenge workers ministering to drug addicts in Argentina, campus evangelism in the Philippines, or missionaries evangelizing nomads in West Africa, accounts of supernatural deliverances and divine guidance have played an important role in reinforcing the spiritual drive of the mission enterprise.[10]

Task Forces

Fraternal participation has been an important component in evangelistic campaigns. One method that has met with considerable success in Latin America has been the use of Task Forces. To expedite church planting in Paraguay, a landlocked country in South America having only a few Pentecostals, Loren Triplett developed a plan for evangelism in 1979 and shared it with Estanislao Candia, superintendent of the Paraguay Assemblies of God. Enlisting his support and that of the national presbytery, together they devised the Paraguay Task Force as "a united, intensive, evangelistic effort involving the national church, resident missionaries, North American missionary-evangelists, Latin American evangelists, pastors from other Spanish-speaking countries, Mobilization and Placement Service (MAPS) workers, Ambassadors in Mission (AIM) teams from several countries, and dedicated friends and churches in the United States."[11] Ministers and laypeople from 12 Latin American countries participated, having as their goal 15 new churches.

To assist in the venture, a coordinator was appointed and specially-designed tents, capable of being enlarged, were purchased. Speed-the-Light provided vehicles and public address systems; Good News Crusades paid for the setting up of the tents, the expenses of the national evangelists coming from other countries, and the printing of promotional materials and song sheets. Added help came from Light-for-the-Lost (Bibles, New Testaments, gospel portions, tracts, ICI evangelism courses) and BGMC (funds for ICI training books and tape recordings of the Gospel of Mark).

The city of San Lorenzo, a suburb of Asuncion, became the site of the first crusade in April 1981. Two years later, 15 crusades were conducted.[12] These combined American–Latin American investments in evangelism and church planting have proven to be especially productive. Task Forces have been promoted for other countries (e.g., Jamaica), as well as specific cities, such as Quito, Ecuador; Mexico City, Mexico; and Santiago, Chile.[13]

Media Ministries

Although radio and television continued to be utilized for evangelism in many quarters, the use of electronic media made rapid progress with the inauguration of STAR Communications in 1979 and International Media Ministries 2 years later. Beginning with pilot video programs produced at First Assembly of God in Lakeland, Florida, in 1978, missionaries Joseph and Margaret Register (Chile, Paraguay) laid the basis for STAR Communications, which received authorization a year later and set up permanent production studios in Lakeland. To assist this new endeavor, Speed-the-Light donated funds for video and audio equipment.

STAR has sought to integrate media and missions. Between 1984 and 1988, it produced and distributed 52,000 audio and video programs, including spot announcements, adult and children's programming, teaching helps, and news reports. Characteristic of other missionary efforts, STAR's operation and effectiveness have received significant contributions from MAPS workers and volunteers. By 1988, 19 television outlets in the U.S. and 18 in Latin America carried STAR programming. Ministry has currently been extended into more than 50 countries.[14] Although generally focusing on Spanish-speaking populations, broadcasts have also been developed in Portuguese and English. In addition to cooperative efforts with Christian Training Network, missionaries and national ministers have used the videocassettes for gospel presentation in auditoriums, homes, and children's Bible clubs. One of STAR's most popular programs, a favorite of thousands of Latin American children and adults, is the Muppet-style gospel children's program *El Lugar Secreto* ("The Secret Place").

STAR programs are not intended to replace the local church. Margaret Register has stated, "Its purpose is to get the attention of the unsaved and point the way to Jesus, so that people will be brought into the church."[15] This strategic investment in media evangelism has significantly contributed to the expansion of Pentecostalism in Latin America.

Coming 2 years later and pursuing a larger scope of operation, International Media Ministries (IMM) set up production facilities in Brussels, Belgium. After graduating from Southeastern College of the Assemblies of God and Florida Southern College, David Lee, later appointed director of IMM, began pioneering a church in Winter Haven, Florida; to support his family, he accepted a teaching position at Lakeland Junior and Senior High School. Several years later, the principal informed Lee that the federal government had selected the school to participate in a project to study the educational use of television. Chosen along with another teacher to direct the undertaking, Lee and his associate set up a television studio in the high school, complete with all of the necessary equipment, and worked in close association with an educational station in Tampa. With growth at the church, Lee resigned his position at the high school, later serving as youth director of the Peninsular Florida District. Through his association with the AIM program, he then became interested in missionary service. After a trip to the 1972 Olympics in Munich, he and his wife took another team to Bogota, Colombia, at Christmastime. Lee recounted, "Through a miracle an ensemble out of the group was invited to sing on television. There was only one television station for 28 million people. We realized then that this was one of the means that God had chosen to reach the masses."[16] Interpreting his previous television training as providential, the Lees traveled to Colombia as appointed missionaries in 1976 and later worked with STAR Communications for a short time before overseeing the development of IMM in 1981.

IMM came into being after a study committee appointed in 1979 (G. Edward Nelson, chair; David Clark, CBN University; Jerry Rose, Channel 38 TV in Chicago; George M. Flattery, ICI; Loren Triplett, DFM; David Lee; Paul Garber, an electronics engineer; and Joe Register, STAR) reported that the Assemblies of God had the largest communications network among evangelical organizations. It also found "much duplication of efforts with expensive equipment and [that the network] could benefit greatly by coordinating . . . various programs."[17] To remedy and coordinate efforts, the agency was designed to focus on the following activities: professional consultation (equipment and software, such as videotapes, films, etc.), production of software (broadcast and education in the language and color standards needed in various regions of the world), training seminars for missionaries and national workers on the use of equipment and the preparation of software, and the building of a catalog and library for distribution of materials for television and radio. IMM also provides a video news service to report missionary activities to the supporting constituency in the U.S., video presentations for promoting large missions projects, and evaluation and servicing of existing equipment.[18]

When national churches and missionaries need assistance in developing radio and television programming, IMM comes to their aid. It has assisted national churches by sponsoring field productions of programs and providing the necessary technicians (e.g., it installed a radio station in Bogota and trained the personnel). Churches in Burkina Faso, Sierra Leone, Botswana, Germany, and Ecuador, among others, have received valuable help. Its ministry, like that of ICI, has also benefited other Christians who want to preach the gospel. In the Netherlands, for example, IMM helped evangelicals obtain free air time on television.

International Ministries and Projects

By 1983 the Division of Foreign Missions had authorized five international agencies to serve as resources for all fields of endeavor: ICI (1967), IMM (1981), Life Publishers International (1946), Center for Ministry to Muslims (1982), and HealthCare Ministries (1983). ICI, called the Bible School of the World, reported in 1988 that 12 million persons in 164 countries have received its initial course, "The Great Questions of Life," 6 million students were enrolled at various levels of study, and more than 6,000 were registered in its collegiate division. Life Publishers International, the oldest of the five agencies, announced that it was sending materials to 43 countries, Bible distribution alone averaging almost 2,000 daily.[19]

Along with the international ministries, the Division of Foreign Missions has approved special projects. Various appeals have been sent by direct mail to the Assemblies of God constituency for projects requiring $10,000 or more. These have included funds for an Arabic radio ministry, a hospital in Calcutta, publishing of Spanish-language Bibles, the Lillian Trasher Orphanage in Egypt, and the production of gospel literature in the Bengali language. An amazing array of other programs have also been promoted: Omega Fund (memorial gifts), Overseas Relief (disaster aid), Overseas Religious Education (assistance for Bible schools), Revolving Loans (church construction), Asia Project 2000 (Far East broadcast ministries), 5th Dimension Projects (another account for large projects), Child Care International (ministry to children), and Paraguay Task Force (evangelism and church planting), to name only a few.[20]

A permanent agency for coordinating and developing programs for Latin America and the West Indies is CLASP (Caribbean–Latin American Special Projects).[21] Initially directed by veteran missionary George Davis, CLASP was founded in 1981. Now directed by C. W. Van Dolsen, it maintains offices in Springfield, Missouri. Among its projects are serving Bible school students with Overseas Library Service, developing a Missionette program in Spanish, preparing ICI materials in Spanish, and offering assistance to missionaries involved in Task Forces. Consistent with the programs listed above, it is supported by financial gifts from the American churches.

Careful financial oversight by the Division of Foreign Missions has reassured contributors that their designated monies are spent accordingly. For example, the Division used only 4.8 percent of its total revenue from offerings and investment portfolio income and 2.2 percent of funds generated from missionary itineration, totaling 7 percent for the costs of administration and promotion in 1987. This represents "the lowest administrative and promotional budget of any major missionary sending body and [is] exceptionally lower than similar budgets for parachurch missionary bodies."[22] Even with the addition of international ministries, fiscal integrity has continued to be a hallmark of the Assemblies of God mission enterprise.

Bible Translations and Distribution

The long friendship between the Assemblies of God and the American Bible Society continued into the 1980s with G. Edward Nelson, secretary of foreign missions relations in the U.S., reporting that "no better partners exist."[23] Through the auspices of this agency and its affiliation with the United Bible Societies, the Division of Foreign Missions has channeled monies for sponsoring and printing Bible translations at affordable costs. These funds have contributed to the production and distribution of Bibles in the Burmese, Cambodian, Chinese, Marshallese, and Polish languages, among others. Because of the Bible's essential role in evangelism, teaching, and discipleship training, the Assemblies of God has become one of the largest users of Bibles printed by the Society.[24]

The relationship of Wycliffe Bible Translators (founded in 1934) with the Division of Foreign Missions originated with the ministry of Marva Strickland Farnsworth, one of the few Wycliffe translators having an Assemblies of God background. After returning home to California from assignment in Papua, New Guinea, the Farnsworths were invited to speak in several Assemblies of God churches. Three of the host pastors indicated interest in contributing to their ministry, but indicated that world missions credit was unavailable for such offerings. When the Farnsworths and executives from Wycliffe approached J. Philip Hogan and other officers of the Division about a joint working agreement in 1983, their suggestions received a positive response.[25] Final approval came a year later with the implementation of a joint sponsorship policy that allows Assemblies of God adherents who secure ministerial credentials with the denomination to work with Wycliffe and itinerate in Assemblies of God churches for their support. By 1988, more than 20 ministers were raising funds to serve as Wycliffe translators.[26]

Missions in the Local Church

Since the founding of the Women's Missionary Council (later Women's Ministries Department), its development, along with that of other support agencies in the General Council, has firmly tied lay involvement to the missions program. Indeed, by the 1970s and 1980s, many overseas endeavors would have been seriously impaired without the funds and volunteers of these agencies. Whether projects of the Women's Ministries Department, Light-for-the-Lost, BGMC, Speed-the-Light, or AIM, every age group can participate in supporting missions. The Assemblies of God Division of Church Ministries claimed, therefore, that "the validity of the needs they seek to meet is one secret of the ongoing vitality of the programs."[27]

Sandra Goodwin Clopine, national secretary of the Women's Ministries Department and herself a former missionary to Africa, speaking on behalf of women's involvement, commented that "women not only pray, they also help supply books, furniture, and appliances for missionary families, Bible schools, and other missions institutions overseas. Every woman who involves herself feels a keen sense of partnership with the missionary process."[28]

Assemblies of God youth continued supporting Speed-the-Light, contributions rising to more than $3.5 million in 1987. The number one church in total giving that year was First Assembly of God in Lancaster, California: Their young people raised an astonishing $93,022 for Speed-the-Light![29]

New Cooperative Ventures

Fraternal cooperation has taken many forms over the years. In some countries, established Pentecostal churches requested assistance from the American Assemblies of God. In Portugal, for example, the Assemblies of God (an indigenous national church organization) invited the Division of Foreign Missions in 1972 to set up a Bible school near Lisbon, citing their lack of resources for such a project. Under the agreement, "the Pentecostal Bible Institute shall be directed and maintained by the American Assemblies of God, and the Portuguese Assemblies shall furnish the students and if needed [sic] be some teachers. At least one or two of the Portuguese Pastors must belong to the school board."[30] Since that time the school has developed one of the finest Bible school campuses overseas, increased student enrollment, and made important contributions to the growth of the Portuguese Assemblies.

A uniquely different arrangement developed when the West German Full Gospel Mission requested assistance with its work in Cameroon, a former German colony in Central Africa. Impressed by the quality of ICI programs for evangelism and training, the West German agency invited Assemblies of God missionary Duane Collins to open an ICI office in the capital city of Douala. Since that time the relationship has remained cordial and avenues for ministry have increased.[31]

One of the largest cooperative efforts in Bible school training has been the Brazilian Extension School of Theology (BEST). The idea for such a school originated with a pilot program initiated by missionary Ronald Iwasko that later gained the enthusiastic support of evangelist Bernhard Johnson. When the program was launched in 1979, over 52,000 Assemblies of God pastors and laymen, many having neither formal Bible training nor means to move away to Bible schools, were overseeing congregations. Taking Bible instruction into local communities at an affordable price became the challenge of BEST. The school offers a 4-year course of study and standard Bible institute courses; classes are taught in specified local churches designated as learning centers. At its inception, over 2,000 men were enrolled and the numbers have steadily increased, making it the largest extension program of its kind in the world.[32] Assistance for BEST came from Speed-the-Light funds, which provided transportation and equipment for producing study materials, as well as MAPS construction teams and volunteers, who provided a variety of services. In 1984 alone, 1,000 pastors and layworkers graduated from the program in 24 graduation ceremonies. By the next year, approximately 8,000 students were enrolled at 225 learning centers in 19 states in Brazil.[33] Since then BEST has grown to more than 15,000 students.

Two important initiatives from American colleges also appeared in the 1980s, signalling new efforts in overseas education. First, Southern California College (SCC), Costa Mesa, California, inaugurated a graduate program leading to an M.A. in Religion (concentrations in biblical studies or church leadership studies) in 1983. Desiring to enrich its educational offerings to students and assist missionaries in Latin America with graduate studies, it opened a summer study program in San Jose, Costa Rica. Since 1985, courses on church leadership have been taught there by SCC faculty members and approved adjunct instructors. Doug Petersen, missionary to Costa Rica, serves as on-site director of the study center. The extension program in Costa Rica specifically attempts "to provide for the academic development and continuing education enrichment of North American students and North American church leaders serving in Latin America with an extension site developed for study in Church Leadership."[34] If national students meet the admission requirements of the college, they can be admitted to the program as well. Plans call for the program to move beyond a summer format to an enhanced calendar of courses, making an M.A. degree available through the center in Costa Rica. Funding for the program is partially provided through gifts from the Bryan S. Smith Institute for World Missions Leadership, an endowment program at SCC "for those who wish to minister interculturally, with a particular emphasis on ministry to the Hispanic people especially in Latin America."[35] Margaret S. Smith serves as the director pro tem of the institute.

The second undertaking has been the linking of North Central Bible College (NCBC), Minneapolis, Minnesota, with the East Africa School of Theology (EAST) in Nairobi, Kenya. In 1981 EAST signed an agreement with ICI to jointly offer a B.A. in Bible-Theology (a nontraditional degree accredited by an American agency). Enhancing its standing further, it also recently entered a working relationship with NCBC. A strategic factor in this new arrangement has been the accreditation of NCBC by a regional accrediting agency in the U.S. According to Dr. Don Meyer, vice-president for academic affairs at NCBC, "These arrangements contribute to the enhancement of the world view which we desire to cultivate in our entire [college] community. . . . We are enacting our philosophy/theology of ministry: to the Lord; to the church; to the world. . . .

The 'soul of North Central' is enriched by these associations."[36] An informal agreement has also been reached with Continental Bible College in Brussels, Belgium, another regional advanced school.

Ministries of Compassion

Background

The historic aim of Pentecostal missions has been the evangelization of the lost before the return of Christ; at the same time, sizable funds and energies have been directed to those with physical needs. Early missionaries such as Esther B. Harvey and Lillian Trasher ministered to widows and orphans through the institutions they founded. Missionaries also cared for lepers and other needy people. Industrial schools were set up to train converts, some of whom had been rejected by their families and needed a trade to support their livelihood. As early as the close of World War I, Assemblies of God church members responded to the appeals of European relief agencies. Etta Calhoun and local chapters of the Women's Missionary Council across America sacrificed and toiled to provide articles of clothing, bedding, bandages, and other essential items for needy people, beginning in 1925. Sponsorship of European refugees grew to such a scale after World War II that the Division of Foreign Missions instituted a relief and rehabilitation program in the 1950s to provide assistance for them as well as for victims of disaster. Since that time, contributions for relief projects have often been directed through the World Relief Commission, an affiliate of the National Association of Evangelicals.[37] Unfortunately, these efforts to alleviate the needs of the suffering have never received the historical investigation and analysis they deserve.

Over the years, appeals to Assemblies of God churches for relief funds have met with positive responses. In the late 1960s, when the Biafrian civil war occurred in Nigeria, General Superintendent Thomas F. Zimmerman, writing in the *Pentecostal Evangel,* stated that "as God-fearing men and women we cannot stand idly by while thousands of Assemblies of God believers die of starvation in a land that for nearly 30 years we have tried to evangelize. . . . We must show them that we love them enough to care about their present suffering."[38] Within a short time, tens of thousands of dollars had been contributed. Not limited to relieving Pentecostal believers, such appeals have included aid for refugees in Thailand, relief efforts in Vietnam, disaster victims in Bangladesh, and famine victims in Africa.

Recent Activities

For missionaries living in underdeveloped Third World countries, the ideal of simply preaching the gospel and training leaders has been tempered by the necessity of addressing the physical needs of the people. Dale Preiser, a missionary to Haiti, reflecting on his ministry there, said, "I want to preach. I know I've been called to declare the Word. But I've been out in the country and preached to an audience of people who couldn't stay awake because they lacked proper nutrition."[39] In an article entitled "Sharing Christ Through Food," missionary Dale Fagerland (Burkina Faso) recounted for readers of *Mountain Movers* his work in distributing grain to starving nomads. He requested readers "to pray that the relief distribution, and soon the seed grain, will be understood by the recipients as a demonstration of the love of God through a lot of caring, loving people."[40] Missionaries have emphasized, however, that such assistance without gospel proclamation is insufficient for one's eternal well-being.

Providing for the physical needs of people has often been spearheaded by individual missionaries in cooperation with the Division of Foreign Missions. Notable ministries have included the ongoing work of the Lillian Trasher Orphanage in Assiout, Egypt, which celebrated its 75th anniversary in 1985.[41] A more recent example can be found in the multi-faceted ministries of the Calcutta Mission of Mercy, founded by missionary Mark Buntain. Through evangelistic activities, Buntain was able to erect an Assemblies of God church in 1959, the first Protestant church to be built there in almost a century. Soon a school was founded, for over 200 children who attended his Sunday school program had been expelled from their private (non-Christian) day schools because of their attendance in the Sunday school. By 1984 six thousand children were enrolled in the school and the church had grown to two thousand in attendance.

The plight of the hungry and the sick, however, challenged Buntain to address their needs. Always active in evangelism, he was distributing tracts in a crowded railway station when three young men said to him: "Sir, give us something for our hungry stomachs; then you can give us something for our hungry souls."[42] Shaken by their response and the later Bengali famine in 1964, Buntain opened food kitchens for the victims. Later, the staggering need for medical attention prompted him to open the Assemblies of God Hospital and Research Center, a 6-story, 120 bed hospital. Opened in 1977 at a cost of $1 million, it is the only full-scale hospital ever sponsored by the denomination. These ministries, including the lately erected West Bengal Bible College (1986), reflect the mixture of evangelism and compassion that characterized the work of missionary Mark Buntain and his wife, Huldah.

Child Care International

As the world's population of children has dramatically increased in recent years, concerns for addressing the physical, educational, and spiritual needs of children have gained considerable attention. Citing the desperate needs of children overseas, missionary Paul Hutsell, area representative for northern South America, observed that "the Assemblies of God is the largest evangelical church in many areas of the Third World. Our national believers and churches are now joining with us missionaries in loving and helping these children in order to influence their lives for Christ."[43] Each of the major fields, therefore, has instituted some type of child care program, collectively called Child Care International. These endeavors raise funds for the care of orphans in Italy, India, Egypt, Japan, and Latin America; Christian school programs (general expenses, school uniforms, hot lunches); and feeding programs (sometimes clothing and medical attention as well).[44] Promotional materials have encouraged church members in the United States to "adopt" a child overseas by pledging to support their care on a monthly basis.

One of the most successful attempts in child care has been in El Salvador, a war-ravaged country in Central America. Missionary John Bueno, pastor of the Evangelistic Center in San Salvador, started a Christian school in 1963 and enrolled 81 children. From this modest beginning the program expanded until 25 years later, 18,231 students were enrolled in 30 schools.[45] The schools are operated entirely by Salvadorans with assistance from American and national donors. Components of their care include education, medical attention, and feeding. Until 1988, one of the largest contributors to the operation was Jimmy Swaggart Ministries, which supported over 6,000 children.[46]

HealthCare Ministries

Although nurses and clinics have been supported for many years, mission leaders have long been wary of founding full-scale hospitals (the Assemblies of God Hospital and Research Center in Calcutta is a notable and recent exception). Reservations about such institutions received reinforcement when an Assemblies of God physician and surgeon, Dr. Jere Melilli, reported in the *Pentecostal Evangel* in 1961 about an extensive trip he had taken through Africa. Stressing the primary value of evangelistic efforts, he questioned the value of medical programs: "[t]hey are very much secondary and many times unnecessary. They have their place, but should never become the prime motive or the first avenue of endeavor in establishing a missionary program. . . . It was my observation that medical missions do not increase the spiritual harvest to a great extent."[47] Even a decade later, concerns about the evangelistic impulse of the enterprise being compromised by the health care of people and the care and funding of medical facilities prompted J. Philip Hogan to write:

> [W]e have not and probably never will become a great institutional mission. By this I mean that we will never establish abroad the kinds of ministries that generally characterized the oldline denominational efforts. I am speaking of institutions such as hospitals, secular school systems, etc. This has meant that we have kept our emphasis at the cutting edge of evangelism and church planting and we have sought for, supported, and appointed the kind of people who can best carry out these tasks.[48]

These sentiments, however, are reactions to the older strategy of American and European churches that promoted institutions overseas, rather than focusing on evangelism and church planting.

With the desperate needs of the physically infirm reaching unprecedented proportions, Assemblies of God church members and missionaries began to voice greater concerns about caring for temporal needs. A dramatic new proposal for increased medical aid was presented by Paul R. Williams, M.D., a pediatrician and Assemblies of God church member, to the Foreign Missions Board in November 1982. From that meeting came a study committee appointed by Hogan, which consisted of Norman L. Correll (chair), Wesley R. Hurst, John Bueno, Ronald A. Iwasko, and Williams.

In November 1983 the committee offered their proposal to the Foreign Missions Board, which, in a historic move, approved the development of HealthCare Ministries, to be directed by Paul Williams. Despite the long record of humanitarian endeavors initiated by Assemblies of God missionaries, this decision by the Board marked a level of endorsement and encouragement not known before. Indeed, the heightened theological emphasis in the denomination on the contemporary presence of the Kingdom of God presents a rich opportunity for integrating the commands of Christ with His compassion—without, however, jeopardizing the commitment to the former.[49]

Rather than following an institutional model, the program envisions a medical outreach that will be "people-centered and national indigenous church-related."[50] The inauguration of this fifth international ministry by the Division of Foreign Missions represents (1) the compassion of Assemblies of God church members for human suffering, (2) a serious attempt to remain faithful to the primary objective of evangelism while caring for physical needs, and (3) the interest of medical professionals within the Assemblies of God desirous of overseas ministry. (The third item also denotes the growing professional sophistication among church members, a sharp contrast to earlier years.) Operating in consultation with missionaries and national church leaders, the agency has these among its goals: serving as an evangelistic aid through providing medical treatment, developing medical educational materials for missionaries and nationals, promoting indigenous medical efforts, assisting the Division on medically-related matters, providing health-care seminars for missionaries, and giving guidance for the use of medical relief monies, supplies, and personnel in the event of disasters.[51]

Reflecting the concern to complement the first priority of evangelism with medical treatment, Williams stated to the Foreign Missions Board, "I can't help but feel that we all believe we are in the last days and the Lord's return is soon. . . . In the last days there are going to be many famines, pestilences, earthquakes, and a lot of different problems. When you have all those kinds of problems, you also have medical needs that come. . . . We can fully express our Pentecostal witness and yet also express the love of Christ through medicine."[52] Through teams of medical volunteers and staff members, HealthCare Ministries has sponsored outreaches around the world. In 1987 alone, 13 countries were visited for the dispensing of medical and dental care. While the patients received medical attention, they were also presented with the gospel message. As a result, the agency reported 3,550 conversions. On the visit to Chihuahua, Mexico, 40 percent of those treated confessed Christ as Savior.[53]

Growing Pains

Unethical Practices

Like all other human institutions, the Division of Foreign Missions and its many far-flung endeavors has been subject to the wiles of unscrupulous individuals. Religious con artists, making false claims about their ministries and sometimes identifying themselves with the Assemblies of God or a fraternally-related church organization abroad, have siphoned off thousands of dollars from well-meaning individuals and churches. In many instances, donors have failed to check with the Division of Foreign Missions or the Missionary Field Fellowship in a particular country before sending their contributions. In a few situations, missionaries who have been disciplined and defrocked for unethical actions have sometimes returned to their fields and generated division among the churches. Unfortunately, some Assemblies of God churches have continued to support them, believing them to be innocent victims of bureaucratic scheming. Such maverick support has actually contributed to serious disorder on certain mission fields.[54]

Jim Bakker and PTL

During 1987 and 1988, the Assemblies of God suffered acute embarrassment from the moral scandals of two of its most prominent ministers: televangelists Jim Bakker and Jimmy Swaggart. Begun in 1974, the PTL television network had grown into a $172 million operation by 1987, including television production studios and Heritage U.S.A. at Fort Mill, South Carolina; the latter comprised a Christian amusement park, dinner theater, time-share condominiums, the Heritage Grand Hotel, a home for unwed mothers, a home for the handicapped, and other associated projects.

Although Bakker[55] readily professed PTL's interest in supporting missions, his actual contributions were miniscule compared with those of Jimmy Swaggart Ministries. Serious problems began on June 13, 1977. While hosting the *PTL Club,* Bakker promised to underwrite a South Korean PTL program, hosted by Paul Yonggi Cho, pastor of Yoido Full Gospel Church in Seoul, Korea. Later in the year, he made a similar promise for a PTL program in Brazil. Through television appeals, Bakker raised $350,000, but subsequently spent the money on bills at home, including expenses for building Heritage U.S.A. Because of this misrepresentation, the PTL network was investigated by the Federal Communications Commission in 1979. Although the charges were serious, the Justice Department declined to prosecute.[56]

In other instances, PTL did lend some assistance to overseas ventures. PTL programs were broadcast on television in Thailand, Korea, Japan, and other countries under the auspices of the missionaries, national churches, and the PTL television network.[57] When Bakker confessed to moral failure on March 19, 1987, these television ministries and the national churches associated with them experienced embarrassment and ridicule simply because of the name identification.

Jimmy Swaggart Ministries

For the cause of world evangelization, however, the most painful tragedy came with Jimmy Swaggart's tearful confession to moral failure on Sunday, February 21, 1988.[58] Coupled with his later refusal to accept the terms of rehabilitation expected of other ministers facing similar charges, as well as his subsequent defrocking, this announcement sent shock waves through the Assemblies of God and created enormous problems for national church organizations.

As an evangelist, Swaggart came to prominence in the mid-1960s. In 1969 he began singing and preaching on the radio and developed a considerable following. His popularity grew to such proportions that before long he was ministering to people in packed-out auditoriums all over America. In 1981 he discontinued his radio ministry and began investing his money and energies in televangelism. Approximately 3 years before going on television, Swaggart had increased his schedule of large overseas crusades. During these years, his telecasts, representing sophisticated television production, took his ministry into the homes of millions around the world. By 1986, he had become an internationally-known evangelist and television personality and his organization's annual receipts had grown to $186 million.

The rise of Jimmy Swaggart Ministries as an independent corporation associated with the Assemblies of God is an anomaly in the history of the denomination. Several factors were responsible for the special latitude his ministry enjoyed. First, Swaggart's singing and preaching styles touched a resonant chord in Pentecostal spirituality, winning him the endorsement of many for his evangelistic emphasis and call for separation from the world.[59] Second, thousands at home and abroad were converted through his crusades and television programs. His crusades markedly affected church growth and provided positive identification for Pentecostals abroad. Third, buoyed financially by successful appeals for funds on television, Swaggart Ministries generously contributed to the designated projects of the Division of Foreign Missions, reaching $1 million per month by 1987. These dollars supported efforts dear to the hearts of his viewers, for example, Child Care International and Calcutta Mission of Mercy. (Missions projects of other Pentecostal denominations, however, were not considered.[60]) Fourth, Swaggart's crusade managers worked closely with national pastors and church leaders in conducting the crusades, planning extensive follow-up procedures for discipleship training of new converts as well. Not surprisingly, Swaggart Ministries strongly supported the indigenous church principles of the Assemblies of God.

Unknown to many television viewers, however, Swaggart's organization depended heavily upon Assemblies of God missionaries to carry out its initiatives: From feeding programs, to television broadcasting, to crusades, its efforts depended on their legwork, a fact sometimes obscured in his promotional materials. So close was the relationship that many missionaries printed both the Assemblies of God logo and the Jimmy Swaggart Ministries logo on their letters to supporters.

However, strains began to develop between Swaggart's organization and the Division of Foreign Missions in the mid-1980s over various issues, including statistical claims about television coverage and viewers. Some church leaders feared that Swaggart was becoming too powerful and could jeopardize the unity of the enterprise. Concerns mounted for several reasons. First, his increasingly strident criticisms of church officials and professed determination to purge the Assemblies of God of alleged spiritual compromise alarmed many within the ranks. Second, Swaggart's assertion that only he could win the world for Christ displayed an unbridled arrogance offensive to observers.[61] Third, certain practices reflected a marked insensitivity to Pentecostals overseas. For example, the special music in crusades, approximately a half hour of each service, was rarely translated into the language of the audience, although the sermons always were. When asked why the music was not translated, one key Swaggart associate replied, "The anointing of the Holy Ghost is so heavy on the musicians that people understand the message of the songs without knowing the words."[62] Recording the music for the American television audience was the primary goal. Fourth, criticism surfaced about his starting a Bible college and seminary—institutions competing with those of the Assemblies of God. Finally, questions arose over Swaggart's personal life-style and the financial integrity of his operation.[63]

Immediately after learning of his admission to moral failure, the Division of Foreign Missions contacted its overseas personnel to cancel contractual obligations dependent on monies from Jimmy Swaggart Ministries. In fact, the organization's contributions to the Division had dropped radically early in 1988 before the scandal broke. In the aftermath, the national churches bore the brunt of the ridicule and criticism. Child Care International lost contributions of about $200,000 per month. And although Assemblies of God church members increased their giving measurably, total missions giving for 1988 was down $1.4 million. In J. Philip Hogan's May 1988 monthly letter to the missionaries, he lamented, "Though time has a way of healing many of these matters, it is my judgment that in some areas the whole foundation of gospel witness has been severely eroded and it is one of those things [for which] we simply must bow our heads in humble contrition and pray that God will keep all of us from being an embarrassment and an offense to the worldwide body of Christ."[64]

Shortly after the national news media began to broadcast the scandal, the funeral service for Melvin L. Hodges, who died February 25, 1988, was conducted in Springfield, Missouri. The memory of his humility, unquestioned integrity, and dedicated service to missions contrasted starkly with the tabloid controversy of the hour. Speakers reminded the mourners that the world mission of the Assemblies of God was based on firmer foundations.

The increase in administrative responsibilities in the Division of Foreign Missions since 1959 has led to the formation of new administrative posts, represented by the following personnel: (front row) Debbie Sherman, Africa field office coordinator; Juanita Evans, special services supervisor; Jean Smith, medical & candidate program coordinator; Esther Smith, Latin America & West Indies field office coordinator; Linda Alexander, finance office coordinator; Brenda Kepley, Eurasia field office coordinator; Rosalee McMain, promotions office coordinator; (back row) Mary Leverett, coordinator for Norman Correll; E. Jane Smith, special services supervisor; Charlene Graves, special assistant for Decade of Harvest; Paul Sherman, supervisor for foreign missions personnel; Robert Freisen, missionary family specialist; Juanita Chastain, Far East office coordinator; Nadine Hicks, research coordinator; Gordon Herron, DFM computer analyst programmer (not pictured)

The office staff of the Division of Foreign Missions has grown considerably since 1959, necessitating the addition of secretaries, editorial assistants, and other workers, numbering 45 in 1989.

Chatting together are (left to right) Fred Cottriel, secretary of foreign missions relations in the U.S.; Paul E. Brannan, secretary of missions support; and Jerry L. Burgess, finance secretary.

Praying for the people in the David Godwin crusade, Sevilla, Spain, 1985

Eurasia Field Director Jerry L. Parsley (center, standing) joins other ministers in ordaining Samuel and Hala Abujaber in Amman, Jordon.

Donald Corbin and his wife, Virginia, participating in the missionary parade at the 1987 General Council meeting in Oklahoma City. Corbin has served as field director for Africa since 1986.

David Lee serves as director of International Media Ministries headquartered in Brussels, Belgium.

International Media Ministries assists national churches in developing their own media productions.

Calcutta Mission of Mercy, founded by missionary Mark Buntain, has developed an extensive ministry to children.

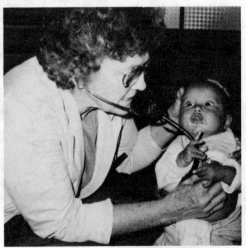

Eloise Judah, a nurse, certified physician's assistant, and appointed missionary with HealthCare Ministries, examining a child on a Latin American visit

Veteran missionary Loren O. Triplett has served as field director for Latin America and the West Indies since 1973.

A respected spiritual leader in the Assemblies of God and an ardent supporter of foreign missions, G. Raymond Carlson was elected general superintendent in 1985.

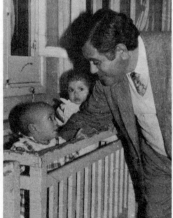

George Assad, the director of the Lillian Trasher Orphanage in Assiout, Egypt, visiting with children. This institution has been one of the best-known charitable ministries supported by the Assemblies of God.

Latin American Child Care provides a Christian education and meals for thousands of underprivileged children.

An innovative program in theological education by extension, the Brazilian Extension School of Theology (BEST) offers courses in specified local churches designated as learning centers in many parts of the country.

14

Preparing for the Decade of Harvest

The year 1989 marked two milestones in the history of the Pentecostal movement: first, the 75th anniversary of the founding of the General Council of the Assemblies of God, the movement's largest organized expression in North America, and, second, the 70th commemoration of the founding of the organization's "Missionary Department" in 1919. With centennial celebrations now just over the horizon, the evangelistic and church planting activism of the Assemblies of God has already pushed it into prominence among other church bodies and mission agencies. While calling for the return of apostolic signs and wonders, it has also recognized the providential hand of God in the arrangement of circumstances at home and abroad.

After midcentury, the national and foreign operations of the denomination were directed by two men of considerable stature, Thomas F. Zimmerman and J. Philip Hogan. Their long tenures enabled them to carry through with vital programs that were initiated during their administrations, minimizing the impact of turnover in other offices.

The fruit of building strong indigenous churches became apparent with the growing number of missionaries sent out by national churches themselves. The sudden surge in their numbers and activities around the world, however, created new problems for coordination and training. Partially to address these needs and to search for cooperative efforts in evangelism before the end of the century, a Decade of Harvest meeting of international church leaders convened in Springfield, Missouri, in 1988.

Personnel

The Hogan Years

The 30-year tenure of J. Philip Hogan as executive director of foreign missions for the Assemblies of God (1960–1989) has had a profound influence on the course of the agency's development and activities.[1] His election on three different occasions to the presidency of the Evangelical Foreign Missions Association signaled his standing as a leader in the Christian world mission, whose perspectives and advice were often solicited. As the longest-serving Pentecostal since Noel Perkin to shepherd a mission agency, he became the dean of Pentecostal mission executives.

Deeply committed to the dynamics of Pentecostal spirituality, Hogan's contributions as director centered on his willingness to pragmatically consider creative initiatives in evangelism, discipleship training, and leadership training. Since he always sought to follow where the Holy Spirit seemed to be guiding, it is hardly incidental that four international ministries were birthed during his administration and have had far-reaching consequences on the entire effort. His firm commitment to indigenous church principles and selection of associates equally committed to them accelerated the building of fraternal ties to national churches.

As an administrator, Hogan exhibited the concerns of a practitioner; at the same time, however, he encouraged and appreciated the missiological labors of Melvin L. Hodges and others who explored the theoretical dimension of the task. A keen student of history, Hogan readily acknowledged the value of historical investigation. During his years in office, the program made great strides in understanding and articulating its objectives and methodologies, fostering continuing education for missionaries, and promoting the endeavor before the supporting constituency—all the while maintaining a remarkable consistency with the original objectives of the enterprise.

Divisional Officers

Important leadership changes occurred in the years after 1978, including the retirement of two field directors and the death of another. Charles E. Greenaway, field director for Eurasia since

1966, retired from office in 1983. Although his missionary service had begun in Senegal, West Africa, he strongly promoted the cause of evangelism in Europe, the Middle East, and Southern Asia before the American constituency. Greenaway has continued his preaching ministry across the country, having preached at over 800 missionary conventions through the years. As field director, he was succeeded in January 1984 by Jerry L. Parsley, a missionary to Bangladesh (1970–1979) and area representative for Southern Asia (1979–1983). Parsley and his wife, Karen, had been engaged in literature evangelism during their earlier missionary service.[2]

An important transition for the Africa field took place in 1985 with the retirement of Morris O. Williams as field director, a position he had held since 1971.[3] (After leaving office, he joined the faculty of the Assemblies of God Theological Seminary as associate professor of missions.) Williams was succeeded in January 1986 by Donald R. Corbin. Along with his wife, Virginia, Corbin began his missionary service in Senegal, later transferring to Ivory Coast in 1974 where he assumed the post of area representative for West Africa.[4]

The untimely death in early 1987 of Wesley R. Hurst, the first officer that J. Philip Hogan appointed when he became executive director in 1960, brought to a close a long and distinguished career in Assemblies of God missions. Hurst had served as a missionary to Africa and later as promotions director and home secretary for the Division of Foreign Missions. As field director for the Far East after 1970, he strongly encouraged the growth of the Far East Advanced School of Theology in the Philippines, the organization of the Assemblies of God Asian Mission Association (a network of Asian national churches working together to evangelize the region), and the establishment of the Asia Project 2000 Commission (a program designed to promote media evangelism).[5] In July 1987, area representative (Northern Area, Far East) Robert Houlihan advanced to the position of field director. Houlihan and his wife, Carolyn, had served as missionaries to Japan for more than 20 years. Prior to their appointment with the Division of Foreign Missions in 1971, they directed the Language Institute for Evangelism in Japan.[6]

Another meaningful change took place in the office of administrative assistant to the executive director. Joseph W. Kilpatrick, who had held the position since 1977, resigned in 1982 to accept an administrative post at Southeastern College of the Assemblies of

God in Lakeland, Florida (he later returned to the Division of Foreign Missions to serve as an appointed missionary). Selected to succeed him was Norman L. Correll, a well-known church leader and missionary. Overseas service for Correll and his wife, Norma, began with two terms in Tanzania. Later missionary activity took them to Brussels, Belgium, where he worked as dean of evangelism and Christian education at the International Correspondence Institute. Interspersed with these assignments were duties at the denominational headquarters in the U.S., assisting in the development of the Mobilization and Placement Service and later directing the national Youth Department. Prior to his appointment as administrative assistant, he served as secretary of missions support, working with candidate and veteran missionaries in itineration and fundraising. In his new administrative capacity under Hogan, Correll's responsibilities have included the direction and coordination of the activities of the missionaries, vice-chairmanship of the Foreign Missions Committee, membership on the Foreign Missions Board, office manager of the division's staff in Springfield, Missouri, and oversight of the five international ministries.[7]

Other key changes included the appointment of G. Edward Nelson as secretary of foreign missions relations in the U.S., a newly created office that partially assumed the duties of home secretary (previously held by David A. Womack).[8] Nelson had formerly pastored an Assemblies of God church and later served as an officer of the American Bible Society. In his post with the Division, he directed the Promotions Department, fund-raising and development activities, and liaison work with districts and churches.[9] When Nelson resigned in 1988 to accept the pastorate of Neighborhood Church in Bellevue, Washington, he was succeeded by Fred Cottriel. A former pastor, evangelist, and missionary, Cottriel gained considerable experience as a missionary in Europe and the Middle East. Most recently, he had completed a term as superintendent of the Southern California District of the Assemblies of God.[10]

Significant transitions took place in other areas as well. Since 1975 Joyce Wells Booze had served as foreign missions editor. Under her supervision, *Good News Crusades* magazine was replaced with *Mountain Movers* (January 1979). This is the chief publication of the division focusing on news reports of overseas activities, the need for intercessory prayer support, and financial needs.[11] Booze was followed by Janet B. Walker (1981–1982) and Beverly Graham (1982–1986); Graham gained missionary appointment to Africa in 1986. With her departure, former pastor Nick Henry accepted editorial responsibilities, receiving the new title of secretary of foreign missions publications. Henry served until February 1989, after which Joyce Booze rejoined the staff, assuming the new title. Sue Montgomery and, more recently, Marilyn S. Jansen have compiled and edited *Happenings* (1984–), a popular newsletter distributed to individual donors and churches.

Giving direction to the complex activities of newly-appointed and veteran missionaries itinerating for financial support is Paul E. Brannan, a long-term missionary to Latin America. Replacing Norman L. Correll in this role, he has served since 1982. Finance secretaries since 1978 have included F. Jesse Hannah (1974–1979), Dewey Hatley (1979–1980), and Jerry L. Burgess, a minister and certified public accountant (1980–).

Structure and Finances

The structural arrangement of the Division of Foreign Missions went through few changes during these years. The General Council, however, did make some minor adjustments and authorized a committee in 1981 to study the responsibilities of the executive director of foreign missions and the administrative costs of the Division.[12] Two years later, the study committee reported that the rising costs of operating the overseas program needed the serious attention of the Council. A representative of the Division had reported:

> [S]ince 1974 we have experienced an inflation rate of 110 percent. During the same time the Division of Foreign Missions has had a net gain of purchasing power of 88 percent, which means that we have lost 22 percent of our purchasing power in the last 10 years. While other movements have been increasing their share of the income for administrative purposes, we have held consistently to the 5 percent, so that we have actually had to cut back in some operations at the level of 22 percent, which is unadjusted over a 10-year period, to accommodate our programs worldwide.[13]

To ameliorate the situation, the Council lifted certain restrictions on the use of undesignated funds for such expenses.[14]

The potential for serious change in the leadership status of the executive director of foreign missions arose at the 1985 General Council when the specially appointed Committee to Study the Feasibility of Executive and National Directors on the Executive Presbytery recommended that all national directors of divisions (Christian Education, Church Ministries, Communications, Home Missions, Publication) receive the title of executive director as well. However, whereas all would become full members of the General Presbytery, none would serve on the Executive Presbytery. Although this would elevate the status of national directors, it would severely diminish the influence of the executive director of foreign missions (and potentially that of the Division) since the office holder would lose the traditional seat on the Executive Presbytery. In the discussion that followed the introduction of the resolution, strong opposition was voiced by delegates who feared that such a move would erode the historic priority of foreign missions in the denomination. By a resounding vote the resolution failed.[15]

Providential Happenings

Through the years Assemblies of God publications, such as the *Pentecostal Evangel, Good News Crusades, Mountain Movers,* and most recently *Happenings,* have carried many stories of conversions, miraculous healings, and deliverances from chemical addictions and unsavory habits as well as satanic oppression. Dramatic testimonies of visions and dreams that contributed to the spread of the gospel message have also been published, emphasizing the supernatural expectations of Pentecostal spirituality.[16] Indeed, Assemblies of God theologian Russell P. Spittler has stated that "the history of Pentecostal missions can be told through stories of persons who sensed the guidance of the Holy Spirit and accordingly took bold, venturesome—some would say foolish—'steps of faith.' "[17] Thus, although some contemporary missiologists have opened the door for emphasis on the gifts of the Spirit and demonstration of signs and wonders in evangelistic undertakings, Pentecostals have a long record of advocacy and experience of such phenomena.[18]

The intense desire to see the demonstrated power of the Holy Spirit has recently kindled interest in the events transpiring in Argentina. Readers of the *Pentecostal Evangel* were startled to find an article in 1986 entitled "Argentina's Pentecostal Outpouring," with a heading that added, "Possibly 500,000 people have been saved in Argentina in the last year." Missionary Richard Nicholson reported on the ministry of Carlos Annacondia, an independent evangelist whose spectacular ministry began on the day that the Argentine battleship *General Belgrano* was sunk by a British submarine during the Falklands War in 1982. Although not the only leader in the revival, Annacondia has been supported by Assemblies of God missionaries and national churches, perceiving him to be "God's man of the hour" for that country.[19] Annacondia has become well-known for "power encounter" with the forces of evil. Challenging the devil in services, he says, "Hear me, and hear me well, Satan. I come against you in the name of Jesus of Nazareth, and I command you to loose these minds and bodies. Leave now!"[20]

Nicholson further observes that the revival, resulting in the conversions of hundreds of thousands of people (even by conservative estimates), has been characterized by four factors: (1) Pentecostal phenomena (conversions, healings, deliverances, baptisms in the Holy Spirit), (2) spiritual encounters with Satan, (3) a breadth of activity that far exceeds the work of Annacondia, and (4) the recognition of spiritual unity among believers, diminishing the isolation caused by denominational walls. Annacondia interprets the revival as a gift of God's love to the nation after their humiliating defeat by Great Britain and the fulfillment of an interpretation of tongues through his wife in which the Spirit said, "Very soon, very soon, very soon, great revival in Argentina—and Argentina will be Mine, saith the Lord!"[21] The revival has also had a marked influence on non-Pentecostal denominations in the country. Although spiritual fervor has continued in other Latin American countries such as Brazil and even in the Marxist-controlled countries of Nicaragua and Cuba, the timing of the spectacular events in Argentina has been attributed to the providential work of God in that nation's history.[22]

Although such dramatic accounts of church growth have caught the attention of many, unusual progress has occurred in other countries as well. On the European scene a unique course of events that began in the early 1970s, attributed to the leading of the Spirit, made a positive impact on the ministry of missionaries Harold and Agnes Schmitt in Munich, Germany. Since any groups outside of the Catholic and Lutheran churches in Germany are regarded as sects, Harold Schmitt reported that "for 5 months my wife and I did little but pray and seek God for an opening in what to us seemed an impregnable wall."[23] At the same time, a young American student at Munich University began ministering to two small charismatic groups in the city. Hearing about the Schmitts, he went to their home and introduced himself, suggesting that he might be able to help them find a ministry among some newly-baptized Christians.

Through the student's influence, Schmitt later received permission from a local Catholic cleric, Abbot Odilo Lechner of St. Boniface Church, to use the stone basement crypt of the church for Sunday evening services. For 15 years (1973–1988), Catholics, Lutherans, Pentecostals, and others attended these services, where hundreds professed Christ as Savior and were baptized in the Spirit; the abbot himself became Spirit-baptized and at different times preached at the meetings. From these services came a permanent congregation in 1980. Known as the Charismatic Center, it recently dedicated new quarters and continues to sponsor evangelistic outreaches in the city.[24]

Assemblies of God missionaries have readily interpreted the arrangement of circumstances favorable to the expansion of the faith as sovereign activities of God. Pentecostal spirituality, which regards highly the individual promptings of the Spirit, has nevertheless left ample room for the more subtle feats of His workings. In Angola, for example, when Assemblies of God missionaries went to help the national church construct a Bible school, church members scrambled to find adequate building materials in their war-torn country. Meanwhile, the front of the property had been turned into a dumping ground for trash and other junk materials by Cuban soldiers stationed nearby. Among the burning garbage the workers discovered a large bale of reinforcing rods for concrete—the Cubans had unwittingly helped them. Area Representative Billy Burr wrote, "This was like discovering a gold mine! We never dreamed we would have steel to reinforce our concrete."[25]

Other examples include the recent contacts with believers in mainland China, stemming from important changes in the political climate there.[26] To this can be added invitations from the governments of Laos and Vietnam to participate in relief work in their countries, important opportunities that may open doors for other forms of ministry.[27]

Third World Missionaries

Rapid church growth in the last several decades has produced several startling results. First, the population center of Christianity is gradually shifting to the Southern Hemisphere. Latin America, Africa, and Asia (including Oceania) will contain the majority of Christians by the year A.D. 2000. Already some churches in the Third World (i.e., developing nations) have dwarfed the size of their parent bodies; the national church organizations that originated through the efforts of the Assemblies of God (U.S.A.) are a case in point. Interestingly, the majority of these Third World Christians will probably be Pentecostal in their spirituality.[28]

Second, the appearance of thousands of Third World missionaries has been a startling development in the 20th century. This event—because of its implications for expediting world evangelization—according to Paul Pierson, Dean of the School of World Mission at Fuller Theological Seminary, represents "the most significant step in mission history since Carey sailed for India in 1793."[29] He further maintains that as the non-Western mission agencies are welcomed into partnership for this task, the entire missionary movement will be enriched: This will (1) contribute to more rapid and effective evangelism, (2) dispel the image that Christianity is a Western religion, (3) increase understanding about the nature of the church, (4) enhance the comprehension of the riches of the gospel, and (5) challenge Western Christians to discover the power of God anew through modeling the servanthood of Christ.[30] One writer suggests that this new enlargement of the missionary landscape points to the arrival of "the last age of missions."[31]

Since at least the 1960s, Assemblies of God mission leaders have increasingly witnessed the sending of missionaries by national churches. Observing in 1969 that the Assemblies of God organizations in Japan and the Philippines had set up their own missions departments, J. Philip Hogan wrote,

> Should our Lord tarry, we expect that within five years the major developing nations where we are privileged to work will themselves be sending agencies. In fact, we are already talking about a day in the not-too-distant future when a vast, world-wide, simultaneous evangelism thrust, including not only

American but those of every Assemblies of God church around
the world, can be realized.[32]

Since the goal of indigenous church principles has been the development of New Testament churches, the interest and capacity of
these bodies to evangelize and send missionaries has been interpreted as a vital sign of their maturity.[33] Indeed, Hogan remarked
that "the Lord of the harvest, who knows the end from the beginning
and who is not the interpreter but the Designer of history, is preparing the national churches of the world to share their part in the
task of making disciples in all nations."[34]

Although the number of missionaries emanating from the national
churches is difficult to ascertain, the groundwork for their appearance had been laid many years before through the founding of Bible
institutes. The emphasis on Bible training, coupled with the practical hands-on experience of pioneering new churches on the week-
ends, has paid rich dividends in church growth in many countries.
Therefore, the sending of missionaries by these younger churches
was a logical step, rather than an unexpected happening. Such initiatives have also been encouraged by the convening of regional
conferences of national churches. Whether through the West African
Conference or the meetings of the Assemblies of God Asian Mission
Association, important strides in cooperative efforts have resulted.[35]

The structure of Third World mission efforts varies. In some
instances, their ministries have been informal and they have not
borne the official designation of missionary. In Burkina Faso, West
Africa, severe economic conditions have forced many of its citizens
to search for employment in other countries. These people have
included Christians who have taken their Bibles, songbooks, and
Sunday school materials with them. Their journeys have subsequently been accompanied by the planting of new churches.[36]

Others have traveled under the auspices of a national church or
even on their own—"by faith" (without pledged support).[37] In some
instances, local congregations have commissioned their own missionaries. Two of the best-known examples are the missions programs of the Calvary Charismatic Centre in Singapore pastored by
missionary Rick Seaward and the Yoido Full Gospel Church in Seoul,
Korea, pastored by Paul Yonggi Cho. In the organization of their
mission initiatives, Calvary Charismatic Centre exemplifies a con-

gregational model (consistent with a mission policy practiced by Pentecostals in many parts of the world) and Yoido Full Gospel Church reflects the hierarchical structure of the South Korean church. Whether informal or appointed, such missionaries have made an important contribution to the expansion of Christianity within a short period of time. Their missiological perspectives and achievements are certain to continue receiving the scrutiny of church growth specialists and missions historians for years to come.

The exploits of Third World missionaries, however, have not been accomplished without difficulties. Lacking adequate financial backing and training on occasion, they have sometimes faced discouraging circumstances. Their activities have sometimes been followed by intense persecution. Although it may be premature to generalize about their methods and effectiveness, they have struggled, like their Western counterparts, with cultural adjustments, paternalism, and relating to national church organizations already in operation in their new fields of ministry.

Decade of Harvest

As the last decade of the 20th century and the end of the second millennium A.D. approached, Christian denominations and mission agencies began planning long-term goals for evangelism and church planting.[38] In the Assemblies of God, the idea and the logo for the coming Decade of Harvest program surfaced at the annual staff retreat of the Foreign Missions Committee in May 1987. A week later, it received the enthusiastic endorsement of the Foreign Missions Board and subsequently that of other officers of the General Council. Three months later at the General Council gathering in Oklahoma City, the specially-appointed Total Church Evangelism Strategy Committee recommended to the General Presbytery that the denomination engage in a bold new strategy of evangelism for the remainder of the century. The suggested goals included the enlistment of 1 million prayer partners, winning 5 million persons to Christ, training 20,000 persons for ministry, and starting 5,000 new churches. The presbyters accepted the proposal with its objectives, and in November 1988 the Executive Presbytery of the Assemblies of God designated the time period the "Decade of Harvest."[39]

Planning for the Decade of Harvest began when the Division of Foreign Missions envisioned the possibilities of such an emphasis overseas. With the increase in Third World missionaries, accompanied by a growing need for consultation and coordination of efforts, J. Philip Hogan announced in late 1987 that a special conference would convene in Springfield, Missouri, the following year for officers of the Division and national church leaders. The objective would be to "formulate ideas for organizing efforts in their respective nations—deciding how they can best accept the challenges of the 1990s and this Decade-of-Harvest effort."[40]

The first Decade of Harvest Conference was held July 11–15, 1988, and drew church leaders from 40 nations. During the sessions, the delegates called for an international fellowship of Assemblies of God church bodies and related Pentecostal churches to help complete the evangelization of the world. Despite the absence of legislative authority over member organizations, such an association could promote important cooperative efforts. Peter Kuzmič, representing the largest group of Pentecostal churches in Yugoslavia, described the gathering as "the highest level of an international Pentecostal leadership working conference ever held. . . . There was a unanimity and a tremendous consensus in the Spirit, not only about the urgency of the task, but also about the necessity of an international network . . . that would facilitate the vision and the spiritual potential that there is in the Assemblies of God Fellowship."[41] The conference then appointed a provisional committee: Kuzmič, Errol Bhola (Guyana), John Bueno (El Salvador), William Cornelius (Canada), Andrew Evans (Australia), Prince Guneratnam (Malaysia), Immanuel Lazaro (Tanzania), Daniel Munshi (Bangladesh), Jean Pawentaore Ouedraogo (Burkina Faso), José Wellington Bezerra da Costa (Brazil), Paul Yonggi Cho (South Korea), and Hogan (chair, U.S.).[42] Since the delegates did not authorize any specific programs, the committee was asked to formulate proposals and submit them to a second Decade of Harvest Conference, to convene August 14–15, 1989, immediately following the General Council meeting in Indianapolis, Indiana.

At the conclusion of this historic first meeting, the participants unanimously adopted the following declaration:

Because we believe that the Great Commission of our Lord

(Matthew 28:19,20; Mark 16:15) commands us to go into all the world and preach the gospel to every creature,

Because we believe that our obedience to this Commission is inextricably linked to the imminent return of our Lord Jesus Christ,

Because we believe that there is no other name under heaven given among men whereby we must be saved and that those who do not know Jesus as their Savior will be eternally lost,

Because we are aware that there is an unprecedented move of the Spirit of God in the world today, giving us encouragement to believe that the evangelistic task can be completed,

Because 2.7 billion people, the majority of the human race, have not yet heard an adequate presentation of the gospel,

And, because we now possess the tools and technology that make it possible for us to communicate with every citizen of earth,

We, therefore, as a body of delegates representing the world-wide Fellowship of the Assemblies of God, assembled in Springfield, Missouri, U.S.A., on this 15th day of July, 1988, do consecrate and dedicate ourselves to work and to pray until we witness the total evangelization of the world.

May God help us be faithful to this, our covenant. Amen, Alleluia![43]

The declaration reflects the historic missiological commitment of the Pentecostal movement and the Assemblies of God in particular to evangelization. Even though it denotes great optimism for the potential accomplishments of the next decade, it nevertheless stops short of predicting a specific time for the return of Christ.[44]

The opportunities that such an international fellowship present are enormous. Closer cooperation, even while preserving the independence of each organization, could make important advances in coordinating the activities of national churches, their missionaries, and the endeavors of the Assemblies of God (U.S.A.) for evangelism and discipleship training. Overlapping efforts, including the sometimes redundant expenditure of resources, could be diminished as the participants close ranks to pursue their common objectives. The conception of the international Decade of Harvest initiative, with its fraternal basis and commitment to Pentecostal spirituality, may herald the final triumph of the venerated indigenous church principles, long held and implemented by the Assemblies of God.

Conclusion

By the 1980s, the growth of worldwide Pentecostalism had caught the attention of many observers who sought to understand the movement's spiritual dynamics and missiological viewpoints. Within the Assemblies of God, the motives for mission have remained the same since the beginning of the endeavor, with ministries of compassion gaining greater approval and recognition than in previous years. Assemblies of God missionaries have credited their successes and those of the national churches to the dynamic empowerment of the Holy Spirit, but closer examination reveals fruitful strategizing as well.

Candidate missionary training continued to evolve in the years after 1978, undergoing some change when the Division of Foreign Missions substituted the shorter Pre-Field Orientation program for the Candidate Graduate Training Program previously offered through the Assemblies of God Theological Seminary. Assemblies of God missiologists made significant contributions through books, articles, and papers. In many instances, their writings reflect a heightened interest in the linkage between the contemporary presence of the Kingdom of God and the role of signs and wonders of the Holy Spirit in evangelism.

Influenced by the growing concern among evangelicals to evangelize "unreached peoples," Assemblies of God missionaries focused renewed attention on them, attention epitomized by the founding of the Center for Ministry to Muslims. The concern to win converts to Christ remained the undiminished priority, evidenced by the planning of Good News Crusades, the development of task forces, and the activities of both new and older international ministries.

The years between 1978 and 1989 saw the rise of two notable independent ministries having close connections to the Assemblies of God: Jim Bakker's PTL organization and Jimmy Swaggart Ministries, both of which exhibited interest in supporting missions. The fall of these ministries tested the ethical resolve of the denomination as well as that of the fraternal churches abroad. The concern for integrity of character and ministry prevailed.

The last 30 years in the history of Assemblies of God missions can also be labeled "the Hogan years." The perspectives of J. Philip Hogan on the mission enterprise and his pragmatic openness to innovation have profoundly influenced the direction it has taken. His long tenure provided stability for the ongoing efforts of the program. Field directors, area representatives, and field fellowship chairmen increasingly shouldered the burgeoning administrative load of the far-flung operation. The fiscal integrity of the Division of Foreign Missions has endured due to careful oversight, only a small fraction of the missionary dollar continuing to be reserved for administrative expenses.

The efforts of Third World missionaries came to prominence as church growth specialists observed their numbers and activities in the decade of the '80s. Although sometimes reflecting the ventures of individuals, congregations, or national churches, their mere existence testified to the stature and vision of Third World Christians and churches. With the relationship between the Assemblies of God (U.S.A.) and the fraternally-related churches overseas now one of partnership, the Division of Foreign Missions sponsored the first Decade of Harvest conference in 1988 to focus renewed attention on evangelizing the world before the end of the century, as well as on the need to explore new means of cooperation to fulfill the task of the Great Commission.

Robert Houlihan, field director for the Far East, visiting crippled children in Vietnam, 1988

Construction of the Bible school in Angola, 1987

Housed in a former synagogue, the Pentecostal Church in Osijek, Yugoslavia, is pastored by Peter Kuzmič. It is the fastest growing and largest Pentecostal and evangelical congregation in the country.

Women attending crafts workshop at Kenya National Women's Convention, Kisumu, Kenya, 1988

Sunday evening charismatic service held in the stone basement crypt of St. Boniface Church, Munich, Germany

Delegates attending the Pacific Latin American District Women's Ministries Annual Seminar in 1988. The theme of the seminar was "Decade of Harvest," and the women had a western session in which the Harvest theme was emphasized.

Norman L. Correll chatting with Anthony Ogba, a Nigerian attending the Assemblies of God Theological Seminary. Correll is a veteran missionary to Africa who has more recently served as administrative assistant to the executive director of Foreign Missions.

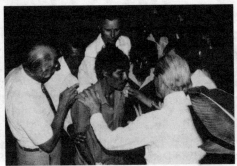

Prayer for the sick has been a hallmark of Good News Crusades.

Tens of thousands have attended the evangelistic campaigns of Carlos Annacondia in Argentina.

Delegates at the 1988 Decade of Harvest Conference in Springfield, Missouri

Epilogue

After 80 years of worldwide Pentecostal expansion, the history of North American Pentecostal mission agencies and their mission churches abroad remains in the infancy stage. The appearance of denominational mission histories, notably Charles W. Conn's *Where the Saints Have Trod* (1957) for the Church of God (Cleveland, Tennessee), Yeol Soo Eim's Fuller Seminary dissertation on the history of Foursquare missions (1986), and my own study of Assemblies of God foreign missions, represent an important beginning. They provide, however, only a small, albeit significant, part of the global picture. Hopefully, other agencies, such as the Pentecostal Assemblies of Canada, the International Pentecostal Holiness Church, and the United Pentecostal Church International, will soon recount and interpret their own pilgrimages.

The work of independent mission boards, congregations (as sending agencies), missionary-evangelists, and the more recent efforts of charismatic missionaries working within the framework of the historic churches represents another significant part of the picture. Their missiological perspectives and the churches they have established abroad have not received the attention they deserve.

Even so, our vision of Pentecostal mission efforts will remain limited by our Western lenses until the mission churches and their independent offshoots begin to tell their own stories. Third World perspectives on the North American agencies, as well as other Western mission enterprises, may be threatening and/or rewarding. Their theological and missiological perspectives may challenge presuppositions and methods that are currently entrenched, serving notice that the Spirit, like the wind, "blows wherever it pleases." In so doing, they may offer a prophetic voice of direction to Western Pentecostals. In any event, the stories of the Third World Pentecostals will be enormously fruitful for all concerned and could build

287

bridges of understanding and cooperation in those places where none currently exists.

Although important advances have been made in analyzing Pentecostal contributions to missiology, much more work needs to be done. A holistic theology of mission that adequately ties the role of signs and wonders in evangelism, ministries of compassion, and social justice to the contemporary presence of the kingdom of God has yet to appear. Faithfulness to the biblical text, dependence on the guidance of the Holy Spirit, openness to what the Spirit is doing in the world today, and recognition of the lostness of humanity without Christ must be foundational to such an endeavor. To these components should be added confidence in the partnership principle of mission as a demonstration of the Spirit's distribution of gifts in the universal church. From this vantage, the future elucidation of Pentecostal missiology can contribute to the continued growth of the church, while maintaining fidelity to the heritage of Pentecostalism.

Endnotes

PART I: PREPARATIONS FOR ADVANCE

Chapter 1: Pentecostal Missions Mature

[1]For further information, see Stanley M. Burgess, Gary B. McGee, eds.; Patrick H. Alexander, assoc. ed. *Dictionary of Pentecostal and Charismatic Movements* (Grand Rapids: Zondervan Publishing House, 1988), s.v. "Azusa Street Revival," by C. M. Robeck, Jr. (Hereafter, this source will be referred to as *DPCM.)*

[2]"Important Pentecostal Manifesto," *Confidence,* 15 August 1908, p. 9.

[3]Gary B. McGee, "Levi R. Lupton and the Ill-Fated Pentecostal Missionary Union in America," paper presented at the 16th meeting of the Society for Pentecostal Studies, Costa Mesa, California, 14 November 1986.

[4]Gary B. McGee, "The Azusa Street Revival and Twentieth-Century Missions," *International Bulletin of Missionary Research* 12 (April 1988): pp. 58–61; for the early expansion of Pentecostalism in China, see Daniel H. Bays, "The First Pentecostal Missions to China, 1906–1916," paper presented at the 18th meeting of the Society for Pentecostal Studies, Wilmore, Kentucky, 10–12 November 1988.

[5]Burgess and McGee, *DPCM,* s.v. "Pentecostal Mission in South and Central Africa," by G. B. McGee.

[6]"General Convention of Pentecostal Saints and Churches of God in Christ," *Word and Witness,* 20 December 1913, p. 1.

[7]*Ripening Harvest* (Toronto: Overseas Missions Department of the Pentecostal Assemblies of Canada, 1974).

[8]Joseph E. Campbell, *The Pentecostal Holiness Church: 1898–1948* (Franklin Springs, Ga.: Publishing House of the Pentecostal Holiness Church, 1951), pp. 350–351; *The World of Pentecostal Holiness Missions* (Oklahoma City, Okla.: World Missions Department, n.d.).

[9]Charles W. Conn, *Where the Saints Have Trod: A History of Church of God Missions* (Cleveland, Tenn.: Pathway Press, 1959); Christopher C. Moree, ed., *Into All the World: Church of God World Missions Anniversary*

Album (Cleveland, Tenn.: Church of God World Missions Department, 1984).

[10]Peggy Humphrey [Scarborough], *J. H. Ingram: Missionary Dean* (Cleveland, Tenn.: Pathway Press, 1966).

[11]Burgess and McGee, *DPCM,* s.v. "Russian and Eastern European Mission," by J. Colletti; Tom Salzer, "The Danzig Gdanska Institute of the Bible," (Part I) *The Assemblies of God Heritage* 8 (Fall 1988): 8–11, 128–29; (Part II) 8 (Winter 1988–89): 10–13, 17–18.

[12]*The Apostolic Faith* (Portland, Ore.: Apostolic Faith Publishing House, 1965).

[13]Burgess and McGee, *DPCM,* s.v. "Pentecostal Church of God," by W. E. Warner.

[14]Burgess and McGee, *DPCM,* s.v. "Pridgeon, Charles Hamilton" and "Evangelization Society, The," by G. B. McGee.

[15]Burgess and McGee, *DPCM,* s.v. "Church of God of Prophecy," by H. D. Hunter.

[16]Burgess and McGee, *DPCM,* s.v. "Church of God in Christ," by C. E. Jones; Carlis L. Moody, "The Church of God in Christ Movement," *World Pentecost,* no. 3 (1977), pp. 22–23.

[17]Burgess and McGee, *DPCM,* s.v. "Fellowship of Christian Assemblies," by J. Colletti.

[18]Burgess and McGee, *DPCM,* s.v. "Independent Assemblies of God International" by J. Colletti.

[19]Burton K. Janes, *The Lady Who Came: The Biography of Alice Belle Garrigus, Newfoundland's First Pentecostal Pioneer* (St. John's, Newfoundland: Good Tidings Press, 1982); *The Lady Who Stayed,* vol. 2 (1983).

[20]Yeol Soo Eim, "The Worldwide Expansion of the Foursquare Church," D. Miss. diss., Fuller Theological Seminary School of World Mission, 1986.

[21]Guy Bongiovanni, "Stepping Ahead with God" and "The Pentecostal Movement in Italy," in *Fiftieth Anniversary of the Christian Church of North America: 1927–1977,* ed. S. Galvano (Sharon, Pa.: Christian Church of North America, 1977), pp. 98–113, 114–118, 122.

[22]Marion Meloon, *Ivan Spencer: Willow in the Wind* (Plainfield, N. J.: Logos International, 1974).

[23]Robert Bryant Mitchell, *Heritage and Horizons: The History of Open Bible Standard Churches* (Des Moines, Ia.: Open Bible Publishers, 1982).

[24]Arthur L. Clanton, *United We Stand: A History of Oneness Organizations* (Hazelwood, Mo.: The Pentecostal Publishing House, 1970).

[25]William F. P. Burton, *God's Working with Them: Being Eighteen Years of Congo Evangelistic Mission History* (London: Victory Press, 1933).

[26]Cornelius van der Laan, "The Pentecostal Movement in Holland: Its Origin and Its International Position," *Pneuma* 5 (December 1983): pp. 30–35.

[27]"Danish Missionary Work," *Pentecost,* no. 2 (December 1947), pp. 11–12; Daniel Hallberg, "Swedish Missionary Outreach," *World Pentecost,* no. 1 (1973), pp. 22–23; Lauri Ahonen, *Missions Growth: A Case Study on Finnish Free Foreign Mission* (Pasadena, Calif.: William Carey Library, 1984).

[28]Harold Lindsell, "The Major Denominations Are Jumping Ship," *Christianity Today,* 18 September 1981, 16–17; cf., Robert T. Coote, "The Uneven Growth of Conservative Evangelical Missions," *International Bulletin of Missionary Research* 6 (July 1982): pp. 118–123.

[29]The attempt of evangelical church historian Earle E. Cairns to include the 20th century Pentecostal movement with other evangelical revival movements of the past reflects the growing acceptance of Pentecostals in evangelical ranks; however, he fails to adequately address its uniqueness and distinctives. See *An Endless Line of Splendor: Revivals and Their Leaders from the Great Awakening to the Present* (Wheaton, Ill.: Tyndale House Publishers, Inc., 1986), pp. 177–184; cf., Peter D. Hocken, *One Lord One Spirit One Body* (Gaithersburg, Md.: The Word Among Us Press, 1987).

[30]Lesslie Newbigin, *The Household of God* (New York: Friendship Press, 1953), 94–95, 108; see also Donald W. Dayton, "The Holy Spirit and Christian Expansion in the Twentieth Century," *Missiology* 16 (October 1988): 397–407.

[31]Henry P. Van Dusen, "Force's Lessons for Others," *Life,* 9 June 1958, pp. 122, 124; for a response to Van Dusen, see Thomas F. Zimmerman, "Where Is the 'Third Force' Going?" *Christianity Today,* 1 August 1960, pp. 15–16, 18.

[32]Donald Grey Barnhouse, "Finding Fellowship with Pentecostals," *Eternity,* April 1958, pp. 8–10.

[33]David J. du Plessis, "Golden Jubilees of Twentieth-Century Pentecostal Movements," *International Review of Missions* 47 (April 1958): p. 194.

[34]For the benefits of membership in the EFMA, see Wade T. Coggins, "What is the EFMA?" *United Evangelical Action* February 1959, pp. 9, 12; for a history of the association, see Wade T. Coggins, "Evangelical Foreign Missions Association: A Brief History," (unpublished ms., 1984).

[35]"Resolutions Adopted at Convention Express ACCC's Position on Issues," *Christian Beacon,* 6 November 1952, p. 4; also, Carl McIntire, *Twentieth Century Reformation* (Collingswood, N. J.: Christian Beacon Press, 1944), pp. 195–196.

[36]Gary B. McGee, *This Gospel Shall Be Preached: A History and Theology of Assemblies of God Foreign Missions to 1959* (Springfield, Mo.: Gospel Publishing House, 1986), 1:202.

[37]J. Philip Hogan, "The World Evangelical Fellowship," *Pentecostal Evangel,* 18 October 1953, pp. 6–7.

[38]Executive Presbytery Minutes, 20 April 1920; Executive Presbytery,

23 May 1950; "Status of Mission Boards and Agencies in the Division of Foreign Missions of the National Council of the Churches of Christ in the U. S. A. As Known to November 25, 1950," *Christian Beacon,* 21 December 1950, 5; Samuel McCrea Cavert, *Church Cooperation and Unity in America* (New York: Association Press, 1970), pp. 50–51.

³⁹For further information on Pentecostal participation in the NAE, see Burgess and McGee, *DPCM,* s.v. "National Association of Evangelicals," by C. M. Robeck, Jr.

⁴⁰*Missionary Manual* (Springfield, Mo.: Foreign Missions Department, 1931), p. 7; Horace McCracken, *History of Church of God Missions* (Cleveland, Tenn.: Church of God Publishing House, 1943), p. 8.

⁴¹Noel Perkin and John Garlock, *Our World Mission: A Survey of Assemblies of God Foreign Missions* (Springfield, Mo.: Gospel Publishing House, 1963), pp. 21–22; unfortunately, elitism survives in Vessie D. Hargrave's *Church and World Missions* (Cleveland, Tenn.: Pathway Press, 1970), p. 54.

⁴²Prudencio Damboriena, S. J., *Tongues As of Fire: Pentecostalism in Contemporary Christianity* (Washington, D.C.: Corpus Books, 1969), vii.

Chapter 2: Foundations for Recent Growth

¹For an excellent discussion of glossolalia, see Burgess and McGee, *DPCM,* s.v. "Glossolalia," by R. P. Spittler.

²For a perspective on the first 50 years of the Pentecostal movement by J. Roswell Flower, a founding father of the Assemblies of God, see "Fifty Years of Signs and Wonders," *Christian Life,* July 1951, pp. 22–24, 28; see also Russell P. Spittler, "Implicit Values in Pentecostal Missions," *Missiology* 16 (October 1988): pp. 409–424.

³Arthur T. Pierson, "Speaking with Tongues," *The Missionary Review of the World,* July 1907, pp. 487–492; Arthur T. Pierson, "Speaking with Tongues—II," *The Missionary Review of the World,* September 1907, pp. 682–684; George B. Cutten, *Speaking with Tongues* (New Haven: Yale University Press, 1927). For the recent perspectives of a social historian, see Robert Mapes Anderson, *Vision of the Disinherited: The Making of American Pentecostalism* (New York: Oxford University Press, 1979); cf., Grant Wacker, "Taking Another Look at the *Vision of the Disinherited,"* *Religious Studies Review* 8 (January 1982): pp. 15–16, 18–20, 21.

⁴Statistics from the office of the secretary of foreign missions relations, U.S., Assemblies of God Division of Foreign Missions, Springfield, Mo.

⁵McGee, *This Gospel Shall Be Preached,* pp. 1:197–198; Maynard L. Ketcham, "The Indigenous Church in the Far East," Our Foreign Mission, no. 3. *Pentecostal Evangel,* 22 May 1966, pp. 19–20; Everett L. Phillips, "The Indigenous Church in Africa," Our Foreign Mission, no. 5. *Pentecostal Evangel,* 17 July 1966, pp. 19–20; Jim Grams, "Poorly Kept Secrets: Reflections of a Former Missionary," *Agora,* Winter 1979, pp. 12–13.

[6]Melvin L. Hodges, "The World Mission of the Assemblies of God," *Pentecostal Evangel,* 29 November 1959, pp. 2–3, 28.

[7]Not surprisingly, Pentecostals have often argued for the longer ending of Mark. See Stanley M. Horton, "Is Mark 16:9–20 Inspired?" *Paraclete* 4 (Winter 1970): pp. 7–12; cf., Burgess and McGee, *DPCM,* s.v., "Mark, Gospel of," by L. W. Hurtado.

[8]Melvin L. Hodges, *The Indigenous Church* (Springfield, Mo.: Gospel Publishing House, 1953), pp. 131–134.

[9]Alan Walker, "Where Pentecostalism Is Mushrooming," *Christian Century,* 17 January 1968, p. 81.

[10]Robert C. Cunningham, "Fulfilling the Great Commission," (editorial) *Pentecostal Evangel,* 15 July 1950, p. 2.

[11]Noel Perkin, "The Secret of Successful Missions," *Pentecostal Evangel,* 29 December 1959, p. 5.

[12]Harmon A. Johnson, "Authority Over the Spirits: Brazilian Spiritism and Evangelical Church Growth" (M.A. thesis, Fuller Theological Seminary, 1969), p. 101; for information on the Independent Assemblies of God, see Burgess and McGee, *DPCM,* s.v., "Independent Assemblies of God International," by J. Colletti.

[13]For information on the salvation/healing movement, see David Edwin Harrell, Jr., *All Things Are Possible: The Healing and Charismatic Revivals in Modern America* (Bloomington, Ind.: Indiana University Press, 1975); Hodges, *The Indigenous Church,* pp. 50–52.

[14]Kenneth Godbey, "Signs and Wonders Follow," *World Challenge,* December 1958, p. 7.

[15]Donald Gee, *Trophimus I Left Sick* (London: Elim Publishing Co., 1952), pp. 9–10; Noel Perkin, "Introduction to the Missions Seminar," *Key,* July–August 1956, p. 6.

[16]For information on Roland Allen, see Priscilla M. Allen, "Roland Allen: A Prophet for This Age," *The Living Church,* 20 April 1986, pp. 9–11.

[17]Alice E. Luce, "Paul's Missionary Methods" (Part 1), *Pentecostal Evangel,* 8 January 1921, pp. 6–7; (Part 2), 22 January 1921, pp. 6, 11; (Part 3), 5 February 1921, pp. 6–7.

[18]General Council Minutes, 1921, pp. 61–64.

[19]J. Philip Hogan, "Harvest Hints," *World Challenge,* January 1957, p. 18.

[20]Melvin L. Hodges, "The Indigenous Church in Latin America," *Pentecostal Evangel,* 20 February 1960, p. 11.

[21]Morris Williams, "The Gulf and the Goal," *World Challenge,* October 1957, p. 5.

[22]Gary B. McGee, "For the Training of . . . Missionaries," *Central Bible College Bulletin,* February 1984, pp. 4–5; for an overview of the development of Assemblies of God higher education, see William W. Menzies,

Anointed to Serve: The Story of the Assemblies of God (Springfield, Mo.: Gospel Publishing House, 1971).

[23]Arthur E. Wilson, *A Visit to Mossi Land* (Springfield, Mo.: Foreign Missions Department, ca. 1932), p. 22.

[24]Arthur E. Wilson, *Mining Black Diamonds in Upper Ivory Coast, French West Africa,* The Assemblies of God in Foreign Lands (Springfield, Mo.: Foreign Missions Department, ca. 1942), p. 45.

[25]H. C. Ball, "They Worship in a Rabbit House Because . . ." *World Challenge,* 25 October 1953, p. 9.

[26]Carl Malz, "The Crowning Missionary Method," *Pentecostal Evangel,* 26 July 1959, p. 4; see also Ralph Williams, "Teach Others Also," *Pentecostal Evangel,* 11 November 1957, pp. 12–13.

[27]Cited in Carl Malz, *Foreign Bible School Survey Report: A Report of the Bible School Program of the Foreign Missions Department of the Assemblies of God* (Springfield, Mo.: The Assemblies of God, 1959), p. 1.

[28]Carl Malz to "Dear Fellow Bible School Administrators," August 1959.

[29]Carl Malz. *Foreign Bible School,* p. 4.

[30]Louise Jeter Walker, "Must We Turn Them Away?" *World Challenge,* 13 February 1955, p. 6; "Touring the Bible Schools," *World Challenge,* November 1955, pp. 4–7.

[31]A "triumphalist" view of history is a self-serving (promotional) perspective that purports to show: (1) the divine origins and purpose of a movement and (2) an optimistic assessment of its progress. This approach, while informative and inspiring, may lack the careful critical assessment necessary for accurate historical analysis. For Pentecostal historiography, see Burgess and McGee, *DPCM,* s.v., "Bibliography and Historiography of Pentecostalism (U.S.)," by G. Wacker.

[32]Flora H. Beaver, "The Little Church With a Big Heart," *Pentecostal Evangel,* 15 June 1958, pp. 10–11; W. S. Graham, "How 'Missions' Works in My Church," *World Challenge,* May 1955, pp. 4–5.

[33]*The WM Leader: Handbook of Leadership Training for Women's Ministries Leaders* (Springfield, Mo.: Gospel Publishing House, 1987), pp. 9–17.

[34]*Declare His Glory: Speed-the-Light—40th Anniversary* (Springfield, Mo.: Youth Department of the Assemblies of God, 1983); McGee, *This Gospel Shall Be Preached,* 1:183–184.

[35]McGee, *This Gospel Shall Be Preached,* 1:184.

Chapter 3: The Transition Team

[1]Menzies, *Anointed,* pp. 167–168.

[2]For further information, see "Gayle F. Lewis 1898–1979," *Pentecostal Evangel,* 21 October 1979, p. 7.

³For an account of his life and ministry, see Leonard Bolton, *China Call* (Springfield, Mo.: Gospel Publishing House, 1984).

⁴"Application for Appointment as Missionary," 1 January 1945, p. 3, J. Philip Hogan File, Editorial Office Files, Assemblies of God Division of Foreign Missions, Springfield, Mo.

⁵"A Life of Faith," *Pentecostal Evangel*, 24 August 1940, p. 8; for further information, see Nettie D. Nichols and Joshua Bang, *God's Faithfulness in Ningpo*, The Assemblies of God in Foreign Lands (Springfield, Mo.: Foreign Missions Department, 1938).

⁶J. Philip Hogan, "Ningpo Enjoys Blessings in Spite of Hardships," *Pentecostal Evangel*, 26 April 1947, p. 6; Letter from J. Philip Hogan to Noel Perkin, 18 November 1947.

⁷J. Philip Hogan, "Our Mission in the Mid-Century Crisis," *Pentecostal Evangel*, 18 November 1951, p. 7; J. Philip Hogan, "I Visited the United Nations," *Pentecostal Evangel*, 14 January 1951, pp. 3–4.

⁸Virginia Hogan, unpublished ms., 30 April 1979. J. Philip Hogan File, Editorial Office Files, Division of Foreign Missions.

⁹For information on their distinguished ministry, see Clarence W. Hall, "Littlest Lady with the Biggest Heart," *Reader's Digest* 81 (July 1962): 159–164; Ruth A. Tucker, *Guardians of the Great Commission* (Grand Rapids: Zondervan Publishing House, 1988), pp. 211–214; Lillian Dickson, *These My People* (Grand Rapids: Zondervan Publishing House, 1958).

¹⁰Among other resources, biographical data on his life can be found in Raymond T. Brock, "Making of an Executive Director," *The Missionary Forum* 32 (January–February 1960): pp. 1–3; "TAIWAN—James Philip and Mary Virginia Hogan—November 16, 1978," unpublished ms. J. Philip Hogan File, Editorial Office Files, Division of Foreign Missions; Burgess and McGee, *DPCM*, s.v. "Hogan, James Philip," by G. B. McGee.

¹¹For information on Emil A. Balliet, see "With Christ," *Pentecostal Evangel*, 30 October 1977, p. 7.

¹²For the election results, see General Council Minutes, 1959, pp. 22, 32, 40.

¹³General Council Minutes, 1959, pp. 24–25.

¹⁴For information on the work of Stephen Walegir, see Marion E. Craig, "Missionary to Missions," *Missionary Forum*, 4th Quarter, 1962, pp. 10–11.

¹⁵Robert T. McGlasson, "Resume for J. P. Hogan of New York Office on Robert T. McGlasson," 1959, pp. 1–5.

¹⁶J. Philip Hogan, "Our Foreign Missions Team," *Pentecostal Evangel*, 20 March 1960, p. 15.

¹⁷For information on Ketcham, see Maynard L. Ketcham, *Pentecost in the Ganges Delta: Being An Account of the Birth and Development of the Assemblies of God Mission Work in Bengal, India* (By the author, 1945);

Maynard L. Ketcham, *Tigers That Talk* (Charlotte, N. C.: PTL Television Network, 1979).

[18]For information on Williams, see Burgess and McGee, *DPCM*, s.v. "Williams, Ralph Darby," by G. B. McGee.

[19]For information on Hodges, see Burgess and McGee, *DPCM*, s.v. "Hodges, Melvin Lyle," by G. B. McGee.

[20]Hogan, "Our Foreign Missions Team," p. 14.

[21]"Everett L. Phillips with Christ," *Pentecostal Evangel*, 6 March 1988, p. 7.

[22]For more information on Greisen, see "Three Men in Missions," *Pentecostal Evangel*, 17 November 1963, p. 18; "Former District Superintendent with the Lord," *Pentecostal Evangel*, 31 August 1980, p. 25.

[23]Raymond T. Brock, "New Faces in Springfield," *Missionary Forum*, March–April 1960, pp. 2, 4; "He Dared to Dream," *Mountain Movers*, April 1987, pp. 6–7.

[24]Hogan, "Our Foreign Missions Team," p. 15.

[25]Ibid.; for his tenure overseas, see Raymond T. Brock, "Nigeria Revisited," *Advance*, July 1974, pp. 10–11.

[26]Ibid.

PART II: GLOBAL CONQUEST (1959–1967)

Chapter 4: Unprecedented Promotion and Progress

[1]Elva Johnson Hoover, "Let's Talk About Missions Education," *Key*, 1st Quarter, 1964, pp. 2–3; for information on the appointment of John Garlock to the post of foreign missions editor, see "New Editor for Foreign Missions Publications," *Pentecostal Evangel*, 24 February 1963, p. 9.

[2]J. Philip Hogan, "Heroes of the Conquest," *Pentecostal Evangel*, 28 January 1962, p. 7.

[3]General Council Reports, 1961, pp. 87–88.

[4]"Gwen Jones Now Education Editor," *Key*, 4th Quarter, 1963, p. 2.

[5]"Meet the New FMD Editors," *Key*, 4th Quarter, 1965, p. 12.

[6]" '63 Training Book to Feature Foreign Missions," *Key*, 3rd Quarter, 1963.

[7]Dorothy Lindgren Johns, *What Is A Missionary?* (children's text), (Springfield, Mo.: Gospel Publishing House, 1965); Dorothy Lindgren Johns, *What Is A Missionary?* (children's teacher supplement), (Gospel Publishing House, 1965); Mary Tregenza, *What Is A Missionary?* (youth text), (Springfield, Mo.: Gospel Publishing House, 1965); Mary Tregenza, *What Is A Missionary?* (youth teacher supplement), (Springfield, Mo.: Gospel Publishing House, 1965); Elva J. Hoover, *What Is A Missionary?* (adult text),

(Springfield, Mo.: Gospel Publishing House, 1965); Elva J. Hoover, *What Is A Missionary?* (adult teacher supplement), (Springfield, Mo.: Gospel Publishing House, 1965).

[8]Rex Jackson, "Educating for Missions," *Key,* 4th Quarter 1965, p. 4.

[9]John Garlock, "College Uses New Missions Study Series," *Key,* 1st Quarter 1966, 1.

[10]Perkin and Garlock, *Our World Witness,* p. 89.

[11]Norman Correll, "Conducting a Missions Convention," *Missionary Forum,* 4th Quarter, 1963, p. 4; for information on Correll see Wilma Jones, "Correll Named Global Conquest Representative," *Key,* 4th Quarter, 1962, p. 4.

[12]Ruth and Noel Wilson, "How We Did It," *Key,* 3rd Quarter, 1961, p. 6.

[13]Wesley R. Hurst, "The Convention and Finances: The Faith Promise Plan," *Key,* 3rd Quarter, 1963, p. 15.

[14]J. Philip Hogan, "More Money for Missions," *Pentecostal Evangel,* 24 February 1963, p. 9.

[15]Wilson, "How We Did It," p. 7.

[16]Wesley R. Hurst, "Interpreting the Statistics," *Key,* 2nd Quarter, 1967, p. 2.

[17]"Global Conquest Day," *Pentecostal Evangel,* 15 October 1961, pp. 8–9.

[18]For the role of publications in the history of the Pentecostal movement, see Burgess and McGee, *DPCM,* s.v. "Publications," by W. E. Warner.

[19]Christine Carmichael, "Assemblies of God Missions Literature," *Pentecostal Evangel,* 21 August 1966, p. 19.

[20]Ibid.

[21]For information on Henry C. Ball, see Burgess and McGee, *DPCM,* s.v., "Ball, Henry Cleophas," by G. B. McGee.

[22]Melvin L. Hodges, "Spanish Language Ministries Division Makes Strategic Move," *Key,* 4th Quarter, 1966, p. 4.

[23]Raymond T. Brock, "Missionary Literature as a Ministry," *Missionary Forum,* November–December 1961, p. 4; see also J. Philip Hogan, "Will Communism Win?" *Global Conquest,* Spring 1962, pp. 8–9.

[24]Carmichael, "Assemblies of God Missions Literature," p. 19; for a tribute to the work of Christine Carmichael, see "Christine Carmichael Retires," *Key,* 3rd Quarter, 1965, p. 15.

[25]Orville Carlson, "Literature Advance in East Pakistan," *Pentecostal Evangel,* 27 November 1960, p. 8; Rex Jackson, "Bookmobile," *Global Conquest,* May–July 1960, pp. 12–13; Harold and Margaret Jones, "Literature Evangelism in West Africa," *Pentecostal Evangel,* 23 April 1961, p. 14.

[26]Floyd Horst, "Literature Evangelism: In the Philippines," *Pentecostal Evangel,* 23 April 1961, p. 14.

[27]D. R. Guynes, "A City-Wide Literature Crusade," *Missionary Forum,* 1st Quarter, 1964, p. 8.

[28]Cited in Carmichael, "Assemblies of God Missions Literature," p. 20.

[29]Richard W. Dortch, "6000 Gypsies Saved," *Pentecostal Evangel,* 20 January 20, 1963, pp. 14–15.

[30]Ralph D. Williams, "Night Bible Schools for Venezuela," *Key,* 3rd Quarter, 1966, p. 11; for information on the distinguished career of Ralph D. Williams, see Burgess and McGee, *DPCM,* s.v., "Williams, Ralph Darby," by G. B. McGee.

[31]Ibid.

[32]Latin American Bible School Committee, "Introspection," *Missionary Forum,* September–October 1960, p. 4.

[33]"Constitution and Bylaws," *Missionary Forum,* July–August 1960, pp. 3, 8.

[34]Ibid., p. 3.

[35]Louise Jeter Walker, "Answers to Questionnaire of Gary McGee," unpublished ms., 1983.

[36]Ralph L. Cimino, "600 Nigerian Preachers," *Pentecostal Evangel,* 20 March 1966, p. 10; Raymond T. Brock, "Training National Workers in Nigeria," *Global Conquest,* Spring 1961, pp. 2–3.

[37]Thomas F. Zimmerman, "Evangelism and Eschatological Imperatives," in *One Race, One Gospel, One Task,* ed. Carl F. H. Henry and W. Stanley Mooneyham (Minneapolis: World Wide Publications, 1967), 2:65.

[38]"Overseas Evangelists Approved for Credit," *Key,* 4th Quarter, 1963, p. 9; J. Philip Hogan, "Do Mass Campaigns Work?" *Global Conquest,* July–August 1965, pp. 6–7.

[39]For example, see Leonard Nipper, "Tokyo Crusade," *Global Conquest,* February 1960, pp. 2–3; Christine Carmichael, "Assemblies of God Metropolitan Evangelism," *Pentecostal Evangel,* 23 October 1966, p. 22.

[40]For example, see Henry Mock, "Reaping Where Nationals Have Sown," *Global Conquest,* Spring 1961, pp. 10–11; Morris Williams, "Things I Learned from Slatiel Zuze," *Pentecostal Evangel,* 6 October 1968, pp. 8–9.

[41]Wesley R. Hurst, "New Currents in the South Pacific," *Pentecostal Evangel,* 17 March 1968, pp. 16–19.

[42]Morris Williams, "Out of the Paw of the Lion," *Pentecostal Evangel,* 28 June 1964, pp. 8–9.

[43]Albert and Tommy Reid, "Victory Below the 38th," *Global Conquest,* November–December 1962, pp. 3–5.

[44]Rico was one of the few Pentecostals invited to address the World Congress on Evangelism in Berlin in 1966; for his address, see José María

Rico, "Evangelism by Groups," in *One Race, One Gospel, One Task,* 2:492–494.

[45]David Womack, "Conquest in Cali," *Global Conquest,* September–October 1962, pp. 4–5.

[46]For example, see Christine Carmichael, "Assemblies of God Metropolitan Evangelism," *Pentecostal Evangel,* 23 October 1966, 21–22; J. Philip Hogan, "The Panama Story," *Pentecostal Evangel,* 17 March 1968, p. 19.

[47]Maynard L. Ketcham, "Will History Repeat Itself in Korea," *Pentecostal Evangel,* 10 April 1960, p. 13; Maynard L. Ketcham, *Tigers That Talk* (Charlotte, N. C.: PTL Television Network, 1979), pp. 99–111; Maynard L. Ketcham, "Seoul Evangelistic Center," *Global Conquest,* Winter 1962, pp. 2–3, 14; Raymond Brock, "One Year of Global Conquest," *Pentecostal Evangel,* 14 August 1960, p. 12; Raymond Brock, "Seoul Evangelistic Center Nears Completion," *Pentecostal Evangel,* 26 November 1961, p. 6; John Stetz, "Korea Field Chairman's Report," *Pentecostal Evangel,* 10 March 1963, pp. 12–13; "Global Conquest Pilot Project," *Global Conquest,* May–July 1960, pp. 2–3.

[48]"LARE Information," unpublished ms., 1962, p. 1; David A. Womack and Paul Finkenbinder, "Latin American Radio Evangelism," *Global Conquest,* March–April 1967, pp. 8–10.

[49]Raymond T. Brock, "A New Dimension in Missionary Evangelism," *Pentecostal Evangel,* 6 November 1960, pp. 12–13. For a recent review of Finkenbinder's ministry, see Daniel B. Wood, "A Message of Conscience," *The Christian Science Monitor,* 30 January 1989, p. 14.

[50]Hugh P. Jeter, "How Shall They Hear?" *Global Conquest,* January–February 1965, pp. 6–7.

[51]For information on the early work of IBRA, see Douglas S. Quy, *Pentecost,* no. 45 (September 1958): p. 5.

[52]D. V. Hurst, "Revivaltime's First Foreign Language Broadcast," *Pentecostal Evangel,* 13 November 1960, pp. 8–9, 30; see also, "Beaming the Gospel to Russia," *Pentecostal Evangel,* 1 June 1980, pp. 6–7.

[53]Christine Carmichael, "Assemblies of God Radio Evangelism," *Pentecostal Evangel,* 20 November 1966, pp. 19–20.

[54]J. Philip Hogan, Large Offering Letter, 10 November 1965.

Chapter 5: The Role of Support Agencies

[1]Elva M. Johnson (Hoover), "She Wanted to Be a Missionary," *Pentecostal Evangel,* 25 September 1960, p. 16; "The Etta Calhoun Story," *WMC Slant,* July–August–September 1966, p. 16.

[2]Gayle F. Lewis, "Mildred Smuland Succeeds Edith Whipple as National WMC Secretary," *Pentecostal Evangel,* 31 January 1960, p. 16.

[3]Ann Ahlf, "District WMC Presidents Plan 'According to the Pattern,' " *Pentecostal Evangel,* 25 October 1964, pp. 18–19.

[4]Mrs. F. J. Walton, "Necessity—The Mother of WMC," *Pentecostal Evangel,* 25 June 1961, pp. 24–25.

[5]Ann Ahlf, "WMC Patchwork Quilts," *Pentecostal Evangel,* 12 June 1966, pp. 20–21.

[6]Ann Ahlf, "Welcome Home," *Pentecostal Evangel,* 28 June 1964, pp. 16–17.

[7]"The Story of the Etta Calhoun Fund," *Pentecostal Evangel,* 10 September 1967, pp. 16–17.

[8]Ann Ahlf, "What Dimes Can Do," *Pentecostal Evangel,* 18 August 1963, pp. 16–17.

[9]Ann Ahlf, "Etta Calhoun Funds March to the Battlefield," *Pentecostal Evangel,* 14 August 1966, pp. 16–17.

[10]"Women's Ministries Giving: 1951–1982," Women's Ministries Department of the Assemblies of God, April 1983.

[11]"Missionette Clubs Prove Valuable," *Pentecostal Evangel,* 26 October 1958, p. 21; see also, "Introducing—The Missionettes," *Pentecostal Evangel,* 18 December 1955, p. 11.

[12]G. F. Lewis, "The Growth and Vision of WMC," *Pentecostal Evangel,* 19 February 1961, pp. 6–7.

[13]Ann Ahlf, "WMC's Serve Around the World," *Pentecostal Evangel,* 6 June 1965, pp. 10–11; see also Martha Jacobson, "Our Hearts Are Made to Wonder," *Pentecostal Evangel,* 27 March 1960, pp. 10–11, 28–29.

[14]Ann Ahlf, "God's Christmas List," *Pentecostal Evangel,* 20 December 1964, p. 19.

[15]Ann Ahlf, "Mrs. M. L. Hodges Visits South American and West Indian WMC's," *Pentecostal Evangel,* 26 July 1964, pp. 10–11; Mrs. Monroe Grams, "CMF in the Mountains and Jungles of Bolivia, South America," *Pentecostal Evangel,* 28 May 1961, pp. 16–17; Mrs. R. D. Williams, "Venezuela CMF Holds Sixth Convention," *Pentecostal Evangel,* 29 July 1962, pp. 16–17.

[16]For further information, see Edith Blumhofer, "The Role of Women in the Assemblies of God," *The Assemblies of God Heritage* 7 (Winter 1987–88): 13–17.

[17]For a historical perspective on the contributions of women in missions, see R. Pierce Beaver, *American Protestant Women in World Mission: A History of the First Feminist Movement in North America* (Grand Rapids: Wm. B. Eerdmans Publishing Co., 1980).

[18]For information on the Full Gospel Business Men's Fellowship, International, see David Edwin Harrell, Jr., *All Things Are Possible: The Healing and Charismatic Revivals in Modern America* (Bloomington, Ind.: Indiana University Press, 1975), pp 146–149.

[19]Everett James, "It Began With a Burden," *Pentecostal Evangel,* 2 December 1962, p. 10.

[20]Ibid., p. 11.

[21]Everett James, "Our Partners in Good News Crusades: Light-for-the-Lost," *Global Conquest,* July–August 1966, pp. 10–11.

[22]Ibid.

[23]Mark Buntain, "Light-for-the-Lost in Calcutta, India," *Pentecostal Evangel,* 10 January 1965, p. 27.

[24]General Council Reports, 1967, p. 121.

[25]Ibid., p. 85.

[26]"Operation Demonstration," *Pentecostal Evangel,* 30 April 1967, p. 24.

[27]John F. Hall, "Speed-the-Light on Four Wheels and Four Hoofs," *Pentecostal Evangel,* 29 April 1962, p. 23.

[28]R. T. McGlasson, "The Matter of Missionary Mobility," *Missionary Forum,* 3rd Quarter (1962), pp. 4–5.

[29]Frances Foster, "BGMC: Little People and a Big Job," *Pentecostal Evangel,* 29 May 1966, p. 26; see also, Raymond T. Brock, "Thank God for BGMC," *Pentecostal Evangel,* 8 January 1961, p. 14.

[30]Frances Foster, "BGMC Around the World," *Pentecostal Evangel,* 27 January 1963, p. 16.

[31]M. L. Hodges, "What BGMC Means to Latin America," *Pentecostal Evangel,* 10 January 1960, p. 28.

[32]General Council Reports, 1967, p. 144.

[33]General Council Minutes, 1963, pp. 15–16.

[34]Ibid., p. 16.

[35]Ibid., p. 17.

[36]Menzies, *Anointed,* pp. 287–288.

[37]Spiritual Life—Evangelism Commission, "Mobilization and Placement Service of the Assemblies of God," (Mimeographed, 1966), p. 1; two names for the program were originally considered: MAPS (Mobilization and Placement Service) and CALL (Christian Action in Labors of Love), D. V. Hurst to Dick Champion, et al., 10 December 1964.

[38]MAPS Committee Meeting Minutes, 3 June 1964, p. 1; for a succinct description of the opportunities offered by the program shortly after its founding, see Norman L. Correll, "IV. Mobilization and Placement Service (MAPS)," *WMC Slant,* Oct., Nov., Dec., 1967. pp. 25–26.

[39]"Field Representative Named for Spiritual Life–Evangelism Commission," *Pentecostal Evangel,* 12 February 1967, p. 28.

[40]"MAPS: Pilot Project," *Pentecostal Evangel,* 10 March 1968, pp. 16–17; "MAPS Project: Grand Bahama Island," *Pentecostal Evangel,* 27 October 1968, pp. 20–21; for information on Gordon Weden, see David A. Womack, "Our First Construction Missionary," *Pentecostal Evangel,* 12 May 1968, p. 21.

[41]For information on the Garr Memorial Church, see Burgess and McGee, *DPCM*, s.v. "Garr Memorial Church," by C. W. Conn.

[42]"Scattered All Over the Map," *Pentecostal Evangel*, 28 September 1969, pp. 16–17.

[43]Mobilization and Placement Service, "Integration of Youth With A Mission into the Mobilization Program of the General Council of the Assemblies of God," 22 December 1964, pp. 1–7, MAPS Office. (Mimeographed.)

[44]Loren Cunningham with Janice Rogers, *Is That Really You, God?* (Grand Rapids: Chosen Books, 1984), pp. 65–67; Foreign Missions Board Minutes, 4 December 1962, p. 2524–L; Executive Presbytery Minutes, 2 June 1965, p. 5542.

[45]Mel Steward, "V. International Youth Witness," *WMC Slant*, Oct., Nov., Dec. 1967, pp. 27–28; "Presenting International Youth Witness," *Pentecostal Evangel*, 12 March 1967, pp. 24–27.

[46]"Knock and It Shall Be Opened," *Pentecostal Evangel*, 29 October 1967, p. 32.

Chapter 6: Missiology and Fraternal Cooperation

[1]J. Philip Hogan, "1966 School of Missions," *Pentecostal Evangel*, 22 May 1966, p. 17.

[2]Noel Perkin, "School of Missions," *Pentecostal Evangel*, 5 February 1961, p. 15; for additional information on the early schools of missions, see "School of Orientation Becomes Annual Event," *Pentecostal Evangel*, 27 September 1959, p. 7; Raymond T. Brock, "Third School of Missions Convenes in Springfield," *Pentecostal Evangel*, 11 June 1961, pp. 20–21; John Garlock, "A Bigger and Better School of Missions," *Pentecostal Evangel*, 4 August 1963, pp. 12–13; Wesley R. Hurst, "Notes and Quotes from the School of Missions," *Missionary Forum*, 4th Quarter, 1966, pp. 4–6.

[3]G. B. Robeson, "1966 School of Missions," *Pentecostal Evangel*, 31 July 1966, pp. 16–17.

[4]"Missions Directors at Work," *Missionary Forum*, 1st Quarter, 1963, p. 13.

[5]Melvin L. Hodges, foreword to *Faculty Training Program for Overseas Bible Schools*, by Louise Jeter Walker (Springfield, Mo.: Foreign Missions Department of the Assemblies of God, 1965), p. iv.

[6]Melvin L. Hodges, "Missions Real Goals," *Global Conquest*, November–December 1964, p. 12.

[7]Wesley R. Hurst, "The Missionary Dimension of the Indigenous Church," *Pentecostal Evangel*, 15 January 1967, pp. 19–20.

[8]For further information, see McGee, *This Gospel Shall Be Preached*, 1:169–171; Finis Jennings Dake, ed., *Dake's Annotated Reference Bible* (Atlanta: Dake Bible Sales, Inc., 1963); John G. Hall, *Dispensations*, 2nd ed. (Springfield, Mo.: Inland Printing Co., 1957). Duane V. Hurst, *Ye Shall*

Be Witnesses (Springfield, Mo.: Gospel Publishing House, 1962); D. V. Hurst and T. J. Jones, *The Church Begins* (Springfield, Mo.: Gospel Publishing House, 1959); Carl Brumback, *What Meaneth This?* (Springfield, Mo.: Gospel Publishing House, 1947); cf., Gerald T. Sheppard, "Pentecostalism and the Hermeneutics of Dispensationalism: Anatomy of an Uneasy Relationship," *Pneuma* 6 (Fall 1984): 5–33.

⁹Stanley Horton, *The Promise of His Coming* (Springfield, Mo.: Gospel Publishing House, 1967), p. 91; Ernest S. Williams, *Systematic Theology,* 3 vols. (Springfield, Mo.: Gospel Publishing House, 1953), 3:95; Ernest S. Williams, "Thy Kingdom Come," *Pentecostal Evangel,* 31 July 1966, p. 8.

¹⁰W. Glenn West, "Triumph of the King," *Pentecostal Evangel,* 22 October 1967, pp. 6–7, 24.

¹¹For the development of evangelical missiology in the post-war period, see Arthur F. Glasser, "The Evolution of Evangelical Mission Theology Since World War II," *International Bulletin of Missionary Research* 9 (January 1985): 9–13.

¹²Noel Perkin, "Has the World Been Reached?" *Pentecostal Evangel,* 28 April 1963, p. 7.

¹³Perkin and Garlock, *Our World Witness;* the single reference is found on p. 64.

¹⁴Melvin L. Hodges, "Mission—And Church Growth," in *The Church's Worldwide Mission,* ed. Harold Lindsell (Waco, Tex.: Word Books, 1966), pp. 141, 145; the earlier portion of this quotation was deleted when the address was edited for publication in the *Pentecostal Evangel* under the title "Mission and Church Growth," 12 June 1966, pp. 16–19.

¹⁵Melvin L. Hodges, *Grow Toward Leadership* (Chicago: Moody Press, 1960), p. 30.

¹⁶For example, see Delmar Kingsriter, "The Relationship Between the Missionary Field Fellowship and the National Church," *Missionary Forum,* 3rd Quarter, 1965, p. 13.

¹⁷Lindsell, ed. *The Church's Worldwide Mission,* pp. 217–237; for assessments of the missiological significance of the Wheaton Declaration, see William R. Hutchison, *Errand to the World: American Protestant Thought and Foreign Missions* (Chicago: University of Chicago Press, 1987), pp. 190–192; Rodger C. Bassham, *Mission Theology: 1948–1975 Years of Worldwide Creative Tension Ecumenical, Evangelical, and Roman Catholic* (Pasadena: William Carey Library, 1979), pp. 210–220; see also David A. Womack, "The Importance of the Wheaton Declaration," *Missionary Forum,* 1st Quarter, 1967, pp. 2–3.

¹⁸Ibid., p. 8; for information on Wesleyan–Arminian theology, see Richard S. Taylor, "Historical and Modern Significance of Wesleyan Theology," in *A Contemporary Wesleyan Theology,* ed. Charles W. Carter (Grand Rapids: Zondervan Publishing House, 1983), 1:55–71.

¹⁹Arthur F. Glasser and Donald A. McGavran, *Contemporary Theologies of Mission* (Grand Rapids: Baker Book House, 1983), pp. 119–120.

[20]Melvin L. Hodges, "Mission—and Church Growth," in *The Church's Worldwide Mission*, ed. Harold Lindsell (Waco, Tex.: Word Books, 1966), pp. 140–150.

[21]J. Philip Hogan, "The Congress on the Church's Worldwide Mission," *Pentecostal Evangel*, 12 June 1966, p. 19.

[22]Assemblies of God speakers included Thomas F. Zimmerman, general superintendent; Paul Finkenbinder, missionary to Latin America; and José María Rico, an international evangelist; other prominent Pentecostals included Oral Roberts, healing evangelist, and Nicholas B. H. Bhengu, South African evangelist; for their addresses, see Carl F. H. Henry and W. Stanley Mooneyham, eds. *One Race, One Gospel, One Task.*

[23]*Like a River* (50th Anniversary Commemorative Book) (Springfield, Mo.: Assemblies of God, 1964), p. 3.

[24]Raymond T. Brock, "Three Unusual Conferences Project Global Conquest Advance," (editorial) *Global Conquest*, March–April 1963, pp. 12–14.

[25]J. Philip Hogan, "Together We Work," *Missionary Forum*, March–April 1960, p. 1.

[26]J. Philip Hogan, promotional letter, 5 June 1963.

[27]Melvin L. Hodges, "The Holy Spirit and a Changing World," *Missionary Forum*, 3rd Quarter, 1965, p. 2.

[28]Hodges, "Mission—and Church Growth," p. 144; see also the articles by McGavran and Hodges in Donald Anderson McGavran, ed., *Church Growth and Christian Mission* (New York: Harper and Row, 1965).

[29]For more information on post-war developments, see Ralph D. Winter, "The Twenty-five Unbelievable Years, 1945–1969," chapter in Kenneth Scott Latourette, *Advance Through Storm: A History of the Expansion of Christianity* (Grand Rapids: Zondervan Publishing House reprint edition, 1970), 7:507–533.

[30]Maynard L. Ketcham, "A New Day Dawns in Missions," *Pentecostal Evangel*, 17 July 1966, pp. 12–13; Glenn Stafford, "Going Home—to Burma!" 30 December 1973, pp. 16–17; Jeanne Anglin, "Asian Leaders Study at FEAST," *Mountain Movers*, August 1982, pp. 8–9.

[31]M. L. Ketcham, "Nationalism, A Force for Good," *Missionary Forum*, March–April 1961, p. 3.

[32]Vernon Metz, "Let Him Walk," *Missionary Forum*, 2nd Quarter 1964, p. 11.

[33]Colleen D. Tipton, "Identify Yourself with Nationals," *Missionary Forum*, 2nd Quarter 1966, p. 15.

[34]Christine Carmichael, "Assemblies of God National Workers," *Pentecostal Evangel*, 19 June 1966, pp. 13–14.

[35]Raymond T. Brock, "Global Conquest" (editorial), *Missionary Forum*, May–June 1961, p. 2.

[36]David A. Womack, "Change of Name: Global Conquest to Good News Crusades," *Key,* 4th Quarter, 1967, p. 7; Wesley R. Hurst, "FMD Policy Changes," *Key,* 1st Quarter 1966, p. 6.

[37]General Council Minutes, 1957, pp. 31–32.

[38]General Presbytery Minutes, 28 August 1964, p. 30; 24 August 1965, p. 27; 2 September 1966, pp. 45–46.

[39]M. L. Hodges, "Historic Conference in Central America," *Pentecostal Evangel,* 24 April 1960, p. 7; J. Philip Hogan, "CADSA," *Key,* 3rd Quarter, 1964, p. 9; Louise Jeter Walker, et al., "Charting the Course," *Pentecostal Evangel,* 27 March 1966, pp. 16–17.

[40]J. Philip Hogan, "Pan-African Conference," *Pentecostal Evangel,* 1 November 1964, p. 9.

[41]Maynard L. Ketcham, "Far East Conference Great Success," *Pentecostal Evangel,* 8 September 1960, p. 14.

[42]Report of the Second Conference of Assemblies of God, 12 June 1967, pp. 2–3; Alfred F. Missen to R. T. McGlasson, 2 April 1970.

[43]Robert C. Cunningham, "Erected to the Glory of God," *Pentecostal Evangel,* 22 April 1962, p. 16.

[44]*Missionary Manual* (Springfield, Mo.: Foreign Missions Department, 1963), pp. 15–16.

[45]For information on Bhengu, see Burgess and McGee, *DPCM,* s.v., "Bhengu, Nicholas Bhekinkosi Hepworth," by G. B. McGee.

[46]M. Williams to P. Hogan, 28 July 1964; difficulties occasionally surfaced on other fields as is evidenced in Allen V. Koop, *American Evangelical Missionaries in France, 1945–1975* (Lanham, Md.: University Press of America, 1986), p. 111.

[47]Donald Anderson McGavran, *How Churches Grow* (New York: Friendship Press, 1959), pp. 88–89.

[48]Donald McGavran, John Huegel, Jack Taylor, *Church Growth in Mexico* (Grand Rapids: William B. Eerdmans Publishing Co., 1963), pp. 114–115.

[49]J. S. Murray, "What We Can Learn From the Pentecostal Churches," *Christianity Today,* 9 June 1967, p. 10.

[50]Ibid., p. 12.

[51]W. Dayton Roberts, "Pentecost South of the Border," *Christianity Today,* 19 July 1963, p. 32.

[52]James D. Crane, "What We Can Learn From the Assemblies of God En [sic] El Salvador," ca. 1962. (Typewritten.)

[53]J. Philip Hogan, "How Do We Compare?" *Missionary Forum,* 3rd Quarter, 1964, p. 7.

Chapter 7: Aspects of Missonary Life

[1]Departmental Reports and Financial Statements, 1963, p. 92.

[2]*Missionary Manual* (Springfield, Mo.: Foreign Missions Department, 1963), p. 15.

[3]Morris Williams, "Things I Learned from Slatiel Zuze," *Pentecostal Evangel,* 6 October 1968, p. 8.

[4]Marion E. Craig, "24 Approved for Foreign Service," *Pentecostal Evangel,* 31 March 1963, p. 8.

[5]*Missionary Manual* (Springfield, Mo.: Foreign Missions Department, 1963), p. 2.

[6]*Missionary Manual* (Springfield, Mo.: Foreign Missions Department, 1969), p. 11.

[7]*Missionary Manual* (Springfield, Mo.: Foreign Missions Department, 1963), pp. 3–4.

[8]*Missions Manual* (Springfield, Mo.: Division of Foreign Missions, 1987), pp. 3-1–3-8.

[9]*Missionary Manual* (Springfield, Mo.: Foreign Missions Department, 1963), p. 5.

[10]J. Philip Hogan, "Uncle Sam and You," *Missionary Forum,* 2nd Quarter, 1962, pp. 4–5; J. Philip Hogan, "Dear Fellow Missionary" October 1965.

[11]John Weidman, "Just Itinerating?" *Missionary Forum,* July–August 1960, p. 6.

[12]Margaret J. McComber, "The Peculiar Problems of Missionaries' Children," *Missionary Forum,* November–December 1960, p. 1.

[13]Ibid., pp. 1–2.

[14]Adele Flower Dalton, "Our Ministry of Hospitality," *Missionary Forum,* 1st Quarter, 1964, p. 3.

[15]Ibid., p. 4.

[16]"The Toll of a Tragic Summer," *Pentecostal Evangel,* 22 September 1968, p. 10.

[17]Ibid.; Sue Schaeffer, *Africa Is Waiting* (Grand Rapids: Baker Book House, 1970).

[18]John Weidman, "Twenty-two Days a Missionary," *Pentecostal Evangel,* 17 February 1963, pp. 8–9.

[19]"Missionaries Attacked in Paraguay," *Pentecostal Evangel,* 25 March 1962, p. 7.

[20]Christine Carmichael, "Colombia," *Pentecostal Evangel,* 15 June 1969, pp. 19–20.

[21]Angeline Tucker, "Crisis Days in the Congo" (Part 2), *Pentecostal Evangel,* 21 February 1965, p. 8; J. W. Tucker's story is told in more detail by Angeline Tucker in *He Is In Heaven* (New York: McGraw-Hill Book Company, 1965).

[22]J. Philip Hogan, "Love's Summit Reached," *Global Conquest,* March–April 1965, p. 11.

[23]David Kensinger, "Divinely Delivered," *Pentecostal Evangel,* 30 July 1961, p. 5.

[24]Debbie Irwin, "Complete Victory on the Way!" *Mountain Movers,* September 1979, p. 7.

[25]Ibid.

[26]Harold Kohl, "A Challenge to Witness and a Call to Suffer," *Pentecostal Evangel,* 29 January 1967, p. 7.

PART III: EVANGELISM, EDUCATION, AND EXPANSION (1968–1977)

Chapter 8: A Forward Movement

[1]For more information on the committee's personnel and progress, see Richard Champion, Edward S. Caldwell, and Gary Leggett, eds. *Our Mission in Today's World: Council on Evangelism Official Papers and Reports* (Springfield, Mo.: Gospel Publishing House, 1968), pp. 10–14.

[2]Ibid., p. 17.

[3]Ibid., p. 212.

[4]Donald Gee, *Toward Pentecostal Unity* (Springfield, Mo.: Gospel Publishing House, 1961), p. 33; for information on Gee, see Burgess and McGee, *DPCM,* "Gee, Donald," by D. D. Bundy.

[5]Champion, *Our Mission,* p. 8.

[6]*Good News Crusades,* November–December 1968, p. 3.

[7]*Good News Crusades,* March–April 1970, p. 2.

[8]"The Message That Counts . . . " *Good News Crusades,* March–April 1977, p. 2.

[9]J. Philip Hogan, "The Bush or the Boulevard," *Good News Crusades,* March–April 1970, pp. 12–13.

[10]Ibid., p. 11.

[11]David A. Womack, "The End of Our Rope!" *Key,* 1st Quarter, 1969, p. 9.

[12]Marl Neely, "Target: Rio de Janiero," *Good News Crusades,* November–December 1968, pp. 10–11.

[13]Bernhard Johnson, "God—Give Us Evangelists Today!" *World Pentecost,* no. 2, vol. 6 (1976), pp. 8–9.

[14]J. Philip Hogan, "Evangelism That Produces," *Pentecostal Evangel,* 25 February 1973, p. 11.

[15]David Irwin, "This Gospel Shall Be Preached," *Pentecostal Evangel,* 24 March 1974, pp. 16–17.

[16]Cited in David A. Womack, "Committed to Sacrifice," *Good News Crusades,* September–October 1967, pp. 2–3.

[17]A. M. Cakau, "Pentecost—The Power for Missions," *Pentecostal Evangel,* 27 December 1970, p. 9.

[18]David Kent Irwin, "How to Make a Christian Lake," *Good News Crusades,* May–June 1972, p. 10.

[19]Paul Wright, "They Came to Gwanzura," *Pentecostal Evangel,* 28 March 1971, pp. 14–15.

[20]Joyce Wells Booze, "The Crippled Man . . . Is Walking," *Good News Crusades,* September–October 1978, pp. 1–3.

[21]William Caldwell, "Sri Lanka Shaken," *Good News Crusades,* September–October 1973, p. 6.

[22]Richard Vinyard, "God's Power Breaks Satan's Stranglehold," *Good News Crusades,* September–October 1973, p. 13.

[23]Jack Willis, "The Djakarta Impact," *Good News Crusades,* March–April 1971, p. 4.

[24]Doyle G. Jones, "Divine Healing and Assemblies of God Foreign Missions," unpublished ms., 1988, pp. 22–24; Doyle G. Jones, "Birth of a Church," *Good News Crusades,* March–April 1977, pp. 12–14; for Jeffery's association with Gordon Lindsay's Native Church Crusade, see G. Lindsay, "The Story of the Native Church Crusade," *Voice of Healing,* June 1963, p. 5.

[25]Bernhard Johnson, "Reverend Johnson . . . 'What's Your Gimmick?' " *Pentecostal Evangel,* 14 April 1974, pp. 16–17; for information on Johnson, see Burgess and McGee, *DPCM,* s.v. "Johnson, Bernhard," by E. B. Robinson.

[26]Bernhard Johnson to Rev. J. Philip Hogan, reprinted in *Good News Crusades,* May–June 1975, p. 9.

[27]Morris Williams, "Why I Do Not Use 'Outside' Funds," *Missionary Forum,* July–August 1960, p. 1.

[28]The activities of some healing evangelists interfered with the missiological strategy of the Assemblies of God at times. This was particularly true of T. L. Osborn's Association for Native Evangelism; see Wesley E. Bjur, "Then What," *Missionary Forum,* 1st Quarter, 1962, pp. 10–12; Melvin Hodges, "On Overseas Evangelists," *Missionary Forum,* 4th Quarter, 1963, pp. 14–15. More in line with Assemblies of God perspectives was Gordon Lindsay's Native Church Crusade; see G. Lindsay, "The Story of the Native Church Crusade," *Voice of Healing,* June 1963, pp. 4–7, 10.

[29]"Ten Year Comparison," *Key,* 2nd Quarter, 1970, p. 3; J. Philip Hogan, "A Review of the 60s," *Pentecostal Evangel,* 26 April 1970, p. 15. Unfortunately, the report in *Key* (the quarterly report to district missionary secretaries), which provided these statistics, referred to them as representing the growth of the "foreign constituency." A better and more accurate label would have been "overseas national constituencies," accurately reflecting the emerging partnerships between the sending agency and the younger churches.

[30]David A. Womack, "What Do Colombia and Korea Have in Common?" *Good News Crusades,* November–December 1967, pp. 12–14.

[31]Paul Brannan, "Good News From the First of the Seven Cities in '70," *Good News Crusades,* July–August 1970, pp. 8–11.

[32]"Birthday in Seoul," *Good News Crusades,* September–October 1969, pp. 6–9; John Stetz, "Church Growth: Korea," *World Pentecost,* no. 3, vol. 7 (1977), pp. 14–15; see also John N. Vaughan, *The World's 20 Largest Churches* (Grand Rapids: Baker Book House, 1984), pp. 35–49.

[33]Paul Y. Cho with R. Whitney Manzano, *More Than Numbers* (Waco: Word Books, 1984), p. 44.

[34]Bethany Bible College, an Assemblies of God institution in Santa Cruz, California, conferred an honorary doctor of divinity degree on Paul Yonggi Cho in 1969. See "Bethany Bible College Honors Cho Yonggi," *Key,* 3rd Quarter, 1969, p. 5; for more information on his ministry, see Cho with Manzano, *More Than Numbers.*

[35]John Bueno, "We Recognize the Lordship of Christ," *Pentecostal Evangel,* 22 August 1976, pp. 20–21; see also John Bueno, "Church Planting and the Evangelist," in *The Calling of An Evangelist,* ed. J. D. Douglas (Minneapolis: World Wide Publications, 1987), pp. 255–260.

[36]Morris Plotts, "Preaching Christ in the Land of the Arabian Nights," *Good News Crusades,* March–April 1971, pp. 6–10; Morris Plotts, "In the Year of King Cyrus 2,500," *Good News Crusades,* July–August 1972, pp. 2–7; David Irwin, Morris Plotts, Morris Williams, "A Cross Without a Church," *Good News Crusades,* November–December 1973, pp. 3–7; for his autobiography, see Morris Plotts, *Bwana Tembo: A Prince with God* (Baton Rouge: Jimmy Swaggart Evangelistic Association, 1980).

[37]For examples of the ministries of Argue and Olson, see respectively Orville H. Carlson, "400 Saved in Suva," *Good News Crusades,* July–August 1968, pp. 4–6; and Herris Heidenreich, "Accent on Accra," *Good News Crusades,* March–April 1968, pp. 11–15.

[38]For example, see Robert C. Cunningham, "Pioneering in the Northern Jungles," *Pentecostal Evangel,* 11 September 1977, pp. 12–13.

[39]Fred Cottriel, "Tragedy Strikes Middle East Missionary Family," *MissioNews,* Winter 1970, p. 7.

[40]For an analysis of Assemblies of God ministry to servicemen in the Far East, see Doyle E. Burgess, Jr., "The Ministry of Assemblies of God Servicemen to the National Church of Asia," unpublished research paper at the Assemblies of God Graduate School, Springfield, Missouri, 1978.

[41]"Revival Fires Linger Following 13th Annual Servicemen's Retreat," *Pentecostal Evangel,* 18 January 1970, p. 28.

[42]"Centurion Foundation Offers Opportunity for Ministry to A/G Servicemen in Europe," *Pentecostal Evangel,* 22 November 1970, p. 28.

[43]Helen Braxton to Gary McGee, 16 September 1988.

[44]Wesley R. Hurst, "We Are There in Vietnam," *Good News Crusades,*

November–December 1974, pp. 2–5; J. Philip Hogan, "Serving Under Two Banners," *Pentecostal Evangel*, 25 June 1972, p. 13; for information on the ministry of Teen Challenge, see Burgess and McGee, *DPCM*, s.v. "Teen Challenge," F. M. Reynolds.

[45]David A. Womack, "Bibles for Burma," *Good News Crusades*, September–October 1969, pp. 10–11; J. Philip Hogan, "Bibles for Burma," *Pentecostal Evangel*, 19 October 1969, p. 23.

[46]David A. Womack, "A New Bible for China," (pamphlet, n.d.).

[47]J. Philip Hogan, "The Bible in Our Time," *Pentecostal Evangel*, 19 July 1970, p. 15.

[48]J. Philip Hogan to "Dear Fellow Missionary," November 1975.

[49]Melvin L. Hodges, "A Pentecostal's View of Mission Strategy," *International Review of Mission* 57 (July 1968): 304–310.

[50]David A. Womack, "The Only Hope for World Evangelization," *Christianity Today*, 20 July 1973, pp. 10–13.

[51]Cited in J. Philip Hogan, "Through an Outsider's Eyes," *Pentecostal Evangel*, 30 January 1972, p. 17.

[52]Donald McGavran, "Korea Asks: Where Shall We Send Missionaries?" in *Readings in Third World Missions*, ed. Marlin L. Nelson (Pasadena: William Carey Library, 1976), pp. 185–186; for information on the relationship between the Pentecostal movement and the church growth movement, see Grant McClung, "From BRIDGES (McGavran, 1955) to WAVES (Wagner, 1983): Pentecostals and the Church Growth Movement," *Pneuma* 7 (Spring 1985): pp. 5–18.

Chapter 9: Missions Education and Missiology

[1]McGee, *This Gospel Shall Be Preached*, 1:167–168, 193–194.

[2]General Council Minutes, 1945, p. 25. For the development of higher education in the Pentecostal movement, see Burgess and McGee, *DPCM*, s.v. "Bible Institutes, Colleges, Universities," by L. F. Wilson; and "Seminaries and Graduate Schools," by C. M. Robeck, Jr.; for higher education in the Assemblies of God, see Richard D. Strahan, "The Development of Education in the Assemblies of God" (M.Ed. thesis, Southern Methodist University, 1949); and Don Paul Gray, "A Critical Analysis of the Academic Evolutionary Development Within the Assemblies of God Higher Education Movement, 1914–1975" (Ed.D. diss., Southwestern Baptist Theological Seminary, 1976).

[3]General Council Minutes, 1949, p. 30.

[4]*Central Bible Institute Bulletin, 1964–65*, pp. 85–86.

[5]"Self-Study Report Submitted to North Central Association of Colleges and Schools, Boulder, Colorado," July 1977, pp. 36–37; see also J. Philip Hogan, "Missionary Candidates," *Pentecostal Evangel*, 16 June 1968, p. 9.

[6]For a historical review of the steps taken toward establishing a seminary, see Menzies, *Anointed*, pp. 366–368.

[7]Assemblies of God Graduate School, "Preliminary Information," February 1973, p. 3.

[8]For biographical information on these two men, see Burgess and McGee, *DPCM*, s.v. "Zimmerman, Thomas Fletcher," by S. M. Burgess, and "Burnett, Cordas Chris," by B. M. Stout.

[9]Assemblies of God Graduate School, *Bulletin, 1974–1975*, pp. 10–11.

[10]"New Position in Foreign Missions," *Pentecostal Evangel*, 21 July 1968, p. 13.

[11]"A/G Graduate School Officially Opened on September 4," *Pentecostal Evangel*, 16 September 1973, p. 29; for more information on the role of the AGGS missions division in the training of missionaries, see "Continuing Education for the Missionaries," *Pentecostal Evangel*, 8 September 1974, pp. 16–17.

[12]J. Philip Hogan, "Graduate Studies in Missions," *Pentecostal Evangel*, 31 March 1974, p. 13.

[13]J. Philip Hogan, "Melvin Hodges—Missions Pioneer Breaks New Ground," *Pentecostal Evangel*, 12 August 1973, pp. 16–17; J. Philip Hogan, "God Prepares Men," *Pentecostal Evangel*, 23 September 1973, p. 17; see also "Faculty Roster Completed for A/G Graduate School," *Pentecostal Evangel*, 25 March 1973, p. 25.

[14]Assemblies of God Graduate School, *Catalog, 1976–1978*, pp. 31–35.

[15]Ibid., p. 34.

[16]See McGee, *This Gospel Shall Be Preached*, 1:167–168; Menzies, *Anointed*, pp. 306, 358.

[17]"Self-Study Report," p. 38.

[18]Ibid., pp. 23–25, 34–35, 39–40, 43.

[19]Ibid., p. 43.

[20]Melvin L. Hodges, *A Theology of the Church and Its Mission: A Pentecostal Perspective* (Springfield, Mo.: Gospel Publishing House, 1977), p. 9; for an important review, see David J. Hesselgrave in *Occasional Bulletin* 3 (April 1979): 82.

[21]Ibid., p. 35.

[22]Ibid., p. 55.

[23]Ibid., pp. 65–70; see also Melvin L. Hodges, "Scriptural Patterns of Church Growth," *Pentecostal Evangel*, 12 March 1972, p. 7.

[24]David K. Irwin, "We Know What Our Business Is," *Good News Crusades* (January–February 1972), pp. 2–3.

[25]Thomas F. Sanders, and Gary L. Leggett, eds., *Adult Teacher*, 2 (September 1972–August 1973), (Springfield, Mo.: Gospel Publishing House, 1972), pp. 25–28, 181–89. At roughly the same time, however, Gospel Publishing House reprinted Frank M. Boyd's *Holy Spirit* (n.d.) as *The Holy*

Spirit Works Today (1970), a study that defines the era of the church as the age of the Spirit but barely mentions the kingdom of God.

[26]Hodges, *A Theology*, pp. 82–83; see also David A. Womack, "Eternal Verities Versus Universalism," *Pentecostal Evangel*, 5 January 1969, pp. 10–12; General Presbytery of the Assemblies of God, "The Eternal Punishment of the Wicked," *Pentecostal Evangel*, 10 October 1976, pp. 6–7.

[27]Ibid., pp. 86–88.

[28]Ibid., pp. 98–126.

[29]Ibid., p. 95.

[30]Ibid.

[31]Ibid., pp. 95–96.

[32]Ibid., p. 96.

[33]Harris Jansen, Elva Hoover, Gary Leggett, eds. *Live in the Spirit: A Compendium of Themes on the Spiritual Life as Presented at the Council on Spiritual Life* (Springfield, Mo.: Gospel Publishing House, 1972), pp. 335–336; see also Joseph R. Flower, "The Charismatic Movement," pp. 200–215, and D. Leroy Sanders, "The Charismatic Renewal in Your Community," pp. 216–221, in the same volume.

[34]J. Philip Hogan, "Ecumenical or Charismatic?" *Pentecostal Evangel*, 25 March 1973, p. 17.

[35]David F. Wells, "Contemporary Evangelism and Neo-Catholicism," in *Theology and Mission: Papers Given at Trinity Consultation No. 1*, ed. David J. Hesselgrave (Grand Rapids: Baker Book House, 1978), p. 131; see also Harold O. J. Brown, "Contemporary Dialogues with Traditional Catholicism" (pp. 147–160), the responses by Wade T. Coggins, Philip E. Armstrong, and Gilbert A. Peterson (pp. 161–66), and the replies by Wells and Brown (pp. 167–170) in the same volume.

[36]For information on the ecumenism between classical Pentecostals and charismatics, see Burgess and McGee, *DPCM*, s.v., "Charismatic Movement," by P. D. Hocken; "Dialogue, Roman Catholic and Classical Pentecostal," by J. L. Sandidge; "Kansas City Conference," by H. V. Synan; "North American Congresses on the Holy Spirit and World Evangelization," by J. R. Zeigler; see also, Peter D. Hocken, *One Lord One Spirit One Body* (Gaithersburg, Md.: The Word Among Us Press, 1987).

[37]For a positive assessment, see David K. Irwin with Sobhi Malek, "Charismatic Renewal Spurs Missions," *Pentecostal Evangel*, 17 March 1974, pp. 14–15.

[38]Paul Hutsell, "Missionaries-in-Residence = Missions Fervor," *Advance*, April 1977, p. 13.

[39]Ibid.

Chapter 10: New Ventures in Education

[1]For information on the history of Pentecostal publishing ventures, see Burgess and McGee, *DPCM*, s.v. "Publications," by W. E. Warner.

[2]J. Philip Hogan, "Twin Emphases," *Pentecostal Evangel,* 27 August 1972, p. 17; Andrew McDearmid,"Key to Indigenous Leadership," *Advance,* September 1971, pp. 28–29. For a philosophy of religious education in the Assemblies of God, see Donald F. Johns, "A Philosophy of Religious Education for the Assemblies of God," Ph.D diss., New York University, 1962.

[3]West Africa Advanced School of Theology, *Catalog,* 1985, pp. 5–6; Christine Carmichael, "Togo," *Pentecostal Evangel,* 14 February 1971, p. 23.

[4]Ibid., p. 4.

[5]John F. Hall, "The Joy of Firstfruits," *Pentecostal Evangel,* 20 April 1975, pp. 18–19.

[6]East Africa School of Theology, *Prospectus,* 1984, p. 12.

[7]Ibid.

[8]Pentecostal Assemblies of Canada (PAOC) missionaries were the first Pentecostals to pioneer in Kenya and developed the largest such organization in the country, known as the Pentecostal Assemblies of Kenya (PAK). For many years a verbal comity arrangement existed with the Assemblies of God (U.S.A.) in East Africa, reserving Kenya for the PAOC and Tanzania for the A/G. In parallel developments, PAK began to establish churches along Lake Victoria in northern Tanzania and in Uganda, while the A/G began to establish fraternal links with churches in Kenya not wishing to identify with PAK; they have since taken (1972) the name Kenya Assemblies of God (KAG). The comity agreement ended in the early 1970s, causing tensions to rise between the organizations, but in recent years the relationships have become cordial. Unfortunately, both sides offer parallel programs and this arrangement has created some confusion in the country. Joint interview with Gerald Morrison, PAOC Africa regional coordinator, and Jimmy Beggs, A/G missionary to Kenya, Nairobi, Kenya, 14 April 1988; *Kenya Field Missionary Handbook* (PAOC), p. 5; Marian Keller, *Twenty Years in Africa: 1913–1933: Retrospect and Prospect* (Toronto: Full Gospel Publishing Co., n.d.).

[9]Southern Asia Bible College, *Prospectus,* n.d., pp. 3, 6.

[10]"Six Churches Begun in India," *Good News Crusades,* March–April 1977, p. 11.

[11]Burgess and McGee, *DPCM,* s.v. "European Pentecostalism," by D. W. Cartwright and P. D. Hocken.

[12]Burgess and McGee, *DPCM,* s.v. "Squire, Frederick Henry," by G. B. McGee.

[13]Burgess and McGee, *DPCM,* s.v. "Toppi, Francesco," by G. B. McGee.

[14]See "Continental Bible College, Brussels, Belgium," *Key,* 4th Quarter, 1968, pp. 4–5. These anonymous, paternalistic, and somewhat anti-European sentiments are difficult to account for since they do not reflect the policies of the Division of Foreign Missions.

[15]Continental Bible College, *Catalog,* 1980–81 to 1981–82, p. 2; see also

Warren Flattery, *Report on Eurasia Education Meeting,* January 21–25, 1974.

[16]Telephone interview with Bill L. Williams, missionary to Western Europe and former president of Continental Bible College, Nice, France, 23 September 1988.

[17]Far East Advanced School of Theology, *Chalice 1984,* pp. 2–3.

[18]Ibid., pp. 4, 6–7, 13; *The President's Annual Report to the Board of Directors,* May 1984, pp. 19–23.

[19]"FEAST Completes Facilities to Train Asians for Ministry," *Pentecostal Evangel,* 29 March 1987, p. 27.

[20]Catie Flowers, "In His Time," *AGAMA News and Notes,* January–March 1982, p. 8; Dora Moses, "Only a Beginning," *AGAMA News and Notes,* January–March 1982, p. 6; telephone interview with William W. Menzies, president of FEAST, Springfield, Missouri, 19 September 1988.

[21]James E. Richardson, "A Study of the Leadership Training Programs of the Assemblies of God in Spanish America," unpublished ms., 1974, pp. 32–41. Richardson's study is an indispensable tool for analyzing the development of ministerial training among Assemblies of God constituencies in Spanish America.

[22]For more information, see *The Basic Plan* (Miami: Program of Advanced Christian Education, Assemblies of God, 1987); Richardson, "A Study," pp. 42–85; Sam Balius, "Watch Out—the Nationals Are Coming!" *Pentecostal Evangel,* 17 February 1974, pp. 16–17.

[23]"Latin America Trains Its Leaders," *Key,* 4th Quarter, 1968, p. 2.

[24]Ibid., pp. 2–3; Richardson, "A Study," pp. 86–107.

[25]Monroe D. Grams, "A New Name for PACE," *Pentecostal Evangel,* January 1, 1984, p. 10; interview with Samuel H. Balius, missionary to Latin America, Springfield, Missouri, 7 July 1988.

[26]Missionaries who have made significant contributions to CTN over the years include Verne A. Warner, Byron L. Niles, Monroe D. Grams, Floyd C. Woodworth, Harold B. Calkins, Samuel H. Balius, and Milton J. Kersten.

[27]For information on earlier correspondence programs overseas, see "Correspondence Schools in the Mission Field," n.d.; Melvin L. Hodges to Charles Greenaway, 7 June 1967; M. L. Ketcham to Charles E. Greenaway, 2 June 1967; Everett L. Phillips to Charles Greenaway, 5 June 1967; Rex Jackson to Charles Greenaway, 1 June 1967; and F. H. Burke, "Evangelical Literature Invasion of Schools of Africa," n.d.

[28]Normal L. Correll, "The Bible School of the World," *Mountain Movers,* July 1987, p. 5.

[29]Dr. George Flattery and J. Philip Hogan, "Conversations," pp. 4–5, ICI, Brussels, Belgium (an abridged edition has been published: Ron Barefield, "ICI's First 15 Years," *World Pentecost* 11 [1982]: 4–6); George Flattery to Gary McGee, n.d.

[30]For further information, see George M. Flattery, "Suggestions for an Assemblies of God Home Study Institute," unpublished ms., 10 March 1967; George M. Flattery, "Correspondence School Program," unpublished ms., 26 July 1967, pp. 1–12. At the request of Hardy Steinberg, chairman of the ICI Domestic Use Committee, Flattery offered a proposal for a stateside school on January 29, 1971. Although the National Correspondence Institute was formed, it did not offer college level programs. Over the years, in response to public demand, ICI also was permitted to work domestically at different times and in various ways. Considerable tension existed over ICI's involvement in the United States. However, in 1985, the last year of Zimmerman's tenure as general superintendent, Berean School of the Bible was upgraded with a collegiate program and renamed Berean College of the Assemblies of God, adding a fourth A/G academic institution in Springfield, Missouri. The entire curriculum of ICI collegiate courses was then utilized for this new program; Berean College has also developed some new courses. For the stateside proposal, see George M. Flattery, "An Extension School for the United States," unpublished ms., 29 January 1971, pp. 1–18, ICI, Brussels.

[31]"New Progress in International Correspondence Institute," *Key*, 1st Quarter, 1969, p. 7; "International Correspondence Institute," *Key*, 4th Quarter, 1967, pp. 8–10.

[32]Foreign Missions Department, "International Correspondence Institute" (promotional brochure), ca. 1969.

[33]Flattery and Hogan, "Conversations," p. 13.

[34]Ibid., pp. 14–16.

[35]George M. Flattery, "Cooperative Multinationalism: An Emerging Philosophy of Missions," unpublished ms., 1969, p. 1.

[36]Ibid., pp. 17–22.

[37]Ibid., p. 25.

[38]Ibid., p. 27.

[39]George M. Flattery, "What ICI Is," unpublished ms., 1978, p. 4.

[40]Correll, "The Bible School," p. 6.

[41]"World Report," *ICI Datelines*, September/October 1987, p. 6.

[42]"ICI Enrolls 10,000th Student in College-level Program," *Pentecostal Evangel*, 29 September 1985, p. 28.

[43]Cited in Helen Braxton, "Alive for the Lord," *Pentecostal Evangel*, 29 March 1987, p. 11.

[44]For information on the Apostolic Church in New Zealand, see Charles Edwin Jones, *A Guide to the Study of the Pentecostal Movement* (Metuchen, N. J.: Scarecrow Press, 1983), 1:421.

[45]"ICI Offices and Directors," *ICI Datelines*, September/October 1987, p. 14.

Chapter 11: Expanding Ministries

[1]J. Philip Hogan, "The Holy Spirit and the Great Commission," *World Pentecost*, no. 1, 1972, pp. 4–5; this article is a significant representation of Hogan's missiological perspectives. For his perspective on his long-term service as executive director, see General Council Minutes, 1975, p. 37. His attitude about unnecessary mission consultations can be found in J. Philip Hogan to "Dear Fellow Missionaries," 1 October 1985.

[2]McGlasson contributed the article "Pentecostal Missions" in the *Concise Dictionary of the Christian World Mission* (Nashville: Abingdon Press, 1971).

[3]"Former Foreign Missions Head McGlasson With Christ," *Pentecostal Evangel*, 22 February 1987, p. 28; "Joe Kilpatrick Named Department Secretary," *Pentecostal Evangel*, 28 August 1977, p. 29; a helpful guide to tracing the changes of personnel in the Division of Foreign Missions is "Division of Foreign Missions Personnel," n.d., prepared by Adele Flower Dalton. (Typewritten.)

[4]David A. Womack, "44 Years for Christ and Asia," *Pentecostal Evangel*, 10 May 1970, pp. 18–19; for more information, see Maynard L. Ketcham, *Tigers That Talk* (Charlotte, N.C.: PTL Television Network, 1979).

[5]Burgess and McGee, *DPCM*, s.v. "Hurst, Wesley Robinson," by G. B. McGee.

[6]J. Philip Hogan to "Dear Members of the African Missionary Family," April 1970.

[7]Burgess and McGee, *DPCM*, s.v., "Phillips, Everett L.," by S. Shemeth, and "Williams, Morris Oliver," by G. B. McGee.

[8]Ibid., s.v., "Triplett, Loren Otis, Jr." by G. W. Gohr; for a helpful survey of Assemblies of God literature ministries abroad in this period, see Nelda Ammons, "Our Worldwide Literature Program," *Advance*, May 1971, p. 32.

[9]"Charles Greenaway Retires; Jerry Parsley Named Eurasia Field Director," *Pentecostal Evangel*, 11 December 1983, p. 20.

[10]Telephone interview with David A. Womack, pastor of Twin Palms Assembly of God, San Jose, California, 11 October 1988.

[11]J. Philip Hogan, "Missionary Candidates," *Pentecostal Evangel*, 16 June 1968, p. 9.

[12]James W. Jones, "Some Factors Contributing to Missionary Withdrawals in the Assemblies of God and Including a Comparative Study with Other Missions (1965–1974)," (unpublished ms., Assemblies of God Graduate School, 1976), pp. 26–27.

[13]Ibid., pp. 28–33; for information on collegiate education for MKs, see Hogan, "Dear Fellow Missionary," October 1970.

[14]Ibid., pp. 61, 64.

15Ibid., p. 65; see also J. Philip Hogan, "Our Ministry—Their Call," *Pentecostal Evangel*, 24 June 1973, p. 87.

16Hogan, "Dear Fellow Missionary," October 1968.

17Delmer R. Guynes, "Touchstone of A/G Foreign Missions," *Advance*, June 1971, pp. 12–13.

18Hogan, "Dear Fellow Missionary," February 1976. The policy with Christian Fidelity Life Insurance Co. had been partially designed by George M. Flattery and dated back to 1963; telephone interview with Cecil L. Barnett, president of the Christian Fidelity Life Insurance Co., Waxahachie, Texas, 13 October 1988; for the history of MBA, see Menzies, *Anointed*, p. 284.

19J. Philip Hogan to "Dear Fellow Missionary," October 1968; interview with Barnett.

20J. Philip Hogan to "Dear Fellow Missionary," July 1976; McGee, *This Gospel Shall Be Preached*, 1:195.

21General Council Minutes, 1965, p. 107.

22Ibid., p. 108.

23General Council Minutes, 1971, pp. 26, 50, 55, 113.

24General Council Minutes, 1973, pp. 92, 106.

25"Suggested Job Description for the *Area Representative*," appended to the following letter, J. Philip Hogan to "Dear Fellow Missionaries," January 1975.

26General Council Minutes, 1955, pp. 30–31.

27General Council Minutes, 1957, pp. 18–19.

28General Council Minutes, 1961, pp. 54, 80.

29Memorandum to All Missionaries, 8 September 1971, Editorial Office Files, Division of Foreign Missions.

30General Council Minutes, 1971, pp. 86–87.

31Memorandum.

32J. Philip Hogan, "International Money and Foreign Missions," *Pentecostal Evangel*, 18 July 1971, p. 11.

33J. Philip Hogan, "The Rising Cost of Missions," *Pentecostal Evangel*, 16 March 1969, p. 11; for explanations about the expenditure of funds, see Robert T. McGlasson, "Administering Foreign Missions," *Pentecostal Evangel*, 21 January 1968, pp. 12–13; David A. Womack, "What Happens to Your Missions Dollar?" *Pentecostal Evangel*, 21 December 1969, pp. 18–19; and Wesley R. Hurst, "Crisis in Office Administration Funds," *Key*, 1st Quarter, 1968, pp. 1–2.

34J. Philip Hogan, "The New Missionary Allowance Program," *Advance*, January 1971, pp. 34–35; see also J. Philip Hogan to "Dear Fellow-Missionary," June 1972.

35J. Philip Hogan to "Dear Fellow Missionary," May 1971.

[36]J. Philip Hogan, "A Gift Multiplied Many Times," *Pentecostal Evangel,* 26 September 1971, p. 17.

[37]Assemblies of God Division of Foreign Missions, *Annual Report 1977* (Springfield, Mo.: Division of Foreign Missions, 1977), p. 15.

[38]J. Philip Hogan, "Editorial Vida Continues to Grow," *Pentecostal Evangel,* 18 May 1969, p. 19; for a brief history of Life Publishers International, see Brenda Smith, "Unseen Employees Enjoy Miami Life," *Onward,* June 1986, pp. 1–2.

[39]"Vida Publishers," *World Pentecost,* no. 4, vol. 7, p. 4.

[40]Burgess and McGee, *DPCM,* s.v., "Teen Challenge," by F. M. Reynolds.

[41]For further information on Foltz's ministry, see "Eurasia Teen Challenge Report," 1977 (Mimeographed).

[42]Reynolds, "Teen Challenge."

[43]Jerry Sandidge as told to Janet Bonham, "As Bright as Our Faith," *Pentecostal Evangel,* 14 November 1976, pp. 18–20.

[44]For example, see Shirley I. Jones, "Missions Giving: Key to Local Church Vitality," *Advance,* September 1977, pp. 10–11.

[45]Louise Jeter Walker, "That's Why We Teach Missions," *Advance,* February 1972, pp. 7–8

[46]"BGMC Day '72, A Twenty-Year Milestone," *Pentecostal Evangel,* 23 January 1972, pp. 20–21.

[47]J. Philip Hogan, "WMC's Adjust to a Changing World," *Advance,* November 1975, p. 16.

[48]J. Philip Hogan, "Women Led by the Spirit," *Pentecostal Evangel,* 20 February 1977, p. 7.

[49]Marian M. Munch, "I Gave My Fat to Missions," *Pentecostal Evangel,* 18 September 1977, p. 3.

[50]Robert C. Cunningham, "A Kingdom Which Cannot Be Moved," *Pentecostal Evangel,* 21 August 1977, p. 16.

[51]Robert C. Cunningham, " 'MAPS' Builds Walls of Love," *Pentecostal Evangel,* 18 September 1977, p. 16.

[52]"MAPS Shares the Rest of the Story," *Advance,* October 1980, p. 7.

[53]"MAPS Foreign Construction 1987," 1987; ACMR Report for 1987. (Typewritten.)

[54]For an example, see David Godwin, "A Solid Foundation on Shaky Ground," *Pentecostal Evangel,* 28 March 1982, pp. 16–18.

[55]Vivian Warren, "Watching MAPS Grow," *Advance,* October 1976, p. 15.

PART IV: INTO THE EIGHTIES (1978–1988)

Chapter 12: Partnership in Mission

¹David B. Barrett, *World Christian Encyclopedia* (Oxford: Oxford University Press, 1982), p. 838; for a recent update, see Burgess and McGee, *DPCM*, s.v. "Statistics, Global," by D. B. Barrett.

²For a definition of classical Pentecostalism, see Burgess and McGee, *DPCM*, s.v. "Classical Pentecostalism," by H. V. Synan. For assessments of worldwide Pentecostalism, see Walter J. Hollenweger, "After Twenty Years' Research on Pentecostalism," *International Review of Mission* 75 (January 1986): 3–12; Mircea Eliade, ed., *The Encyclopedia of Religion* (New York: Macmillan Publishing Co., 1987), s.v. "Pentecostal and Charismatic Christianity," by Robert Mapes Anderson.

³Barrett, *World Christian,* p. 838; Milton T. Rudnick, *Speaking the Gospel Through the Ages: A History of Evangelism* (St. Louis: Concordia Publishing House, 1984), p. 220.

⁴Earle E. Cairns, *An Endless Line of Splendor: Revivals and Their Leaders from the Great Awakening to the Present* (Wheaton, Ill.: Tyndale House Publishers, Inc.), p. 177.

⁵Terry Muck, "Spiritual Lifts," *Christianity Today,* 16 October 1987, p. 15.

⁶W. Richie Hogg, "The Role of American Protestantism in World Mission," in *American Missions in Bicentennial Perspective,* ed. R. Pierce Beaver (South Pasadena, Calif.: William Carey Library, 1977), p. 390.

⁷Rudnick, *Speaking the Gospel,* p. 220.

⁸David J. Hesselgrave, *"Today's Choices for Tomorrow's Mission: An Evangelical Perspective on Trends and Issues in Missions* (Grand Rapids: Zondervan Publishing House, 1988), p. 118.

⁹The papers presented at the 1988 gathering of the American Society of Missiology may be found in the November 1988 issue of *Missiology.*

¹⁰For an analysis of post-World War II developments, see Ralph D. Winter, "The Twenty-five Unbelievable Years, 1945–1969," in *A History of the Expansion of Christianity,* by Kenneth Scott Latourette (Grand Rapids: Zondervan Publishing House, reprint ed., 1970), 7:507–533. See also Harold Lindsell, "The Major Denominations Are Jumping Ship," *Christianity Today,* 18 September 1981, pp. 16–17; cf., Robert T. Coote, "The Uneven Growth of Conservative Evangelical Missions," *International Bulletin of Missionary Research* 6 (July 1982): 118–123.

¹¹Tim Stafford, "Testing the Wine from John Wimber's Vineyard," *Christianity Today,* 8 August 1986, pp. 17–22; for the report of the faculty task force at Fuller Seminary, see Lewis B. Smedes, ed., *Ministry and the Miraculous* (Pasadena: Fuller Theological Seminary, 1987).

¹²L. Grant McClung, Jr., "Why I Am Optimistic About the Future of

Pentecostal Missions," *The Pentecostal Minister* (Winter 1987), p. 7. This valuable issue of the magazine focuses exclusively on world evangelization.

[13]For example, see Vinson Synan, "A Vision for the Year 2000," *Charisma,* August 1987, pp. 42–44, 46.

[14]J. Philip Hogan, "Critical Issues," *Advance,* May 1987, p. 4.

[15]For statistical studies, see Burgess and McGee, *DPCM,* s.v. "Statistics, Global," by D. B. Barrett; s.v. "Church Growth," by C. P. Wagner; and Vinson Synan, *The Twentieth-Century Pentecostal Explosion* (Altamonte Springs, Fla.: Creation House, 1987), pp. 5–13. Appraisals of the charismatic renewal can be found, among other treatments, in Arnold Bittlinger, ed., *The Church is Charismatic* (Geneva: World Council of Churches, 1981); Burgess and McGee, *DPCM,* s.v. "The Charismatic Movement," by P. D. Hocken; Rex Davis, *Locusts and Wild Honey: The Charismatic Renewal and the Ecumenical Movement* (Geneva: World Council of Churches, 1978); Russell T. Hitt, *The New Wave of Pentecostalism: A Second Look* (booklet, n. p., 1975); Edward D. O'Connor, C.S.C., *Pentecost in the Modern World* (Notre Dame, Ind.: Ave Maria Press, 1972); Synan, *The Twentieth-Century*; and Peter D. Hocken, *One Lord One Spirit One Body* (Gaithersburg, Md.: The Word Among Us Press, 1987).

[16]"A/G Overseas Constituency Doubling Every 5 Years," *Pentecostal Evangel,* 3 August 1980, p. 12.

[17]Noel Perkin, "The Four-Fold Challenge," *The Missionary Challenge* (January–March 1944), p. 4.

[18]For an exposition of the theme, see G. Edward Nelson, "Jesus—No Other Name," *Advance,* March 1980, pp. 4–5; see also his "Lift Jesus Higher," *Advance,* January 1982, p. 13.

[19]This statement of purpose is printed in each issue of *Mountain Movers*; for example, see the July 1986 issue, p. 2. For the origin of this statement, see Adele Flower Dalton, "From These Beginnings," *Mountain Movers,* January 1989, p. 14. Although the Assemblies of God mission enterprise has increasingly addressed the need for ministries of compassion overseas (children, the hungry, refugees, disaster victims, etc.), it has studiously avoided identification with social issues, fearing that the truth of the gospel would be compromised by political involvement; an example of this stance by a national church official can be found in "Interview with Motsatse," *Mountain Movers,* April 1987, pp. 12–13. For more information, see Hodges, *A Theology,* ch. 6; also, Lidia Susana Vaccaro De Petrella, "The Tension Between Evangelism and Social Action in the Pentecostal Movement," *International Review of Mission* 75 (January 1986): 34–38. For love for Christ as motivation, see Dale Preiser, "The Cross—Focal Point of Missions," *Pentecostal Evangel,* 2 October 1983, p. 11.

[20]Thomas F. Zimmerman, "Absolute Certainty for a Time of Uncertainty," *Pentecostal Evangel,* 2 October 1983, pp. 3–6; see also Melvin L. Hodges, "Reaffirming the Mission of the Church," *Pentecostal Evangel,* 16 October 1983, p. 13. For tributes to the work of Thomas F. Zimmerman as general

superintendent, see "We Salute You, Brother Zimmerman!" *Advance,* December 1985, pp. 4–5; "Tribute to a Great Leader," *Pentecostal Evangel,* 29 December 1985, pp. 6–9. For information on the 1985 General Council, which elected G. Raymond Carlson as Zimmerman's successor, see Steve Maynard, "Zimmerman Steps Down as Head of Assemblies of God," *Houston Chronicle,* 17 August 1985, pp. 1, 3.

[21]David Godwin, "Evangelism: A Matter of Life and Death," *Mountain Movers,* March 1988, p. 11.

[22]For an account of Bonnke's ministry, see R. W. Bonnke, "Africa—God Did It Again," *World Pentecost,* vol. 9, no. 4 (1979,) pp. 12–13; also Burgess and McGee, *DPCM,* s.v. "Bonnke, Reinhard Willi Gottfried," by H. V. Synan, and "Church Growth," by C. P. Wagner.

[23]J. Philip Hogan, "Critical Issues," *Advance,* May 1987, p. 5. For a historical analysis of the decline in eschatological expectancy in the Assemblies of God, see Howard N. Kenyon, "An Analysis of Ethical Issues in the History of the Assemblies of God" (Ph.D. diss., Baylor University, 1988), pp. 401–403; cf., Edith L. Blumhofer, "Divided Pentecostals: Bakker vs. Swaggart," *Christian Century,* 6 May 1987, pp. 430–31.

[24]For example, see the editorial "Then . . . Shall the End Come," by Nick Henry, secretary of Foreign Missions publications, in *Mountain Movers,* August 1988, p. 3; Daniel E. Johnson, "Please Don't Tamper With the Blessed Hope," *Pentecostal Evangel,* 24 August 1980, pp. 4–5; G. Edward Nelson, " 'Closure' and Christ's Second Coming," *Mountain Movers,* August 1988, pp. 4–11; and Richard L. Dresselhaus, *What We Believe: A Series of 16 Messages on Our Statement of Fundamental Truths* (Springfield, Mo.: Spiritual Life–Evangelism Office, 1986), pp. 38–42, 50–54.

[25]David K. Irwin, "Intercessory Prayer," *Advance,* June 1985, p. 5.

[26]Jerry Sandidge, "How to Pray for Missionaries," *Mountain Movers,* January 1981, p. 5.

[27]John Thannickal, "The Holy Spirit in Today's Conflicts," *World Pentecost,* vol. 10, no. 2 (1980), pp. 9–11; William W. Menzies, "The Value of Being Baptised in the Holy Spirit," *World Pentecost,* vol. 8, no. 4 (1978), pp. 16–17; "Evangelizing Urban Masses: The Case for Pentecostal Power," *Mountain Movers,* August 1987, pp. 5–13; Donald Stamps, "Signs, Wonders, Miracles, and Deliverance," *Mountain Movers,* April 1988, pp. 10–11; Bob Hoskins, *The World's Greatest Need* (Miami: Life Publishers International, 1984).

[28]Jim Grams, "Poorly Kept Secrets: Reflections of a Former Missionary," *Agora* 2 (Winter 1979), p. 13.

[29]John M. Miller, review of *The Indigenous Church and the Missionary,* by Melvin L. Hodges, In *Missiology* 7 (April 1979): 269–70; Lloyd E. Kwast, review of *The Indigenous Church and the Missionary,* by Melvin L. Hodges, in *Evangelical Missions Quarterly* 15 (January 1979): 60–61. See also, Melvin L. Hodges, "Facing the World of the 1980s," *Pentecostal Evangel,* 12 August 1979, pp. 8–10.

³⁰For more information on Williams, see Burgess and McGee, *DPCM*, s.v. Williams, Morris Oliver," by G. B. McGee.

³¹Morris O. Williams, *Partnership in Mission: A Study of Theology and Method in Mission* (Springfield, Mo.: Assemblies of God Division of Foreign Missions, 1986), p. 161; see also his "Where the Philosophical Rubber Hits the Road of Reality," paper presented at the 1982 School of Missions, Springfield, Mo., 1982 (Mimeographed). For the perspectives of J. Philip Hogan on partnership, see J. Philip Hogan to "Dear Missionary Family," April 1983. For the perspective of the general superintendent of the Assemblies of God in Burkina Faso, West Africa, see Jean Pawentaore Ouedraogo, "Indigenous Church Principles at Work," *Mountain Movers*, January 1988, p. 4.

³²Williams, *Partnership*, pp. 266–272; see also Morris Williams, "Making the Indigenous Church Our Goal," *Mountain Movers*, February 1988, pp. 10–11; Morris Williams, "Partnership is Working," *Advance*, October 1978, pp. 24–25.

³³Morris Williams to Gary B. McGee, 11 September 1988.

³⁴Harold R. Carpenter, "A Universal Purpose," *Mountain Movers*, February 1986, p. 4.

³⁵"Why Missions?" *Mountain Movers* (January 1986), p. 6. The complete series of articles in *Mountain Movers* under the heading "The Biblical Basis of Missions," by Harold R. Carpenter, are the following: "Why Missions?" (January 1986), p. 6; "A Universal Purpose," (February 1986), p. 4; "A Patriarch's Family," (March 1986), p. 10; "A Harlot's House," (April 1986), p. 9; "An Unwilling Missionary," (May 1986), p. 10; "A Messianic Kingdom," (June 1986), p. 23; "A Mission Fulfilled," (July 1986), p. 10; "The Mission of the Church," (August 1986), p. 10; "The Church in Action," (September 1986), p. 10; "A Willing Missionary," (October 1986), p. 22; "A Theology of Missions," (November 1986), p. 10; "A Commitment to God," (October 1986), p. 31.

³⁶Ruth A. Breusch, "The Church and the Kingdom," *Mountain Movers*, July 1987, p. 9; see also Stanley M. Horton, *What the Bible Says About the Holy Spirit* (Springfield, Mo.: Gospel Publishing House, 1976), pp. 194–95.

³⁷"Thine is the Power," *Mountain Movers*, September 1987, p. 10. Her other articles are the following: "The Lord's Prayer," (March 1987), p. 10; "Thine is the Kingdom," (April 1987), p. 10; "Jesus and the Kingdom," (May 1987), p. 9; "Jesus and the Kingdom," (June 1987), p. 10; "The Church and the Kingdom," (July 1987), p. 9; "Servants of the Kingdom," (August 1987), pp. 14–15; "The Spirit and the Last Days," (October 1987), p. 9; "The Supreme Strategist," (November 1987), p. 9; "Thine is the Glory," (December 1987), p. 10.

³⁸Burgess and McGee, *DPCM*, s.v. "Kingdom of God," by P. Kuzmič.

³⁹Peter Kuzmič, "History and Eschatology: Evangelical Views," in *In Word and Deed: Evangelism and Social Responsibility*, ed. Bruce J. Ni-

cholls (Exeter, UK: Paternoster Press, 1985), pp. 135–164. In reference to Assemblies of God responses to ethical issues, see Kenyon, "An Analysis."

[40]For example, see Grady W. Manley, "Prepare the Way!" *Pentecostal Evangel,* 13 February 1983, pp. 20–21; G. Edward Nelson, "Let Jesus Reign," *Advance,* February 1981, pp. 22–23.

[41]Report of the Total Church Evangelism Strategy Committee to the General Presbytery of the Assemblies of God, 1987, p. 1. (Mimeographed.)

[42]"Statement of Basic Values," (Springfield, Mo.: Division of Foreign Missions), 16 March 1988, pp. 3–4.

[43]Wayne A. Detzler, review of *The Third Force in Missions,* by Paul A. Pomerville, in *Journal of the Evangelical Theological Society* 31 (June 1988): 230–31; Walter J. Hollenweger, unpublished review, 1988; Gary B. McGee, review of *The Third Force in Missions,* by Paul A. Pomerville, in *Paraclete* 22 (Spring 1988): 31–32.

[44]Paul Anthony Pomerville, "Pentecostalism and Missions: Distortion or Correction? The Pentecostal Contribution to Contemporary Mission Theology" (Ph.D. diss., Fuller Theological Seminary, 1982).

[45]Paul A. Pomerville, *The Third Force in Missions* (Peabody, Mass.: Hendrickson Publishers, 1985), p. 3.

[46]Ibid., pp. 47–52.

[47]Ibid., pp. 25–35, 74–78.

[48]Ibid., p. 79; for an explanation of post-Reformation scholasticism, see Robert Preus, *The Theology of Post-Reformation Lutheranism,* 2 vols. (St. Louis: Concordia Publishing House, 1970); Bengt Hagglund, *History of Theology* (St. Louis: Concordia Publishing House, 1968); and Jaroslav Pelikan, *From Luther to Kierkegaard* (St. Louis: Concordia Publishing House, 1950).

[49]Ibid., p. 149.

[50]For more information, see Burgess and McGee, *DPCM,* s.v. "European Pietist Roots of Pentecostalism," by D. D. Bundy.

[51]Pomerville's departure from the Assemblies of God in 1984 forfeited the opportunity for further influencing the development of missiological perspectives in the Division of Foreign Missions.

[52]"The CLSC Springfield Statement," (Springfield, Mo.: Christian Leadership Summit Conference), 5 December 1986, p. 2.

[53]Ibid., p. 2. Historical analysis, however, has not borne out the conclusion of the Christian Leadership Summit Conference that premillennialists have been in the forefront of social reformation; see Kenyon, "An Analysis;" Timothy P. Weber, *Living in the Shadow of the Second Coming: American Premillennialism, 1875–1925* (New York: Oxford University Press, 1979), pp. 93–104, 183–84; Dwight Wilson, *Armageddon Now! The Premillenarian Response to Russia and Israel Since 1917* (Grand Rapids: Baker Book House, 1977); Lidia Susana Vaccaro De Petrella, "The Tension Between Evangelism and Social Action in the Pentecostal Movement," *International Review of*

Mission 76 (January 1986): 34–38. For responses to liberation theology, see Ronald A. Iwasko, "Liberation Theology—Pathway to Liberty or Slavery," *Advance,* February 1985, pp. 9–11, and Gary B. McGee, "Which Way to Liberation?" *Pentecostal Evangel,* 9 November 1986, pp. 11–12.

[54]George O. Wood, *"Kingdom Now* and Missions," *Mountain Movers,* June 1988, pp. 10–11; cf., William A. Griffin, "Kingdom Now: New Hope or New Heresy?" paper presented at the 17th meeting of the Society for Pentecostal Studies, Virginia Beach, Virginia, 14 November 1987.

[55]Hugh P. Jeter, *The Local Church and World Evangelization* (Hereford, Ariz.: by the author, 1984).

[56]David E. Godwin, *Church Planting Methods* (DeSoto, Tex.: Lifeshare Communications, 1984).

[57]Delmer R. and Eleanor R. Guynes, *The Gospel of the Ascension* (Kuala Lumpur, Malaysia: Calvary Church Press, 1986).

[58]Everett A. Wilson, "Sanguine Saints: Pentecostalism in El Salvador," *Church History* 52 (1983): 186–198.

[59]Benjamin Prasad Shinde, "Animism in Popular Hinduism; Survey of the Literature and a Viewpoint" (D.Miss. diss., Fuller Theological Seminary, 1975); Chelliah Zechariah, "Missiological Strategy for the Assemblies of God in Tamil Nadu" (D.Miss. diss., Fuller Theological Seminary, 1981).

[60]Koichi Kitano, "Spontaneous Ecumenicity Between Catholics and Protestants in the Charismatic Movement: A Case Study" (Ph.D. diss., Centro Escolar University, 1981); Ronald A. Iwasko, "An Integrated Program for Training First-Term Missionaries of the Assemblies of God" (D.Miss. diss., Trinity Evangelical Divinity School, 1984); Delbert H. Tarr, Jr., "Indirection and Ambiguity As A Mode of Communication in West Africa: A Descriptive Study" (Ph.D. diss., University of Minnesota, 1979); Dwayne E. Turner, "Toward Identifying and Developing Essential Teaching Competencies for Faculty Members of Assemblies of God Bible Institutes in the Philippines" (D.Min. diss., Denver Conservative Baptist Seminary, 1988); and Harold R. Carpenter, "An Introduction to Assemblies of God Missions for Use at Central Bible College" (D.Miss. diss., Trinity Evangelical Divinity School, 1988).

[61]George M. Flattery, *Current Frontiers in Theological Education: A Missions Strategy* (n.p.: by the author, 1986).

[62]Derek Lionel Eaton, "Bibles for Berbers: Communicating the Good News to the Berber Minorities of North Africa," Assemblies of God Graduate School, unpublished ms., 1978; Beth Grant, "Ethnomusicology: A Study of the Music in the South India Assemblies of God Churches" (M.A. thesis, Assemblies of God Graduate School, 1979).

[63]"Graduate School Establishes Perkin Chair of World Missions," *Pentecostal Evangel,* 17 August 1980, p. 12. Hodges retired in 1985 due to poor health and received the title of professor emeritus in the following year; for further information, see "Melvin Hodges Named Professor Emeritus of A/G Seminary," *Pentecostal Evangel,* 24 August 1986, p. 28.

[64]J. Philip Hogan to Thomas F. Zimmerman, 14 February 1983; for a historical perspective on the relationship between the Division of Foreign Missions and the Assemblies of God Graduate School, see J. Philip Hogan to "Dear Fellow Missionary," May 1978.

[65]"A Self-Study Report Submitted to the North Central Association of Colleges and Secondary Schools, Chicago, Illinois," (Springfield, Mo.: Assemblies of God Graduate School, 1982), p. x, and addendum.

[66]"Official Division of Foreign Missions Position Statement Concerning the Assemblies of God Graduate School (AGGS)," February 1982; cf., Del Tarr to Dr. Gary McGee, 21 December 1988.

[67]J. Philip Hogan to "Dear Missionary Family," November 1986.

[68]For the "steps to the mission field" prior to the development of Pre-Field Orientation, see Ronald Iwasko, "Becoming a Missionary," *Mountain Movers,* April 1980, pp. 8–10; see also his "How to Grow A Missionary," *Advance,* April 1986, pp. 10–11.

[69]Ronald A. Iwasko, "A Plan to 'Grow' Our Own Missionaries," *Mountain Movers,* August 1983, pp. 9–11.

[70]G. Edward Nelson, "The Unreached—Who, Where, and Why?" *Advance,* December 1986, p. 8.

[71]Ralph D. Winter, "The Highest Priority: Cross-Cultural Evangelism," in *Let the Earth Hear His Voice.* Official Reference Volume: Papers and Responses, ed. J. D. Douglas (Minneapolis: World Wide Publications, 1975), pp. 213–241. J. Philip Hogan gave one of the responses to Winter's paper, see Philip Hogan, "Response to Dr. Ralph Winter's Paper," pp. 242–245 in the same volume. There appears to have been no fundamental difference in the opinions of Winter and Hogan on the role of the Holy Spirit in cross-cultural evangelization.

[72]Beverly Graham, "The Unfinished Task," *Mountain Movers,* January 1983, p. 3.

[73]David Leatherberry, "Crossing New Frontiers," *Mountain Movers,* January 1980, pp. 8–9; "The World in Missionary Perspective," *Mountain Movers,* January 1983, pp. 8–9; Gerald L. Falley, "Unreached Peoples," *Advance,* February 1988, pp. 14–15; see also Foreign Missions Board Minutes, October 9–10, 1979.

[74]George M. Flattery, "The Other Half of the World—The Illiterate," *Mountain Movers,* June 1987, pp. 12–13.

[75]David K. Irwin, "The Center for Ministry to Muslims," *Advance,* February 1983, p. 10; see also "David Irwin Named Coordinator of Ministry to Muslims," *Pentecostal Evangel,* 25 July 1982, p. 29.

[76]David K. Irwin, "Islam Is An Unplanted Field," *Mountain Movers,* December 1984, pp. 5–6, 10.

[77]"David Kent Irwin—With Christ," *Pentecostal Evangel,* 26 August 1984, p. 5.

[78]"Jumaa" is Arabic for Friday, the Muslim day of prayer. Members of

the Jumaa Prayer Fellowship (presently numbering 23,000) agree to pray for Muslims on Friday, fasting the noon meal.

[79]"Born Out of Miracles," *Mountain Movers,* July 1987, p. 12.

[80]"Testimonies," (n.d.) Files at Center for Education, Malaga, Spain. (Mimeographed.)

[81]Interview with Sobhi W. Malek, missionary to the Middle East/North Africa, 20 October 1987, Malaga, Spain; for further information, see Sobhi Malek, "Changing the Wrapping on the Gift," *Mountain Movers,* January 1980, pp. 5–6; Sobhi Malek, "Jesus, If You Are the Son of God, Reveal Yourself to Me," *Pentecostal Evangel,* 10 February 1985, p. 11; "Muslim Ministries: Bridging the Gap," *Pentecostal Evangel,* 10 February 1985, p. 10.

[82]For example, see "In Memory of Daniel," *Mountain Movers,* September 1984, p. 3.

[83]Delmar Kingsriter, "Muslims Are People," *Mountain Movers,* May 1987, p. 4.

Chapter 13: The Undiminished Priority

[1]For qualifications, see Melvin L. Hodges, "Is Our Standard Too High?" *Pentecostal Evangel,* 20 March 1983, pp. 16–17; Ronald A. Iwasko, "The Making of a Missionary," *Mountain Movers,* August 1983, pp. 8, 11. On the categories of foreign missionaries see *The Missions Manual* (Springfield, Mo.: Division of Foreign Missions, 1987), pp. 2-1–2-35.

[2]"Our Mission for the 90s," (interview with G. Raymond Carlson) *Decade of Harvest Quarterly,* 1 January 1989, p. 4.

[3]"A Third Generation of Missionaries," *Pentecostal Evangel,* 17 October 1982, p. 21; see also J. Philip Hogan, "A Costly Operation," *Pentecostal Evangel,* 24 September 1972, p. 17.

[4]Don Corbin, "Building Power!" *Mountain Movers,* April 1979, p. 9.

[5]Statistics from the office of the secretary of foreign missions relations, U.S., Assemblies of God Division of Foreign Missions, Springfield, Mo. For understanding the methodology used by the Division of Foreign Missions in calculating statistics, see "Key to Statistics," *Mountain Movers,* December 1986, p. 5.

[6]G. Raymond Carlson, "A Call to Prayer," *Advance,* January 1989, p. 4.

[7]For information on Good News Crusades, see "Currents and Challenges," *Mountain Movers,* March 1986, p. 23; Donald Exley, "Good News Crusades Work," *Pentecostal Evangel,* 22 March 1987, p. 16; Beverly Graham, "Good News Crusades Are GOOD NEWS!" *Mountain Movers,* March 1983, pp. 4–7.

[8]Ben Tipton, "Binding the Strong Man," *Mountain Movers,* April 1988, p. 29.

[9]Loren Triplett, "We're Ganging Up on the Devil," *Mountain Movers,* December 1986, p. 21.

[10]Norbert Schenhals, "New Hope for Argentina's Drug Crisis," *Pentecostal Evangel,* 25 January 1987, pp. 20–21; Tyrone and Cina Silva, "Campus Fellowship Reaches Out With Agape," *Pentecostal Evangel,* 24 February 1985, p. 18; Donald Tucker, "We're Reaching the Nomads," *Mountain Movers,* February 1984, pp. 4, 14–15; Morris Plotts, "Born Free," *Mountain Movers,* February 1979, pp. 3, 5–6.

[11]Janet Hedman, "This Is the Paraguay Task Force," *Mountain Movers,* October 1983, p. 5.

[12]Ibid., p. 6.

[13]"Quito Task Force 1985–86," Springfield, Mo.: Division of Foreign Missions, n.d.

[14]"STAR Communications Dedicates Facilities," *Mountain Movers,* May 1988, p. 8.

[15]Margaret Register, "Listen, World, Jesus Loves You!" *Mountain Movers,* June 1979, p. 8.

[16]William David Lee, [Biographical Sketch], 23 February 1988, p. 2. (Typewritten.) See also, "David Lee Directs Media Ministries," *Pentecostal Evangel,* 26 December 1982, p. 29.

[17]G. Edward Nelson, "Behind IMM," *Mountain Movers,* February 1983, p. 4.

[18]David Lee, "IMM Reaches Our World Through the Electronic Media," *Advance,* December 1983, p. 10; see also David Lee, "IMM: Electronic Evangelism," *Mountain Movers,* October 1985, pp. 4–7.

[19]"International Ministries: Sending Our World the Message of Christ," *Mountain Movers,* December 1988, pp. 20–21; Normal L. Correll, "The Bible School of the World," *Mountain Movers,* July 1987, pp. 5–7. For 1987 ICI statistics, see Gene Schachterle, Director of Network Services (ICI) to Rosalee McMain, Promotions Office Coordinator (DFM), 28 November 1987.

[20]For more information on some of the programs listed, see *All About Missions: A Guide to Foreign Missions Programs* (Springfield, Mo.: Division of Foreign Missions, 1987); see also G. Edward Nelson, "What is 'ORE'?" *Advance,* June 1981, p. 11.

[21]"CLASP Helps Latin American Missionaries," *Council Today,* 8 August 1987, p. 20.

[22]Assemblies of God Division of Foreign Missions, *1988 Annual Report,* p. 24.

[23]G. Edward Nelson, "No Better Partners Exist," *Advance,* October 1978, p. 9.

[24]J. Philip Hogan, "Open the Word for the World," *Advance,* December

1980, p. 6; J. Philip Hogan, "The Tide is In," *Advance,* November 1982, p. 6.

[25]"Background to the Agreement Between Wycliffe Bible Translators and the Assemblies of God," (n.d.), Editorial Office Files, Division of Foreign Missions. (Typewritten.)

[26]"Wycliffe and the Assemblies of God," *Pentecostal Evangel,* 25 December 1988, p. 11.

[27]"Missions For The Entire Family," (promotional brochure) (Springfield, Mo.: Division of Church Ministries, 1986).

[28]Sandra Goodwin Clopine, "Women's Ministries: Making It Happen," *Mountain Movers,* June 1988, p. 27; for biographical information on Clopine, see Assemblies of God Office of Information Media Release/ '88; also, "Additional Biographical Resource for Your Information," n.d.

[29]"1987 Speed-the-Light Statistics," Springfield, Mo.: National Youth Department, 1988.

[30]The Lisbon Assembly of God to Reverend Samuel Johnson, Missionary to Spain, 24 May 1972; see also The Lisbon Assembly of God to Reverend Samuel Johnson, 24 May 1972; "The Assemblies of God in Portugal: Reaching Out," *Pentecostal Evangel,* 28 July 1985, pp. 16–19.

[31]John Treherne, "ICI Finds an Open Door in Cameroon," *Pentecostal Evangel,* 24 June 1984, pp. 19–20; David Njemo, "Help Us Reach Our Country," *Pentecostal Evangel,* 24 June 1984, p. 19.

[32]Karen Braithwaite, "In Brazil It's BEST," *Mountain Movers,* November 1979, p. 10.

[33]"BEST Graduates 1,000 Christian Workers," *Advance,* September 1985, p. 30.

[34]"Questions and Answers About the Graduate Program in Costa Rica," (n.d.) (Mimeographed.); for general information about the Southern California College Graduate School, see *Southern California College Graduate Program, 1988–1990* (Costa Mesa, Calif.: Southern California College, 1988).

[35]"The Bryan S. Smith Institute for World Missions Leadership Funded by a Grant from Margaret S. Smith," (n.d.) Office of Graduate Studies, Southern California College. (Mimeographed.)

[36]Don Meyer, vice-president for academic affairs, to Dr. Gary McGee, 11 August 1988.

[37]For more information on the World Relief Commission, see Bruce L. Shelley, *Evangelicalism in America* (Grand Rapids: William B. Eerdmans Publishing Co., 1967), pp. 104–108.

[38]Thomas F. Zimmerman, "Our People Are Dying in Biafra," *Pentecostal Evangel,* 18 August 1968), p. 17; see also "RELIEF for a Starving People," *Key,* 4th Quarter, 1968, pp. 6–7.

[39]Dale Preiser, "Reflections From the Field," *Mountain Movers,* February 1987, p. 4.

[40]Dale Fagerland, "Sharing Christ Through Food," *Mountain Movers,* November 1985, p. 13.

[41]"Lillian Trasher Orphanage Begins 75th Year," *Mountain Movers,* February 1985, pp. 3–5; for a valuable review of medical programs in Assemblies of God missions, see "Report of DFM Medical Missionary Program Study Committee," 11 May 1983, Appendix A.

[42]Mark Buntain, "Give Them One Chance!" *Pentecostal Evangel,* 22 May 1983, p. 6.

[43]Paul Hutsell, "Help Us Love the Children," *Mountain Movers,* November 1981, p. 4.

[44]G. Edward Nelson, "Putting Christianity Into Action!" *Advance,* December 1985, pp. 13–14.

[45]"Latin America and the West Indies," *Mountain Movers,* December 1988, p. 17.

[46]John Bueno, "Now We Want to Sponsor A Child," *Mountain Movers,* January 1985, pp. 6–9.

[47]Jere Melilli with Wesley Hurst, "A Doctor Looks At Missions," *Pentecostal Evangel,* 27 August 1961, p. 20.

[48]J. Philip Hogan, "Men Behind the Lines," *Pentecostal Evangel,* 20 September 1970, p. 17; see also Perkin and Garlock, *Our World Witness,* pp. 29, 55–56; David A. Womack, "Pentecostal Impact on World Missions," *World Pentecost,* no. 3 (1974), pp. 4–6; David A. Womack, "In These Crucial Days," *World Pentecost,* no. 2 (1976), pp. 24–25.

[49]For example, see Arthur Chestnut, "In the Midst of Tragedy, We Are Helping Build His Kingdom," *Pentecostal Evangel,* 11 November 1983, p. 8.

[50]"Report of DFM Medical Missionary Program," p. 2.

[51]Ibid., pp. 3–4.

[52]Foreign Missions Board, "Medical Missions Program Dialogue," November 1983, pp. 3–4.

[53]"International Ministries: Sending Our World the Message of Christ," *Mountain Movers,* December 1988, p. 21; for more information on HealthCare Ministries, see *Caring Across Cultures—Medical Missions* (Springfield, Mo.: Division of Foreign Missions, n.d.); *HealthCare Ministries* (Springfield, Mo.: Division of Foreign Missions, n.d.).

[54]G. Edward Nelson, "Drop-ins and Con Artists on the Mission Field," (Springfield, Mo.: Division of Foreign Missions, n.d.).

[55]For more information on Jim Bakker, see Burgess and McGee, *DPCM,* s.v., "Bakker, James Orsen ('Jim'), and Tammy Faye (La Valley)," by S. M. Burgess.

[56]Charles E. Shepard, "Bakker Misled PTL Viewers, FCC Records Show," *The Charlotte Observer,* 26 January 1986, pp. 1A, 9A; "Promises Prompted

Years of Controversy, Investigation," *The Charlotte Observer,* 26 January 1986, p. 11a.

[57]Bruce Mumm, "PTL Club Thailand," *Mountain Movers,* February 1983, pp. 8–9.

[58]For more information on Jimmy Swaggart, see Burgess and McGee, *DPCM,* s.v., "Swaggart, Jimmy Lee," by B. M. Stout; Jimmy Swaggart with Robert Paul Lamb, *To Cross A River* (Baton Rouge, La.: Jimmy Swaggart Ministries, 1977). For his confession, see Elizabeth Leland, "Swaggart Confesses, Steps Down," *The Charlotte Observer,* 22 February 1988, pp. 1A, 4A.

[59]For an excellent analysis, see Edith L. Blumhofer, "Divided Pentecostals: Bakker vs. Swaggart," *Christian Century,* 6 May 1987, pp. 430–431.

[60]Interview with Jimmy Swaggart, president of Jimmy Swaggart Ministries, Tegucigalpa, Honduras, 17 January 1988; interview with James B. Woolsey, International Ministries director of Jimmy Swaggart Ministries, Tegucigalpa, Honduras, 16 January 1988; Mike Schilling, "Swaggart Provides Millions to AG," *The News-Leader,* 21 February 1988, pp. 1A, 5A.

[61]Jimmy Swaggart, "World Evangelism?" *The Evangelist,* September 1987, p. 6.

[62]Interview with Woolsey.

[63]Peter Applebome, "Scandal Triggers Interest in Critic Swaggart's Own Finances," *The Charlotte Observer,* 28 February 1988, p. 21A; "What Profits a Preacher?" *Newsweek,* 4 May 1987, p. 68.

[64]J. Philip Hogan to Dear Fellow Missionaries, May 1988; see also "Statement of Foreign Missions Committee," 25 February 1988, Editorial Office Files, Division of Foreign Missions.

Chapter 14: Preparing for the Decade of Harvest

[1]For the announcement of Hogan's retirement, see J. Philip Hogan to "Dear Missionary Family," February 1989.

[2]"Charles Greenaway Retires; Jerry Parsley Named Eurasia Field Director," *Pentecostal Evangel,* 11 December 1983, p. 20.

[3]"A Tribute to Morris Williams," *Mountain Movers,* December 1985, pp. 12–13.

[4]"Africa Field Director Morris Williams Retiring; Missionary Donald Corbin to Succeed Williams," *Pentecostal Evangel,* 27 October 1985, p. 29; see also "Don Corbin 1988 Alumnus of the Year," *Central Bible College Bulletin* (June 1988), pp. 1, 6.

[5]"He Dared to Dream," *Mountain Movers,* April 1987, pp. 6–7; J. Philip Hogan to "Dear Fellow Missionaries," February 1987.

[6]"Hogan Announces New Far East Field Director," *Mountain Movers,* September 1987, pp. 8–9.

[7]"N. L. Correll Named Administrative Assistant," *Pentecostal Evangel,* 27 June 1982, p. 28; see also J. Philip Hogan to "Dear Fellow Missionary," April 1982.

[8]J. Philip Hogan to "Dear Fellow Missionary," March 1978.

[9]"G. Edward Nelson Joins Foreign Missions Staff," *Pentecostal Evangel,* 26 November 1978, p. 29; see also J. Philip Hogan to "Dear Fellow Missionary," July 1978.

[10]"Interim Head of Foreign Missions Promotions Named," *Mountain Movers,* June 1988, p. 8.

[11]Joyce Wells Booze, "A Time for Change," *Good News Crusades,* November–December 1978, p. 15; Division of Foreign Missions, "How to Use *Mountain Movers* in Your Church," (n.d.).

[12]General Council Minutes, 1981, pp. 79–87.

[13]General Council Minutes, 1983, p. 79.

[14]Ibid., p. 81; see also "All About Missions: A Guide to Foreign Missions Programs," (Springfield, Mo.: Division of Foreign Missions, n.d.), pp. 24, 31.

[15]General Council Minutes, 1985, pp. 17–21, 22; see also [Jimmy Swaggart] "An Open Letter to the Assemblies of God," *The Evangelist,* July 1985, p. 56.

[16]For a recent example, see Marilyn Ford, "The Red-Faced Mzungu," *Mountain Movers,* September 1985, pp. 4–7.

[17]Russell P. Spittler, "Implicit Values in Pentecostal Missions," *Missiology* 16 (October 1988): 415.

[18]Burgess and McGee, *DPCM,* s.v., "Third Wave," by C. P. Wagner.

[19]Richard Nicholson, "Argentina's Pentecostal Outpouring," *Pentecostal Evangel,* 16 February 1986, pp. 10–11.

[20]Ibid., p. 11.

[21]Ibid.; see also Gary Royer, "Flesh of a New Color," *Mountain Movers,* April 1988, pp. 4–5; Daniel G. Grasso, "A New Awakening," *Pentecostal Evangel,* 25 January 1987, pp. 16–17.

[22]For a survey of recent activities in Latin America and the West Indies, see Loren Triplett, "Latin America: Revival in the Midst of Despair," *Pentecostal Evangel,* 9 November 1986, pp. 8–10. Reports on the Assemblies of God in Brazil, Nicaragua, and Cuba, are reported in "The Brazilian Revival" (interview of Evangelist Bernhard Johnson by Reginald Klimionok), *World Pentecost,* vol. 11, no. 2 (1981), pp. 18–21; Loren Triplett, "A Victory and A Fresh Burden," *Pentecostal Evangel,* 25 October 1987, pp. 16–17; Floyd Woodworth, "Whatever Happened to the Nicaraguan Church?" *Pentecostal Evangel,* 25 October 1987, pp. 18–19; Loren Triplett, "The Cuban Assemblies: A Church Triumphant," *Pentecostal Evangel,* 28 June 1987, pp. 16–17. On the development of the work in Cuba before the

revolution, see Louise Jeter Walker, "Memories of Cuba: Revival & Revolution," *Pentecostal Evangel,* 28 June 1987, pp. 18–19.

[23]Harold Schmitt, "The Munich Story," *Pentecostal Evangel,* 29 May 1977, p. 15; see also Peter Johnson, "Munich—A Spiritual Battleground," *Pentecostal Evangel,* 31 August 1986, pp. 16–17, 19.

[24]Peter K. Johnson, "Catholics Part of Charismatic Renewal in West Germany," *New Covenant,* June 1987, pp. 26, 28; "Charismatic Center Dedicated in Munich," *Mountain Movers,* May 1988, p. 9.

[25]Billy Burr, "This Is the Way We Build A School . . . in Angola," *Pentecostal Evangel,* 30 December 1984, p. 19.

[26]J. Philip Hogan, "The Church in China," *Mountain Movers,* September 1987, pp. 12–13.

[27]"Foreign Missions Delegation Visits Vietnam," *Mountain Movers,* March 1988, pp. 8–9; Robert W. Houlihan, "Ministry Opportunities in Laos," Report to the Foreign Missions Board, October 1988.

[28]Spittler, "Implicit Values," pp. 410–411. For a discussion of the meaning of "Third World," see Lawrence E. Keyes, *The Last Age of Missions* (Pasadena, Calif.: Wm. Carey Library, 1983), pp. 9–16. See also Burgess and McGee, *DPCM,* s.v., "Statistics, Global" by D. B. Barrett.

[29]Paul Pierson, "Non-Western Missions: The Great New Fact of Our Time," in *New Frontiers in Mission,* ed. Patrick Sookhdeo (Grand Rapids: Baker Book House, 1987), p. 10; see also J. Herbert Kane, " 'The White Man's Burden' Is Changing Colors," *Christianity Today,* 17 July 1981, pp. 62–64.

[30]Ibid., pp. 10–13.

[31]Keyes, *The Last Age,* pp. 109–121.

[32]J. Philip Hogan, " 'Foreign' Missions," *Pentecostal Evangel,* 9 February 1969, p. 11.

[33]J. Philip Hogan, "A Cause for Optimism," *Pentecostal Evangel,* 20 July 1969, p. 17.

[34]J. Philip Hogan, "The Designer of History," *Pentecostal Evangel,* 28 October 1973, p. 17.

[35]Rocky Grams, "Learning to Lead," *Pentecostal Evangel,* 25 January 1987, p. 19; Don Corbin, "Churches on Mission Fields Sending Out Missionaries," *Pentecostal Evangel,* 3 October 1982, pp. 10–11.

[36]Don Corbin, "We've Grown to the Point Where We Can Grow," *Mountain Movers,* December 1986, pp. 8–9.

[37]Beverly Graham, "A 'New' Breed of Missionaries," *Mountain Movers,* September 1986, pp. 12–13, 22.

[38]Thomas Wang, "By the Year 2000," *Mission Frontiers,* May 1987, pp. 3–5.

[39]"Executive Presbyters Declare 'Decade of Harvest,' " *Pentecostal Evangel,* 7 February 1988, p. 12; "Declaration of a Decade of Harvest,"

Sunday School Counselor, June 1988, p. 16; see also "Our Strategy for the 1990s," (Springfield, Mo.: U. S. Decade of Harvest, 1988).

[40]"Hogan Announces Plans for Major Overseas Evangelism and Church-Planting Thrusts for the 90s," *Mountain Movers,* January 1988, p. 8; J. Philip Hogan, "Evangelizing the World by A. D. 2000," *Advance,* July 1988, p. 10.

[41]"Delegates from 40 Nations Gather to Pray, Plan Strategies at Decade of Harvest Conference," *Pentecostal Evangel,* 4 September 1988, p. 13; "Delegates Meet for *Decade of Harvest* Conference," *Mountain Movers,* October 1988, p. 8.

[42]Ibid.

[43]Division of Foreign Missions press release, July 1988.

[44]For a less cautious statement, see G. Edward Nelson, " 'Closure' and Christ's Second Coming," *Mountain Movers,* August 1988, pp. 4–11.

Selected Bibliography

Manuscript Collections

Springfield, Mo.: The Assemblies of God Archives
Springfield, Mo.: The Assemblies of God Collection, Central Bible College
    Library
Springfield, Mo.: Editorial Office Files, Assemblies of God Division of
    Foreign Missions
Springfield, Mo.: The General Secretary's Office Files

Periodicals

Advance
Agama News and Notes
Agora
Assemblies of God Heritage
Christian Century
Christianity Today
The Council Today
Evangelical Missions Quarterly
The Evangelist
Global Conquest
Good News Crusades
Happenings
ICI Datelines
Intercede
International Bulletin of Missionary Research
International Media Ministries Report
International Review of Mission
Key
MAPS News
Missiology
Missionary Challenge
Mission Frontiers
Missionary Forum

Mountain Movers
Occasional Bulletin of Missionary Research
Onward
Paraclete
Pentecostal Evangel
Pneuma
Rapport
World Pentecost

Published Works

Assemblies of God Division of Foreign Missions. *The Missions Manual.* Springfield, Mo.: Division of Foreign Missions, 1987.

Barrett, David B. *World Christian Encyclopedia.* Oxford: Oxford University Press, 1982.

Basic Plan, The. Miami: Program of Advanced Christian Education, Assemblies of God, 1973.

Bassham, Rodger C. *Mission Theology: 1948–1975 Years of Worldwide Creative Tension Ecumenical, Evangelical, and Roman Catholic.* Pasadena, Calif.: William Carey Library, 1979.

Beaver, R. Pierce, ed. *American Missions in Bicentennial Perspective.* South Pasadena, Calif.: William Carey Library, 1977.

Blumhofer, Edith Waldvogel. *The Assemblies of God: A Popular History.* Springfield, Mo.: Gospel Publishing House, 1985.

Booze, Joyce Wells. *Into All the World: A History of Assemblies of God Foreign Missions.* Springfield, Mo.: Division of Foreign Missions, 1980.

Bosch, David J. *Witness to the World: The Christian Mission in Theological Perspective.* Atlanta: John Knox Press, 1980.

Boyd, Frank M. *The Holy Spirit Works Today.* Springfield, Mo.: Gospel Publishing House, 1970.

Brumback, Carl. *What Meaneth This?* Springfield, Mo.: Gospel Publishing House, 1947.

Burgess, Stanley M., and McGee, Gary B., eds.; Alexander, Patrick H., assoc. ed. *Dictionary of Pentecostal and Charismatic Movements.* Grand Rapids: Zondervan Publishing House, 1988.

Cairns, Earle E. *An Endless Line of Splendor: Revivals and Their Leaders from the Great Awakening to the Present.* Wheaton, Ill.: Tyndale House Publishers, Inc., 1986.

Carpenter, Harold R. *Mandate and Mission: The Theory and Practice of Assemblies of God Missions.* Springfield, Mo.: CBC Press, 1988.

Champion, Richard G.; Caldwell, Edward S.; Leggett, Gary; eds. *Our Mission In Today's World: Council on Evangelism Official Papers and Reports.* Springfield, Mo.: Gospel Publishing House, 1968.

Cho, Paul Y., with Manzano, Whitney R. *More Than Numbers.* Waco: Word Books, 1984.

Cunningham, Loren, with Rogers, Janice. *Is That Really You, God?* Grand Rapids: Chosen Books, 1984.

Dake, Finis Jennings, ed. *Dake's Annotated Reference Bible.* Atlanta: Dake Bible Sales, Inc., 1963.

Damboriena, S. J., Prudencio. *Tongues As of Fire: Pentecostalism in Contemporary Christianity.* Washington, D.C.: Corpus Books, 1969.

Declare His Glory: Speed-the-Light—40th Anniversary. Springfield, Mo.: Youth Department of the Assemblies of God, 1983.

De Leon, Jr., Victor. *The Silent Pentecostals: A Biographical History of the Pentecostal Movement Among the Hispanics in the Twentieth Century.* By the Author, 1979.

Douglas, J. D., ed. *Let the Earth Hear His Voice. Official Reference Volume: Papers and Responses.* Minneapolis: World Wide Publications, 1975.

Dresselhaus, Richard L. *What We Believe: A Series of 16 Messages on Our Statement of Fundamental Truths.* Springfield, Mo.: Spiritual Life–Evangelism Office, 1986.

Du Plessis, David J. *The Spirit Bade Me Go.* rev. ed. Plainfield, N.J.: Logos International, 1970.

Flattery, George M. *Current Frontiers in Theological Education: A Missions Strategy.* By the Author, 1986.

Gee, Donald. *Trophimus I Left Sick.* London: Elim Publishing Co., 1952.

Glasser, Arthur F., and McGavran, Donald A. *Contemporary Theologies of Mission.* Grand Rapids: Baker Book House, 1983.

Godwin, David E. *Church Planting Methods.* DeSoto, Tex.: Lifeshare Communications, 1984.

Guynes, Delmer R., and Guynes, Eleanor R. *The Gospel of the Ascension.* Kuala Lumpur, Malaysia: Calvary Church Press, 1986.

Hall, John G. *Dispensations.* 2nd Ed. Springfield, Mo.: Inland Printing Co., 1957.

Harrell, David Edwin. *All Things Are Possible: The Healing and Charismatic Revivals in Modern America.* Bloomington, Ind.: Indiana University Press, 1975.

Hembree, Ron. *Mark.* Plainsfield, N.J.: Logos International, 1979.

Henry, Carl F. H., and Mooneyham, W. Stanley, eds. *One Race, One Gospel, One Task.* Minneapolis: World Wide Publications, 1967.

Hesselgrave, David J. *Today's Choices for Tomorrow's Mission: An Evangelical Perspective on Trends and Issues in Missions.* Grand Rapids: Zondervan Publishing House, 1988.

_____, ed. *Theology and Mission: Papers Given at Trinity Consultation No. 1.* Grand Rapids: Baker Book House, 1978.

Hodges, Melvin L. *Grow Toward Leadership.* Chicago: Moody Press, 1960.

_____. *The Indigenous Church.* Springfield, Mo.: Gospel Publishing House, 1953.

_____. *A Theology of the Church and Its Mission.* Springfield, Mo.: Gospel Publishing House, 1977.

Hoover, Elva J., ed. *The WM Leader: Handbook of Leadership Training for Women's Ministries Leaders.* Springfield, Mo.: The Women's Ministries Department of the Assemblies of God, 1980.

Horton, Stanley M. *The Promise of His Coming.* Springfield, Mo.: Gospel Publishing House, 1967.

————. *What the Bible Says About the Holy Spirit.* Springfield, Mo.: Gospel Publishing House, 1976.

Hoskins, Bob. *The World's Greatest Need.* Miami: Life Publishers International, 1984.

Hunt, Dave, and McMahon, T. A. *The Seduction of Christianity.* Eugene, Ore.: Harvest House Publishers, 1985.

Hurst, Duane V. *Ye Shall Be Witnesses.* Springfield, Mo.: Gospel Publishing House, 1962.

Hurst, D. V., and Jones, T. J. *The Church Begins.* Springfield, Mo.: Gospel Publishing House, 1959.

Hutchison, William R. *Errand to the World: American Protestant Thought and Foreign Missions.* Chicago: University of Chicago Press, 1987.

Jansen, Harris; Hoover, Elva; Leggett, Gary, eds. *Live In The Spirit: A Compendium of Themes on the Spiritual Life as Presented at the Council on Spiritual Life.* Springfield, Mo.: Gospel Publishing House, 1972.

Jeter, Hugh P. *The Local Church and World Evangelization.* Hereford, Ariz.: By the Author, 1984.

Kane, J. Herbert. *Wanted: World Christians.* Grand Rapids: Baker Book House, 1986.

Ketcham, Maynard L. *Tigers That Talk.* Charlotte, N.C.: PTL Television Network, 1979.

Keyes, Lawrence E. *The Last Age of Missions.* Pasadena: Wm. Carey Library, 1983.

Koop, Allen V. *American Evangelical Missionaries in France, 1945–1975.* Lanham, Md.: University Press of America, 1986.

Like A River (50th Anniversary Commemorative Book). Springfield, Mo.: Assemblies of God, 1964.

Lindsell, Harold, ed. *The Church's Worldwide Mission.* Waco: Word Books, 1966.

Malz, Carl. *Foreign Bible School Survey Report: A Report of the Bible School Program of the Foreign Missions Department of the Assemblies of God.* Springfield, Mo.: The Assemblies of God, 1959.

McGavran, Donald Anderson. *How Churches Grow.* New York: Friendship Press, 1959.

————, ed. *Church Growth and Christian Mission.* New York: Harper and Row, 1965.

McGavran, Donald; Huegel, John; and Taylor, Jack. *Church Growth in Mexico.* Grand Rapids: William B. Eerdmans Publishing Co., 1963.

Menzies, William W. *Anointed to Serve: The Story of the Assemblies of God.* Springfield, Mo.: Gospel Publishing House, 1971.

Nicholls, Bruce J., ed. *In Word and Deed: Evangelism and Social Responsibility.* Exeter, UK: Paternoster Press, 1985.

Perkin, Noel, and Garlock, John. *Our World Mission: A Survey of Assemblies of God Foreign Missions.* Springfield, Mo.: Gospel Publishing House, 1963.

Plotts, Morris. *Bwana Tembo: A Prince With God.* Baton Rouge, La.: Jimmy Swaggart Evangelistic Association, 1980.

Pomerville, Paul A. *The Third Force in Missions.* Peabody, Mass.: Hendrickson Publishers, 1985.

Rudnick, Milton T. *Speaking the Gospel Through the Ages: A History of Evangelism.* St. Louis: Concordia Publishing House, 1984.

Sanders, Thomas F., and Leggett, Gary L., eds. *Adult Teacher: 2* (September 1972–August 1973). Springfield, Mo.: Gospel Publishing House, 1972.

Schaeffer, Sue. *Africa Is Waiting.* Grand Rapids: Baker Book House, 1970.

Shelley, Bruce L. *Evangelicalism in America.* Grand Rapids: William B. Eerdmans Publishing Co., 1967.

Smedes, Lewis B., ed. *Ministry and the Miraculous.* Pasadena: Fuller Theological Seminary, 1987.

Smith, Jr., W. Douglas. *Toward Continuous Mission: Strategizing for the Evangelization of Bolivia.* South Pasadena, Calif.: William Carey Library, 1978.

Sookhdeo, Patrick, ed. *New Frontiers in Mission.* Grand Rapids: Baker Book House, 1987.

Swaggart, Jimmy, with Lamb, Robert Paul. *To Cross a River.* Baton Rouge, La.: Jimmy Swaggart Ministries, 1977.

Synan, Vinson. *The Twentieth-Century Pentecostal Explosion.* Altamonte Springs, Fl.: Creation House, 1987.

Tucker, Angeline. *He Is in Heaven.* New York: McGraw-Hill Book Co., 1965.

Tucker, Ruth A. *From Jerusalem to Irian Jaya: A Biographical History of Christian Missions.* Grand Rapids: Zondervan Publishing House, 1983.

Vaughn, John N. *The World's 20 Largest Churches.* Grand Rapids: Baker Book House, 1984.

Wagner, C. Peter. *Look Out! The Pentecostals Are Coming.* Carol Stream, Ill.: Creation House, 1973.

Walker, Louise Jeter. *Faculty Training Program for Overseas Bible Schools.* Springfield, Mo.: Foreign Missions Department of the Assemblies of God, 1965.

Wead, Doug. *The Compassionate Touch.* Carol Stream, Ill.: Creation House, 1977.

Williams, Ernest S. *Systematic Theology.* 3 vols. Springfield, Mo.: Gospel Publishing House, 1953.

Williams, Morris O. *Partnership in Mission: A Study of Theology and Method in Mission.* Springfield, Mo.: Assemblies of God Division of Foreign Missions, 2nd Ed., 1986.

Winter, Ralph D. "The Twenty-five Unbelievable Years, 1945–1969." *Advance Through Storm, vol. 7: A History of the Expansion of Christianity,* by Kenneth Scott Latourette, pp. 507–533. Grand Rapids: Zondervan Publishing House reprint edition, 1970.

Wise, Robert, et al. *The Church Divided: The Holy Spirit and A Spirit of Seduction.* South Plainfield, N.J.: Bridge Publishing, Inc., 1986.

Womack, David A. *The Wellsprings of the Pentecostal Movement.* Springfield, Mo.: Gospel Publishing House, 1968.

————. *Breaking the Stained-Glass Barrier.* New York: Harper and Row, 1973.

Minutes and Reports

Division of Foreign Missions. Annual Reports, 1959–1988.

————. Field Director's Reports, 1959–1988.

————. Foreign Missions Board Minutes, 1959–1988.

————. Foreign Missions Committee Minutes, 1959–1988.

General Council of the Assemblies of God. Executive Presbytery Minutes, 1959–1988.

————. General Council Minutes, 1959–1987.

————. General Presbytery Minutes, 1959–1988.

————. Reports and Financial Statements, 1959–1987.

Personal Interviews

Balius, Samuel H. Missionary to Latin America. Interview with author. Springfield, Missouri, 7 July 1988.

Brankel, Donald L. Associate Evangelist, Jimmy Swaggart Ministries. Interview with author. Tegucigalpa, Honduras, 17 January 1988.

Braxton, Helen. Editor/Promotions Coordinator for the Spiritual Life–Evangelism and Mobilization and Placement Service. Interview with author. Springfield, Missouri, 23 September 1988.

Cagle, Judy. Missionary to Guam-Marianas. Interview with author. Brussels, Belgium, 17 October 1987.

Clark, Douglas F. Area Representative for the Middle East and North Africa for the Division of Foreign Missions. Interview with author. Springfield, Missouri, 7 July 1988.

Corbin, Donald R. Field Director for Africa. Interview with author. Springfield, Missouri, 1 March 1988.

Correll, Norman L. Administrative Assistant to the Executive Director of the Division of Foreign Missions. Interview with author. Springfield, Missouri, 30 November 1988.

Dalton, Adele Flower. Senior Editorial Assistant for the Division of Foreign Missions. Interview with author. Springfield, Missouri, 20 September 1988.

De Ment, H. H. "Spud," and De Ment, Joyce. Missionaries to Africa. Interview with author. Nairobi, Kenya, 13 April 1988.

Dudley, Roland Q. Missionary to Portugal. Interview with author. Loures, Portugal, 20 October 1987.

Flattery, George M. President of the International Correspondence Institute. Interview with author. Brussels, Belgium, 17 October 1987.

Ford, Glenn. Missionary to Africa. Interview with author. Nairobi, Kenya, 13 April 1988.

Headley, L. Lamar. Mobilization and Placement Service Coordinator. Interview with author. Springfield, Missouri, 16 October 1988.

Hogan, J. Philip. Executive Director of the Division of Foreign Missions. Interview with author. Springfield, Missouri, 6 December 1988.

Hoggard, Terry L. Missionary to Italy. Interview with author. Rome, Italy, 2 June 1987.

Iwasko, Ronald A. Personnel Secretary for the Division of Foreign Missions. Interview with author. Springfield, Missouri, 1 December 1988.

Jones, Wilma. Secretary to the Special Services Coordinator, Division of Foreign Missions. Interview with author. Springfield, Missouri, 10 October 1988.

Lotter, Dorothea J. Registrar for the Assemblies of God Theological Seminary. Interview with author. Springfield, Missouri, 1 September 1988.

Malek, Sobhi W. Missionary to the Middle East/North Africa. Interview with author. Malaga, Spain, 22 October 1987.

McMain, Rosalee. Promotions Office Coordinator, Division of Foreign Missions. Interview with author. Springfield, Missouri, 28 December 1988.

Missionary to Middle East (name withheld). Interview with author. Middle East, 1987.

Morrison, Gerald. Area Regional Coordinator for Africa for the Pentecostal Assemblies of Canada. Interview with author. Nairobi, Kenya, 14 April 1988.

Ogg, E. Jerald. Crusade Director, Jimmy Swaggart Ministries. Interview with author. Tegucigalpa, Honduras, 16 January 1988.

Parsley, Jerry L. Field Director for Eurasia. Interview with author. Springfield, Missouri, 23 September 1988.

Richardson, James E. Associate Professor of Missions. Assemblies of God Theological Seminary. Interview with author. Springfield, Missouri, 5 December 1988.

Sandidge, Jerry L. Senior Pastor of Evangel Temple Christian Center. Interview with author. Springfield, Missouri, 25 September 1988.

Schmitt, Harold, and Schmitt, Agnes. Missionaries to Europe. Interview with author. Munich, West Germany, 10 April 1988.

Spain, Gerald I. Missionary to Africa. Interview with author. Nairobi, Kenya, 13 April 1988.

Swaggart, Jimmy L. Evangelist and President of Jimmy Swaggart Ministries. Interview with author. Tegucigalpa, Honduras, 17 January 1988.

Triplett, Loren O. Field Director for Latin America and the West Indies. Interview with author. Springfield, Missouri, 25 October 1988.

Williams, Morris O. Field Director for Africa, Retired; Associate Professor of Missions, Assemblies of God Theological Seminary. Interview with author. Springfield, Missouri, 12 September 1988.

Woolsey, James B. International Ministries Director of Jimmy Swaggart Ministries. Interview with author. Tegucigalpa, Honduras, 16 January 1988.

Telephone Interviews

Barnett, Cecil L. President of Christian Fidelity Life Insurance Co. Interview with author. Waxahachie, Texas, 13 October 1988.

Burgess, Jerry L. Finance Secretary for the Division of Foreign Missions. Interview with author. Springfield, Missouri, 3 January 1989.

Guynes, Delmer R. Missionary to the Far East. Interview with author. Waxahachie, Texas, 15 October 1988.

Hoover, Elva J. Former National Secretary of the Women's Ministries Department of the Assemblies of God. Interview with author. Springfield, Missouri, 20 July 1988.

Tarr, Jr., Delbert H. President of California Theological Seminary. Interview with author. Fresno, California, 30 November 1988.

Williams, Bill L. Missionary to Europe. Interview with author. Nice, France, 23 September 1988.

Womack, David A. Pastor of Twin Palms Assembly of God. Interview with author. San Jose, California, 11 October 1988.

Index

Abbott, Robert, 234pl.
Abujaber, Hala, 261pl.
Abujaber, Samuel, 261pl.
Advance, 130, 197
Advanced Ministerial Training Institute (AMTI), 173
Africa, 109, 239
  field directors: Corbin, D., 238, 261pl., 268; Phillips, E., 42, 50, 56pl., 187; Williams, M., 187–188, 203pl., 268
  missionaries, 181pl., 204pl.
  women, 204pl.
Ahlf, Ann, 82
Ajah, Paul O., 179
Alexander, Linda, 259pl.
Allen, A. A., 70
Allen, Roland, 33, 39pl., 132, 293n.16
Ambassadors in Mission (AIM), 197, 241, 243, 246
  and Global Conquest, 105, 122
  history of, 90–93
American Association of Bible Colleges, 151
American Bible Society, 142, 245
American Council of Christian Churches, 24
Amitié, Alfred, 152pl., 171
Angola, 273, 28lpl.
Annacondia, Carlos, 272, 286pl.
Apostolic Faith, 19
Apostolic Faith Movement (Portland, Oregon), 21

Appleby, Blanche, 60
Area representatives, 280
Argentina, 132, 138, 272, 286pl.
Argue, Watson, 71, 140, 309n.37
Assad, George, 264pl.
Assemblies of God, 24, 108
  50th anniversary, 104
  headquarters, 109, 111, 153, 23, 95pl.
  influences on, 33, 35
  missiology, 21, 29, 31–34
  missionaries, 21, 29
  policies, 30
  publications, 167, 271, 312n.1
  75th anniversary, 237, 266
  support agencies, 81–93
Assemblies of God Archives, 11
Assemblies of God Graduate School (*see* Assemblies of God Theological Seminary)
Assemblies of God Hospital and Research Center (Calcutta), 251–252
Assemblies of God Theological Seminary, 285pl., 311n.6
  accreditation, 153
  anti-intellectual sentiments, 152
  DFM, relation to, 325n.64, 325n.66
  establishment, 129, 150, 153, 189
  groundwork, 99
  instructors, 154, 156, 164pl., 165pl., 188, 201, 223–224, 268, 279

343